Because I Said So

*Wisdom I never wanted from
lessons I needed to learn*

Shauna J. Pinneo

Because I Said So
Copyright © 2015 by Shauna J. Pinneo

ISBN-13: 978-0-578-17019-0

Printed in USA by 48HrBooks (www.48HrBooks.com)

Dedication

To my husband without whose insistence, encouragement and belief, this Bucket List moment would never have been realized. You have always believed in me more deeply, passionately and fiercely than I would ever dare to believe in myself. You have taught me to reach for the extraordinary in everything. You are my sense of adventure and the place where my heart is at home. We have travelled to hell and back and I would do it all over again for the gift of a life spent loving you. I look back without regret and look forward with hope and purpose. You are the love of my life and I will neither wish nor want for anything but Us until "The End of Time."

Acknowledgements

Generally acknowledgements involve a list of staff, resources and support systems that help one accomplish the wonderful, yet daunting task of putting the pages of a book together. For me, I would only wish for the opportunity to thank my family for the love, support, inspiration and tireless cheerleading they have done on my behalf. It has meant more to me than I could ever express.

And to my children. You are the brightest lights in my life. a constant beacon that calls me to work harder and do better today than I did yesterday because in spite of all my shortcomings you deserve the best me I can become, if only so I can be that for you. Every-day you are my Every-thing. You have been the endless source of joy, laughter, challenge, motivation, and pure, uncompromising love through the best and worst of it all. EVERY SINGLE DAY I learn from each one of you. Lessons that are surprising, poignant, delightful and deeply transforming. At the end of it all, if I can do right by you, I will consider my life beautifully lived. Being your Mom has been the greatest blessing I have ever known. Thank you for the lessons you have taught me, the joy you have brought me and the gift of knowing with unwavering certainty, that pure, unconditional love continues to exist.

Introduction

I'm not sure if I started writing out of inspiration or exasperation. I think, perhaps, it was both. Suffice it to say that life, thus far, has consisted of one unforeseen "circumstance" after another. The word circumstance seems kinder than the word "crisis" which is probably more accurate. I think some people thrive with copious amounts of drama in their lives and as such they seek it, create it or conjure it up consistently. But it's not my thing. Yet somehow, and for some reason, it has, in large part defined my life, my learning and my journey thus far.

For each and every one of us our life is a story. A unique string of events woven from our experiences, our joys, our frustrations, our learning, our laughter, our hurts and our hope for the future. Every person who picks up these pages has a different tale to tell but I am convinced that at the end of day, there are certain truths...assorted ideas that hold true for all of us including those who would deny that any conventional wisdom could possibly apply to them. The truth is that we all long for joy. We all crave relationships that bring us a sense of connection and belief that in this big crazy world we matter deeply to someone. In a world of millions of different people doing millions of different things we need to feel like we belong somewhere and with someone. We silently long to feel valued and to offer something of importance that will, in ways large and small, somehow make a difference.

But here is what is happening instead. We are tethered to a sense of manic overwhelm and frustration is a feeling constantly simmering under the surface of our carefully constructed image. While we long for relationships and connection, families are flung to the far corners of the country and rarely live near one another. And if they do, they are often of the mind that if their in-laws lived in an alternate universe it might still be too close for comfort.

Divorce is an epidemic and there is scarcely a household that isn't in some way affected by the disease. "Blended families" are more common than smoothie shops and the "for better or worse" we lovingly committed to has been taken to the extremes of human tolerance. We have become dual income or single parent households and as a result our kids are being raised by someone we pay to provide the supervision they need if not the nurturing they deserve. We are struggling to keep up with commitments, expectations, and appearances and falling short on all fronts.

But the beauty that I continue to see is that the human heart is breathtakingly resilient. The fact that we struggle and fail and feel besieged by responsibilities and beleaguered by frustration speaks of something utterly magnificent to me. We feel these things because in spite of everything that comes our way, we continue to hope. We are frustrated because someplace in our soul we know there is something spectacular that we continue to long for. And that longing is the life we are intended to live. I have had the privilege of more than my fair share of bumps in the road. What I know now is that these events didn't happen *to* me, they happened *for* me. They happened so that I could learn, grow and embrace the person I was supposed to become. For myself, for my family and for those whose path I was allowed to cross that might find comfort in knowing that they aren't merely heard, they are truly and deeply understood. They happened so that I could earn a level of true understanding and resolute compassion that I never would have had or known before. They happened so that I could, perhaps, be fortunate enough to help others better understand their own journey. While some people earn PhD's and an array of truly impressive credentials, my life has been my learning ground and I could defend my thesis on how to both survive and thrive and with both certainty and great aplomb. I've seen too much and pulled up my bootstraps far too many times to not assert my credentials. Credentials of insight and perspective that can be a welcome short cut through everything from toddler temper tantrums to a true understanding of how to choose, joy, abundance and accomplishment in life, business, relationships and family. Credentials that range from starting and running a business, to negotiating rocky relationships, to creating a thriving marriage, to finding your balance on the tight rope between work and family, to the absolute gift of raising of five utterly spectacular and unique kids. For better or for worse there aren't many stones I haven't been outrageous enough to overturn. The struggles don't deserve the spot light, but without them none of us can feel the exhilaration of triumph and the realization that we have earned the wisdom that will bring us the life of imperfect bliss that I daresay we all deserve.

Whether life just needs a few tweaks or a major overhaul, there is surely a story here for you. I have also discovered that if we smugly believe that advice or experiences don't apply to us, it a sure bet that one of these days they will, in fact, apply to us or someone we love. Best to get a jump on things. So if more joy, more calm, more balance, abundance, authenticity and achievement sound like they may be of interest to you, read on my friend. Perhaps we can share a story, shed a tear, laugh out loud, learn something, try something, and discover what is possible once again.

Proverbs 24:14

Table of Contents

Because I Said So

Shauna J. Pinneo

Personal Branding

Right now it's a pretty safe bet y'all think I'm talking about marketing, media and the effort to establish your position, image and impression in your chosen field. Well then consider this a Bait and Switch masterfully accomplished. I'm actually talking about tattoos.

Allow me to explain myself. Actually, I suppose this is really a suggestion that you consider explaining YOURself...in the form of expertly applied artwork to your birthday suit. While I am not advocating that everybody should go out and get themselves permanently inked, it does beg the question; what do you believe in so strongly...so absolutely that you would actually consider branding yourself with that belief?

I think for many of us our belief system is somewhat negotiable. We are generally wired to please and avoid conflict and as such, we can, at times, be accused of altering ourselves in order to be appealing, agreeable and well, um...liked. And while this isn't necessarily a bad thing, more often than not, its practice is more than just a bit questionable. A belief system ceases to be a belief system if it comes and goes depending on the company we keep. A belief system in something steadfast and unwavering. It is a conviction, a code, a creed that we live by at all times and through all things. We've all heard the joke about the atheist who goes off to war and the minute enemy fire surrounds him, he's praying to God like no body's business. Odd, semi-funny jokes

1

aside, I think that if we were required to have what we believed in deeply or knew to be true tattooed to our body, we'd REALLY want to be committed to the idea. If a guy gets "Mama" and a huge heart tattooed on his chest and he hasn't been home for a visit or a Sunday dinner in ten years that just false advertising. If a guy has the Sanskrit word for Peace emblazoned on his bicep and is prone to frequent road rage, there is a conflict of interest afoot. If a gal gets her boyfriend's name and the word Forever provocatively tattooed on her shoulder but six weeks later breaks up with him because he lost his job, we could all safely assume she didn't have the fine print of conditions which must be met for her to actually commit to "forever" tattooed as well.

Now, I well realize that an impressive percentage of tattoos were inspiration born out of alcohol induced initiative. "Sure! A tattoo of Mini Mouse on my ass seems like a fantastic idea!" says an inordinate amount of vodka shots in Las Vegas. And low and behold you wake up the next morning with a perky mouse on your fine derriere. But what if…what if, when we had all our whits about us, we purposefully choose something of deep importance that we would abide in forevermore and branded ourselves with that belief. Do you know what it would be? Would you hesitate and ask yourself if you're certain enough to permanently declare it? What, or who, do you believe in with such strength, certainty and fierce resolve that you would actually endure significant pain to proclaim it. Yes, getting a tattoo hurts like hell. But so does standing up for what you believe in. I think it is nearly a given that if we choose something that we will defend with the whole of who we are, it's going to cost us. There WILL be times where we will be criticized and condemned or demonized and dismissed because we daringly choose to hold the line. We live in a world that surrenders so easily and expects us to do the same. Do we quietly comply and adjust ourselves in order to be agreeable or are we willing to stand on the firing line of criticism and contempt

2

not because we are brave, but because we are certain. As Yoda so sagely insisted, "Do or do not. There is no try." Do we TRY to stand for something or do we stand strongly by and for our beliefs...no matter what.

I have referenced before a program that ran briefly on cable TV called "Whale Wars." When I heard the tag line of the show it felt like I'd had the wind knocked out of me. It declared that, "You haven't lived until you've found something worth dying for." Do you have that something? Do you know what it is?
Personal branding is essentially the practice of marketing yourself to create an image or impression on the marketplace. But how are you marketing yourself to the world? What are you insisting that others know, with absolute certainty about you? Businesses, trends and areas of interest and expertise will come, go and evolve across time, as they should. But Who you are. What you believe in. Your Purpose. These are the things we must choose with steadfast courage and a fierceness that never wavers. Are you devoted enough to your ideals to wantingly be branded by them?

I'm not (necessarily) encouraging you to immediately pencil in a trip to the tattoo artist of your choosing. But I am insisting that you find and know what you believe in so resolutely that you are willing to declare it fearlessly and forever.

While Donald Trump remains the undisputed King of personal branding, each of us chooses our own Kingdom. In other words, who we are and all that we stand for builds our life around us. The people we love, the character we live, the principles we are loyal to. Choose with courage. Declare with strength and humility. Believe with the whole of who you are. Allow these gifts to be the enduring mark...the brand, you leave on the world.

Enough about me, what do you think about me?

Let me start off by saying "please don't answer that." But I thought it a mildly sarcastic way to begin a rather important dialog about who we fancy ourselves to be and how we share ourselves with the rest of the world. Due to both recent and alarmingly frequent experiences I realize that the way we see ourselves, what we are offering the world by way of our undeniable awesomeness isn't always what other people take away from their time with us. Hard as it is to believe, the way we see ourselves may not be the end product we were hoping for in other people's minds. There is a sliver of a chance that our image of ourselves, our actions and our impact is not in keeping with how others experience our one-of-a-kind incredible selves. In a world that exalts independence and applauds "being yourself", "you being you", and enthusiastically embraces the belief that we each have a unique contribution we were meant to

4

offer the world around us, concerning ourselves with what OTHERS think of us sounds like horrifically bad advice. But hear me out... I'm as committed as one could possibly be to the notion of blazing your own trail and refusing to allow your life to be altered or defined by what other people may think. Without hesitation, I'm on Team Authentic and hope it always beats the crap out of Team Ordinary. But here's the deal; if we aren't conveying the Self we want to be. If we aren't being experienced for all those things that are soulfully important to us then we need to adjust. Adjust to other people's expectations? Nope. Adjust to our commitment of contributing to the world that which we adore and intend. If it is deeply important to me to be seen as a compassionate person, is that, in fact, what others see in me and from me? It is in the commitment to our own important contribution that we need to evaluate whether or not we are actually delivering the goods.

Our nine year old daughter LOVES anything dramatic. Parties, performances, acting, apparel! If it attracts attention she's in! She'd wear opera gloves to bed if given half a chance. What is deeply true about her is that she delights in giddy laughter, and celebration. She lives for relationships and unencumbered joy. Sharing and experiencing this with others is astonishingly important to her. When her sister growls at her invitations to frivolity she is both shocked and hurt. How POSSIBLY could you not want to bedazzle everything in your closet?! So while Rain sees herself as light-hearted and impossibly enthusiastic, her sister would consider her irritatingly effervescent. With kids, it is a parent's job to encourage their individuality while insisting that they be considerate of one another. But who manages this dance when we are adults? Who gives us feedback on not just what we are doing, sharing and giving, but on how, exactly, we are affecting others? Does our opinion of ourselves allow for a difference of opinion from others?

By way of example I can claim the following experiences and then some. I had a conversation with a highly respected businessman. He is incredibly accomplished and impressively credentialed. His impression of himself is that he is tactful, diplomatic and astute. My impression was more along the lines of aloof and condescending. Now I can guarantee that is not how he would like or intend to be perceived. I can say with certainty it is fundamentally important to him to be experienced by others as a benevolent intellectual. A power house of cerebral prowess combined with inspiring ideals. So at what point do we tune our antennae to the possibility that the person we are fiercely committed to being may or may not be the person we are in the world? I can assure you none of us would have to look far to name someone who declares themselves a Christian but our experience of them screamed self-righteous and judgmental. How ironic that truly Christian people rarely need to proclaim their moral turf, they simply live in a way that loves, accepts and inspires others. They live with humility and kindness and not the haughty high ground of those who would rather claim a label than practice a way of life. As they say, "claiming you are a Christian because you go to church is like insisting you are a car because you stood in a garage." Hard to argue the logic really.

It may be our hearts desire to be an accomplished professional, an incredible spouse, a phenomenal parent, or a loyal friend. But are we honestly delivering the goods? Are the elements of ourselves we so desire to be and give what we are actually sharing with the world? In this regard, what YOU think about me is the greatest feedback mechanism I could ever have. You may want to be the consummate professional but others register you as having all the warmth and sensitivity of a Siberian security guard. You may fancy yourself a devoted disciplinarian with your kids but the word tyrant might come more readily to their young minds. If you consider yourself an incredible friend when did you last make a call, send a note or share a laugh?

Now I can share with you that it is deeply and intensely important to me to be a person of tender compassion, soulful wisdom, uncompromising integrity and relentless commitment to Faith, Family and Friends. Now I can SAY I want to be all these lofty things until you and I are both sick of my drivel. But is that necessarily what others experience? If the answer is "no," I am wonderfully obligated to adjust. This isn't to suggest we can be all things at all times. Only errant thinking would presume we will never act unprofessionally, yell at our kids for no reason or get so consumed with our to-do list that reaching out to others is left for an unnamed tomorrow. The point is simply that in order to put forth with conviction and certainty the parts of who we uniquely and wondrously are, to offer the world and those we love what they need from us, in order to be the very best ME I can find, I need to know if YOU feel the ways I want to touch your life. In other words, while I will never do anything but praise each and every one of us living our singular, unique verse in the world, we can only be said to have accomplished our intention if YOU have felt the purpose of ME. If you have lived better, learned more, been loved more deeply or been given the encouragement to be unafraid then, and only then, can I say I have done what I was uniquely meant to do.

Two Wrongs Don't Make a Right.

As a kid growing up, if I heard this phrase once I heard it a thousand times. I remember my mother saying it more often than perhaps I should admit and I always thought it sounded like a bunch a mumbo jumbo. A thought that confused me and seemed above my adolescent pay grade. And because I didn't really get it, I chose to ignore the concept for the most part. I went about my business continuing to proclaim things as the need arose like "he hit me first" or "so and so did it too!" Like if you're committing a juvenile crime in someone else's company your errant ways don't count. If someone else did it too how could I POSSIBLY be in trouble?! As kids we often act with impunity and believe that our behavior need only be as noble as the trouble makers around us.

But as an adult I have thought long and hard about this phrase…this truth. The sad reality is we don't seem to outgrow our stupidity. The bigger we are, the bigger problems we seem to be able to cause. And we are never far from our need for retribution. If someone hurts or harms us, we almost view it as our duty as much as our instinct to fight back. The Wild West may be no more, but we're still a bunch of gun slingers when it comes to our involuntary need for vengeance. I'm as guilty of this as the next guy but over time I have realized this reflexive revenge never, ever makes me feel any better. In fact, so very much the opposite. It inevitably makes me feel less. Less compassionate, less intelligent, less certain and less noble than I would like or fancy myself to be. And so I have grown to not just recite this philosophy, but to understand it in very real and poignant ways.

I was recently on the outskirts of a conflict and I watched in this sad and somewhat helpless way, the unnecessary harm that we have the ability to inflict on one another. Someone stated a position that while the words expressed disdain, it was obvious that the statement, the position, was the unwelcome offspring of deep hurt and sadness. But the admittedly understandable response was a verbal right hook. You hurt, offended, and insulted me, now getting back becomes some twisted game of wounding one-upsmanship. And before you know it we had mudslinging going on that would make a politician proud. When someone lashes out at us, hurts our feelings, injures our pride or calls our character and intentions into question, it is only human to go about engineering our reprisal. We could make an impressive argument for the fact that we are just defending ourselves and in this light, firing the next shot seems downright courageous. But I have never found this volley of hurts to create any understanding and nobody ever ends up better off for the battle. Perhaps we dig in, wanting to shout our position believing that our rightness, our impressive correctness will be heard above the din of someone else's lack of enlightened perspective. Um yeah. Good luck with that. So the question becomes, when a wrong has been done, how DO we make it right?

I read something in a book by John Gottman one time that I thought was a beautiful visual. It said that when we are fighting, the task before us is to pry open the others fist and see what is really inside. Very rarely is anger a "what you see is what you get" proposition. It is complex and deep seated and when something strikes a nerve and evokes our anger and bitterness, there is much going on that desperately wants to be understood. Now I am not suggesting that this Gandhi-like approach is easy. Personally I am wired to act more along the lines of "the best defense is a good offense" than to have my actions reflect the understanding that offense does not defend, it divides. To divulge even more of my instinct, I remember watching the Dr. Phil Show ages ago and he turned and asked a guy, "do you want to be right or do you want to be happy?" And IMMEDIATELY what flashed through my indignant mind was "how could someone possibly be happy if they aren't right!?!"

But across time, space and experience I have come to understand that happiness and more importantly Peace will never be a product of being right, it will only be the product of patience and compassion. The truth of our nature is that we are complex. Each of us arrives into relationships, conflicts and conversations with the history of who we are. It is simplest and undeniably true to say that there are ALWAYS two sides to every story. But the important part is that we are all, indeed, a Story. An intricately woven tapestry of our experience of the past and our hopes for how we want to be seen, respected and understood in the future.

To this end, I would encourage us all, myself as much as any, to never stray far from the Truth that two wrongs, never have and never will make a right. We want to leave a mark on the world and those we encounter, not battle scars from our cutting and cunning ways. The interesting reality is that what is right, never needs to be defended. The more saber rattling we have to do, the less likely it is that we've got it all figured out. I never have and am convinced I never will, discover a situation where the bridge between battle positions is not built upon compassion. I don't have to agree with you, but if I throw my heart and my intentions into understanding you, everything changes. When we stop doing wrong and cease our need to be right, the magical thing we are left with is Wisdom. And wouldn't we all consider it infinitely better to be remembered for the Wisdom we earned rather than the wounds we inflicted? Taking the High Road isn't easy, but it's the only path we will ever admire.

Your Resume.

Down here in the desert the school year wraps up insanely early. Likely because it is hotter than Hades and everyone is trying to get out of the insufferable heat and find an alternative venue for the summer months. But as the school year came to a close, it marked a significant weigh point in our lives. Our oldest daughter graduated from eighth grade and this incredible milestone ushered in an immense amount of pride and also an important pause and wonderful reflection on what has been my life's work thus far.

If I might indulge myself for a moment, our oldest daughter was awarded what her school refers to as the Pillar Award. It is the highest honor the school bestows on the students and is given to one male and one female student in each grade. Interestingly, the faculty who used to decide on who was deserving of this honor, years ago realized that in truth, the students are far more aware of their own. It is the students that truly know best who among them represents these qualities across both time and circumstance. The Pillar award carries added enormity in the kids eighth grade year as these are the two kids who give a speech, addressing students, faculty and family at the graduation ceremony.

Everest, knowing she needed to write and give this speech sat down to create and craft the message she wanted to share. And in doing so she was adamant about not discussing it, disclosing it or divulging any of her thoughts to her doting and overly curious parents. Even a comment free proof reading couldn't be negotiated. No matter how hard I tried to wiggle my way into her thoughts she was unswayed by my inquiries and I stopped just shy of begging. Now I know my daughter. She has always been my beloved Old Soul. Wise beyond her years and astonishingly unaffected by what the world is doing around her. She has always been beholden to only her own compass and awes me with her ability to forgo "fitting in" in exchange for feeling true to all and everything she is. The irony was most certainly not lost on me that the girl who doesn't care what anyone else thinks is the girl that everyone else admires. Hmmm. Interesting…

But it got me thinking about our resume. Not our fluffed up, occasionally exaggerated, intentionally impressive business resume, but our life resume. I will hazard a guess that most of us have written a work related resume. A few pages of fact and perhaps a little fiction intended to convince would-be employers of our immense abilities and inestimable value to any organization lucky enough to write us a paycheck. But when was the last time we sat down to take stock of our life accomplishments? When have we reflected, on our inventory of "moments?" How often have we spent time dwelling on what we have accomplished in life, love, relationships, and memories? Have we bullet pointed how we have given, cared, celebrated, shared, laughed and lived? Have we made note of the times where we have risen to a challenge, overcome our fears, shown tender kindness and generous care? Have we commemorated those moments of connection, belief, faith, hope, spontaneity, and joy? Have we dared to risk and reveled in the thrill, not of success, but of simply and wonderfully, trying? Trying to both believe in the extraordinary and find our own way to BE extraordinary. Have we given as much mention to each triumph, no matter how small, as we have to every time we have fallen short of our best intentions. In other words, how does our life resume look so far?

With a new baby in the house, I will admit that I toggle between feeling blissfully immersed in the "moment," allowing my senses to be filled with the absolute magic and wonder of the here and now. Every coo and grin swells my heart in ways I will never be able to explain or tell tale of. But the sublime joy of savoring this precious tiny life wrestles with the whip cracking in my mind insisting on accomplishments, achievements and being "productive." And the truth is, I'm desperately drawn to both. And while it would be alarmingly easy to say these two endeavors are at odds – patiently nurturing a child - unglamorous work that doesn't provide trophies, bonuses, a gold watch, a promotion or a trip to Hawaii. A career path whose success is measured in report cards, pleases and thank you's and parental pride is not made or meant to be compared with the business "accomplishments" we pursue with such vigor. Are we offering as much energy and importance to the pursuit of achievements that measure our soul or our salary? Do we throw ourselves equally into making a living as we do our determination to making life worth living?

I heard a great quote recently, "as parents we can't take all of the credit or all of the blame." So as I watched Everest address a room of over 300 people with confidence, poise and grace, I was left utterly and wonderfully speechless as I witnessed in full and glorious version the person she was and is becoming. I realized that there is no honest way I can take the credit for the girl I was witnessing before me. But I also knew that if my life's resume included only this very moment I would feel blessed beyond words. I would feel as though I had done something worthy and right and that such a thing is the greatest accomplishment any of us could hope for.

I desire and demand much out of life and myself. But I also realize that a life's work that seeks out the spouse, the parent, the friend, the daughter or son, sister or brother we are able to be – this is the accomplishment of a lifetime. When we place not just our heart, but the whole of our purpose in these things…in these relationships we have touched upon all that is good and lovely in this world and no other accomplishment or purposeful achievement will ever be so extraordinarily worthy of praise.

True Grit

I mentioned in a recent blog something I have thought a great deal about and not just lately. It has been a topic, a question, that I have wondered on many a time. And my wondering ways have led me to nostalgically inquire, "Where has our "grittiness" gone?"

I have been watching with worry and a growing alarm what seems to be a lack of grit, determination and resolve that have become the concerning norm. Just last week our oldest daughter was interviewing her grandma Mimi. Asking her questions and listening to her childhood remembrances of WWII. The call was on speaker phone and I couldn't help listening with no small degree of astonishment as she recollected a time and experiences most of us can scarcely imagine. Now I have read books that paint an impressively vivid picture of that part of our history, but hearing someone recount first-hand what they remember, what their life and experiences were like took my intrigue off of distantly penned pages and into the here and now. And as Mimi was sharing her stories, her life, I couldn't help but wonder if we, now, are capable of enduring such hardship. I truly believe it is nearly impossible for younger generations to imagine war. War in a way that affects every single aspect of their life, their thoughts, their actions, their very being. Stories of everything from sirens, and riveting airplanes to rationing rubber bands. Stories of a collective suffering in the grips of both fear of what may come and the immense, indescribable grief that reached its insidious hands into every home, and every heart. We live in a world where even post 9/11 we seem to take our ease, our comfort and our safety for granted. It is profoundly humbling to dwell on a time when the entire world knew nothing of such things. They knew hardship, devastation and loss. And yet, for them and in them, was a collective strength. A resolve that seemed to be born out of hardship. Character that seemed inspired by the conflict, and an enduring, beating sense of integrity that grew out of unimaginable adversity.

These days, we consider it a hardship if our Wi-Fi doesn't work or we can't get a latte made with almond milk. We have not been forced to contend with fear, uncertainty, and challenges that test the very fiber of our being. My dad did several tours in Vietnam and what he saw time and time again was that war accelerated who and what we already were. Circumstances forced men and women to become the most extreme version of who they were able to be. Those who were steady and strong found courage of the most uncommon kind. They became leaders, supporters, friends, helpers and heroes. Those whose temperament was not so intact struggled more violently with the ravages of war.

So it begs the question. When our mettle is being tested. When our character is to be revealed through sorrow, struggle and circumstance, WHO are we? Do we go with the flow or mind our own business in the face of a wrong or injustice? Or do we speak up and stand the ground that our character rightly claims? Would we endure hardship with honor, nobility and strength or would we collapse in the face of challenge and adversity? When life and

17

circumstances push us, do we push back or would we qualify as more of a pushover? Do we take advantage of opportunities to serve others or do we take advantage of others to serve ourselves? It was of no small interest to me to learn that HOPE is not an emotion. It is a way of thinking that is born out of resilience. If we are given the opportunity to struggle, to fail, to fall and to overcome THEN we have learned how to hope. We hope because we know we can endure. We do not FEEL hope, we EARN hope. We hope because we realize that hardship and strife does not happen TO us, it happens FOR us. It happens so that we may have the opportunity to learn, to grow, to find grace, compassion and strength that we may never have known without being forced into the fire. And that very fire can either burn us into something bitter and resentful or it can warm the embers of our resolve. It can light the flame of our own courage, resilience and belief not just in what is possible, but in what WE are capable of doing, overcoming, and achieving.

Growing up as an army brat, many of the guys I was friends with would say that they hoped there would be a war in their lifetime. As stunned as I was to hear this, I listened to the reality that what they really craved was to know, really know, without a shadow of a doubt what they were made of. Were they crafted out of courage, valor and dignity or would they be immobilized by their fears.

The reality is that we don't need a war to realize who and what we are. Life itself offers far too many battlefronts already. If we are willing to see them as such, life offers countless opportunities to show our grit. Do we quit the job that's too hard? Do we fight for our relationships or lay waste to hearts that needed to be held with gentle devotion? Do we surrender our values or abide by them no matter what it costs? Do we abandon our dreams because believing is just too hard? Do we forfeit our character to be liked by our peers? Do we parent our children or placate them? Do we commit to the importance of others or live in a fortress of busyness with no time to reach out and no place for others to reach in? Do we volunteer our time, our resources and our understanding or do we abandon our best intentions to excuses of overwhelm? Do we pursue excellence relentlessly or crumble at the slightest critique? Do we abide by our faith or concede it for convenience?

Every day we must wage war on complacence and mediocrity. Every day we are destined to reveal our character, our integrity and our courage. And every day a kind word, a gentle touch, a silent promise or a strong yet simple act of grace offers us a chance to be brave enough to make it all matter.

Conflict Resolution

First and foremost, it is important for me to say that the inspiration for these thoughts did not come to me in the car, in the shower or in some ethereal, enlightened dream. With a five week old infant, the car is chaos, showers are taken with appalling irregularity and sleep seems some hazy recollection of something wonderful but currently forbidden. No, in this case, I am borrowing a notion that was recounted to me by a dear friend after her Pastor spoke about it in church and I found it so fascinating that I couldn't help but be both curious about the topic and vexed by its presence all at once.

It seems to me that people, for the most part, fall into one of only two categories when it comes to conflict. Either they have an aversion to conflict that is so absolute they would rather eat fried scorpions on a stick than argue over whether or not that is a reasonable culinary adventure. On the flip side you have those folks who seem to take on argument with the zealousness of a professional sporting event. Not only are they not averse to conflict they seem to seek it out just to flex their disagreement muscles and keep them in "fighting shape." The more reps the better. These are the people who often seem as though they have an uncanny radar to find anything to bicker, squabble or quarrel about. You could tell them there are seven days in the week and they'd argue about it. I'd encourage us all to find that splendid middle ground. For those who steer clear of conflict, find what expectations, passions and principles are worth taking a stand for and be willing to fight for them with all you are and everything you've got. For those who seem to live on the front lines – always ready to slug it out; the world is not a battle field. Decide which hills you're going to die on and then spend all that excess energy creating something besides hard feelings.

As charming as we may find the latter, most people avoid conflict as vehemently as pre-adolescent boys avoid bathing. We work up a sweat attempting to avoid confrontation in all forms. We wouldn't send cold soup back to the kitchen at a restaurant much less confront someone about a principle, a belief system, an ethical oversight, or any other challenging, trying topic because we have internalized a belief system that views confrontation as being aggressive, unpleasant and terribly out of line. But what exactly are we so afraid of? I think that at the heart the matter we are terrified of not being liked. And if we don't feel "liked" we then see ourselves tumbling uncontrollably into feelings that we are unappealing, unworthy or don't belong. We have become so fragile and needy for approval that anything that puts our perceived pleasantness in jeopardy is cause for alarm and avoidance. What will the waiter think of me if I send my soup back? What will the parents think of me if we don't tell ALL the kids on the team that they are Winners and give them each a trophy? What will the moms and dads think of me if I actually tell them their child is lazy and irresponsible with their school work? What will my kids think of me if I actually act like a parent instead of a pal? What will my employees think if I hold them accountable instead of holding their hand? What will my family think if I dress differently, think differently, parent differently, and believe differently? Answer: Who the hell cares!?!

Apparently we do...A LOT! But again I contend that if we believed in ourselves, in our worth, in our viewpoints, and our values, we wouldn't look at confrontation with such profound foreboding. If we were certain of ourselves, we would concern ourselves with how well we LIVE not how well we are LIKED. What if there was more than one way to view confrontation? To again credit the above inspiration, the current Webster's definition of Confrontation is: A situation in which people, groups, etc., fight, oppose, or challenge each other in an angry way. But is this the best, most productive view of confrontation? Hard to believe that in the original Webster's dictionary confrontation was defined as: The act of bringing two persons into the presence of each other for examination and discovery of truth. WHAT!?! If you're anything like me you reread those definitions four times.

So what if, instead of viewing confrontation as opposing each other in an angry way, we chose to believe the process was about the discovery of truth. Our truth. What if we choose to view confrontation without anger but rather as an opportunity to live, act and express our most profound truths and beliefs? So our first order of business is to know what our beliefs are and to stand by them with strength, conviction and a sense of honor. Once we know who we are and what we believe, we become far less anxious about confrontation. It ceases to threaten our "likability" because likeability is no longer our utmost concern. Once our most passionate and pressing concern is knowing who we are, what we stand for, and what we believe in, then any sort of "confrontation" simply delivers to us an opportunity to discover, explore, express our Truth and to hear one another, without feeling threatened.

The reality is that life these days requires a not so insignificant amount of grittiness. It requires purpose, resolve and determination. It requires us to honor and defend our beliefs and to approach the journey with the humility of heart that is always working to learn, to live, and to love better than before. And so might I suggest that Confrontation is a gift. A profound opportunity to realize we are brave enough to defend our Truth and to discover, with reverence and regard all we have yet to learn.

"Busy" is bulls**t…

Okay. So admittedly that may be a bit too provocative, but I stand by my claim that "busy" is akin to a synonym for disorganized and unproductive. So truly have I come to realize this, that I have quit, cold turkey, using the phrase, "I'm busy." And for someone who has spent the vast majority of her adult life not just feeling but emphatically claiming my busyness, this is not an insignificant epiphany. Prior to my busyness detox program, if I was a boy scout, I'd have a busyness badge. If I was a girl scout I'd have a pin of some sort for achieving consistent overwhelm. And if I was a betting man I'd confidently wager on the chances of me feeling frazzled, and fed-up with my insurmountable to-do list. That is, of course, until I went cold-turkey and gave up being busy forevermore. And it's amazing just how much I now get done in a day.

I'm not sure when, precisely my "A-Ha moment" arrived but it didn't just leave a lasting impression, it altered my entire way of thinking. I realized the people I most respect aren't busy they are incredibly productive. They are focused, on task and able to achieve far more than the busiest person I know could ever hope to accomplish. They are purposeful rather than constantly panicked and never seem to exude that air of absolute chaos that seems to travel alongside so many incredibly "busy" people. But here is the rub. Being productive and not busy requires incredible amounts of organization and copious amounts of calm. Productive people rarely seem flustered or frantic. Instead they wear a focus and concentration not seen in many mortals. They have a resolute centeredness that they hold to as steadfastly as a toddler holds a teddy bear. Have you ever tried to pry the object of a child's affection from their arms? It nearly requires the Jaws of Life and I wouldn't recommend the endeavor under any circumstances. So too do productive, purposeful people grab their vision with a vice grip that would never surrender much less be distracted. Prior to my epiphany, I could be distracted by the need to organize paper clips according to size or to put post-it notes on recipes that I will never, in my life time, cook or create. There is a quote I have enjoyed stating that, "there is nothing so useless as doing well that which shouldn't be done at all." And to this point, I have confessed that I have "busied" myself with alphabetically organizing canned goods in my pantry. In other words, I have done exceedingly well, a task that never should have been done at all. How could making sure Green beans come before Kidney beans possibly be worthwhile?! The answer is, it's not, unless I am determined to be busy which nearly always comes at the cost of being productive about something of meaning and consequence. To be clear, canned goods will never, ever, have meaning or consequence.

What does, or most certainly should, have importance are people, and relationships. How we care for and invest ourselves with others should be our utmost concern. One of Greg's mentors was fond of saying, "if it's convenient, it's not giving." And, with every fiber of my being, I passionately agree. Giving is not required to be easy, on our way, or efficient. And being busy should NEVER, EVER be an excuse for not extending ourselves to care about others in ways that feel meaningful and important

TO THEM. We cannot claim that something or someone is important to us if we don't SHOW this in both word and especially deed. Congratulating someone on an impressive milestone or accomplishment is as useless as my alphabetically organized pantry if I have not invested and shared the journey they have set their sights upon. Acknowledging a personal or professional accomplishment simply because it happens to be big and flashy enough to catch your attention or stir your sense of obligation is a hollow, unworthy and unwelcome exercise. But if instead, along the way, we have simply and sincerely engaged. We have typed an email, made a call, written a card. We have said and shown that we are not, and never will be, too busy to show our heartfelt care with interest and enthusiasm. Now we are producing a life of Purpose rather than flaunting our busyness like some false sense of being exceedingly important because we simply have SO much to manage.

And how is this relevant you ask? I have accepted the reality that for a period of time, I was so exceedingly, inordinately busy that I ceased to be purposeful in my attentions and intentions. My parent's birthdays are five days apart and one year I forgot them both. You would think that my absolute mortification over missing the first one would compel me with great urgency to over deliver on the next one. Nope. I forgot that one too. Why? Because I was so damned busy.

So that is why I KNOW, I know as certainly as the sun rises in the East, that busy is bulls**t. But the business of great accomplishment, the work of being effective and impacting, the focus on our purpose and passion are all the reward for boycotting our busyness. If we could all choose to be productive…productive in our business, in our lives, in our relationships, everything would change. We would no longer be agitated and overwhelmed. We would no longer be stressed and stretched to the limit. We would be content. Content that our vision is certain and undeniable. Content that our time is spent on what and who we truly treasure. Content that we are in charge of our life and our time rather than racing to keep up with relentless demands and obligations. Content in all we are giving because we have chosen to care deeply and sincerely. Content because we are no longer busy, we are benefitting from a life rich in meaning and abundant with purpose. Content because we have chosen relationships over reacting to endless demands. Content because we have been blessed with the ability to shed our busyness and wear the wonder of living, loving and caring...completely.

Who the hell do you think you are?!?

This question can come to us in a multitude of ways. At times it is downright hostile or judgmental, other times shrewdly snide and condescending. Occasionally it is actually spoken yet more often than not, we feel in a discomforting, uneasy way that even though someone else may not be speaking this question to us, they are asking it in their own mind more often than not packaged in not so subtle but always charming, criticism and contempt. The self-righteousness and hypocrisy with which we are capable of treating one another can be downright astounding.

Now I am painting a rather bleak picture to make a point of the provocative and nearly amusing irony that arises from the fact that we often encounter the harshest and most scathing criticism when we are about the business of doing and achieving our very best. I have yet to meet a single soul that is as seethingly critical of another's' failure as they are of another's success. I am not entirely certain why we find ourselves so threatened by the success of others. Maybe we feel the sting of the have and have not mentality. Perhaps when others expect and achieve more for their lives we internalize a personal feeling of being less. Maybe it is as cliché as "misery loves company" and maybe the reality is we crave the freedom to pursue abundance and feel slighted when someone else has the courage to actually DO that which we have done little more than DESIRE. I cannot claim to have exhaustively researched the reason for this phenomenon. But I do know that the cure for the condescension is to know with absolute, unapologetic certainty whose opinion matters to you.

To be sure, EVERBODY has an opinion, at the same time we all realize it is the world's safest bet that we cannot please everyone. Therefore, I have acknowledged in life that there are a handful of extraordinary people whose opinion really and truly matters to me. People whose thoughts, wisdom and judgement I admire and esteem as wonderful measures for my own life and choices. Their lives, their inspiration, their achievement, soulfulness and compassion raise the bar; calling me like a siren song to become better than I am. If they were to call my attention to something I could and should do better I will absorb their input like water in the desert, realizing their thoughts come from a place of care rather than critique. Now the most important truth here is that I am not seeking their approval and they are never looking to pass judgement. Seeking approval is akin to being a lap dog. Constantly chasing the next "Atta boy" or hoping someone will scratch you behind the ears and say "good job."

If we want to create excellence and abundance in our life we need to surround ourselves with those who inspire and encourage that journey. Those who would block our way and malign you for your "selfishness" for your uncompromising commitment to the extraordinary are, in truth, hungry for your vision. Let's look at it this way: can we imagine a parent who asked their seven year old what they wanted to be when they grew up and when the child said, "a doctor, an astronaut, an Olympic athlete or the president," that parent responding to their child with a reprimand for being so selfish as to envision the extraordinary. Can you imagine a football coach scolding his team for demanding excellence of both themselves and their teammates? Can we visualize a teacher berating a child for getting and "A" on their math test? "How selfish of you to work hard and excel! Who do you think you are? Are you trying to make all the other kids feel badly?!? It's all utterly preposterous.

Yet for as ludicrous as this all is and sounds, somewhere along the line we begin to cater to the critics and lessen ourselves, our goals, our dreams and our vision of possibility so as not to offend. Now, does pursuing excellence entitle any of us to become so absorbed with our own achievement that we are dismissive or unconcerned with others? Of course not. But anyone who achieves at the expense of others is not pursuing excellence they are chasing undeserved applause.

We all have our unsteady, uncertain moments. Moments where we doubt ourselves, our ability and our right to the extraordinary. Moments when we look around to see who is watching and concern ourselves with what they might think about our life, our purpose, our choices. Those that want the best for you will encourage you to believe in the abundance, joy and achievement you deserve. They will support you through your failures and encourage you to in your wildest hopes and dreams. They will remind you of your calling toward character, kindness and steadfast principles and never tolerate you being anything short of astonishing in these regards. So, "who the hell do you think you are?" The answer is anything you want to be. Just know who matters and what matters. Empty your pack of the burden of influences that cause you to doubt, question and agonize over their approval. Leave behind the wondering and the worrying. Exhaustive efforts toward winning the approval of a crowd of critics is a fool's errand. Once you believe in your Why and your worth…now ANYTHING is possible. Now you have made the changes that will allow you to change the world.

Good help is SO hard to find!

It's cliché but incredibly true nonetheless. Contrary to what we would all believe or wish to be true, great people are rare and often illusive beings. Akin to enchanted creatures of folklore and fairytales. We have wished for their existence but reluctantly discovered that they only exist in the realm of alluring legend and fantastical imagination. They are stubbornly hiding somewhere undiscovered as we wrestle with seemingly endless frustration, hiring's, firings, and one disappointment after another. Either that or we just numbly settle for the notion that a half-assed effort is good enough and we stop expecting and demanding the extraordinary. Why? Because it's easier and we are too exhausted from our frustration to seemingly throw any more effort after foolishness. We often fall back onto the territory that, it is easier to do it myself than it is to expect awareness, engagement, proactivity, and self-direction from others.

How many of us could claim that in professional circles we are constantly stumbling across amazing, talented, hard-working, absolutely impressive people? Ummm…almost never. In fact, when we do encounter someone who strikes us in this way, we are quite literally left in awe. It is truly an experience so rare and unexpected that it instantly becomes a topic of conversation. Having the pleasure of engaging with someone that is enthusiastic, professional and committed to delivering something of impressive value is quite literally a blog worthy event these days. Second-rate efforts in both life and work have somehow become the prevailing norm. Why are good people so hard to find? I certainly have my theories. I think part of it is that we've stopped believing that life can be extraordinary so we've stopped BEING extraordinary.

Add to this the reality that simply put, our lives, our relationships, our businesses cannot expand without help...good help. While historically we lived in tribes, clans and large extended families that offered cooperation and contribution, times, to be sure have changed and we now need to outsource our support system. If we want to prioritize our spouse, (or simply our sanity for that matter) chances are we need a baby sitter. I don't care if it's the warm arms of a willing grandmother or you're paying someone, this MUST be a part of your relationship life. DO NOT tell me you can't afford to have someone watch your kids one evening a week so you can have time with your significant other. The reality is you can't afford NOT to make this an absolute priority. If you are wanting a growing, thriving business, you are going to need incredible quality help. What that looks like to some degree depends on your need. For example, I HATE, and I mean truly LOATHE asking for "help." So while I well realize I have much to personally overcome in this department, I, personally, need someone who is incredibly attentive, self-directed and aware. To my way of thinking, if I notice something needs to be done...so should you. So I function best with someone who takes copious amounts of initiative and needs little direction. Greg on the other hand is astonishingly good at delegating. I honestly envy the ease with which he is able to direct others. He well realizes the absolute need to spend his time doing what ONLY he can do and is fantastic about insisting that his time be laser focused in this direction and no other. He doesn't flinch, compromise or equivocate...he understands where he needs help and insists on it.

The moral of the story is that we all need good help in various aspects of our life. It is unarguably essential to growth and abundance in ANY aspect of our experience and achievement. If we have lofty expectations for our life, our relationships and our business, it is more than fair to have elevated expectations of others. Any compromise you make here will only add disappointment and frustration to your days. The minute you surrender your ideals and expect less of your life, your relationships, your business, you will then get exactly what you deserve...less. We need to invite others into our world that are honest, hard-working, attentive, devoted and non-judgmental. If you feel as though every request you make of someone who works for you is being subjected to some sort of moral evaluation on their part, move on as instantly has humanly possible. If someone you hire takes it personally when you offer correction or instruction, you have the wrong person. The undeniable fact of the matter is that we are ALL in a constant state of learning, failing, growing and changing and if you hesitate to correct someone because you fret over whether they might take it personally you have some adjustments to make. Every day, I humbly learn lessons and discover through difficulty how to do and be better. So should anybody else you welcome into your world be exempted from this same journey? Of course not. In fact I would see it as a great disservice. We are all both teachers and students. Needing to share what we know and have learned so that others may benefit and ever and always open to the wisdom and changes our own life needs. Another requirement Greg and I share is the need to be efficient. Efficient in both work and communication. If you are moving through your day like your ass is on fire, you aren't going to blend well with someone who lacks a sense of focus and urgency. As well, we need the freedom to communicate economically. I realized in the past how much time I have wasted couching my requests. "When you have a minute…" "If you wouldn't mind…" "I know it's a hassle but could you…" We need to speak our need and move on during the course of the day. Having said that, I will also state that Greg and I place immense value on having a strong relationship with the people who work with us. For as much as we expect, we also have an impossibly deep appreciation for the essential role others play in our lives. The fact of the matter is we simply could not do what we do without them. We know it and we make sure they know how valued and appreciated they are. We are intimately connected to the lives and families of the people who have worked for us. And as we have placed such esteem and value on this relationship, we remain very involved with people even when they no longer work for us. If our care about one another goes no farther than a paycheck I truly believe we are selling ourselves horribly short of what can and should be.

To be sure, good help is indeed incredibly hard to find but we have a responsibility to persevere. If we desire joy, accomplishment, abundance and balance, none of us can fly this journey solo. Life does indeed take a village. While we could wallow is some sort of martyrish mindset that suggests we are somehow less capable or less able because we need help, I would strongly assert the opposite. I am of the firm opinion that we are giving far less than our best if we don't acknowledge, and understand that we all need incredible help in order to get about the business of what we are here to offer, accomplish and contribute. So whether it is something as simple as swapping out child-care with a friend so you can carve out some time for yourself and your spouse or you are hiring employees to help you grow and expand your business, we will never accomplish what we are capable of without the assistance and influence of others . We are all called upon to have outrageously high expectations for what we are capable of and can contribute. Similarly, once we demand this of ourselves and offer that to the world and those around us, we can and should expect an equal level of devotion to the extraordinary from those we surround ourselves with. It would be nothing short of shameful to settle or compromise on any front of your life. Demand the exceptional and extraordinary of yourself and also of others. Life and time are far too precious to spend our moments on anything less.

Going the Extra Mile…

Not exactly a novel, original and enticing thought. I don't think it's a stretch to agree on the general meaning of the phrase. The words imply our willingness to give something an extra, even unexpected, level of effort or dedication. A reasonably noble, if not uncommon concept. So what exactly got me thinking about this ideal? A Target™ parking lot.

Allow me to explain. So I'm leaving Target the other day after having acquired the prerequisite Valentine's Day paraphernalia for the kid's classroom celebrations. Quaint little cards for them to share with their classmates along with some other token of holiday cheer. In our case bubbles because I am so sick and tired of candy being the go to holiday accessory. But that's another story. As the kids and I were walking to our car, I couldn't help but notice that the parking lot was abundantly littered with shopping carts. They were absolutely everywhere! What gives?

Now I'm not referring to my noticing that those tidy little parking lot chutes meant to corral run-away carts were full. What caught my attention was the fact that those handy little drop zones were largely unoccupied while the rest of the parking lot was abundantly scattered with the unmistakable red carts. And all I could think to myself was, "what is wrong with people?" Is it REALLY too much to ask for you to walk twenty additional paces to put the cart where we all know it to belong? REALLY? And as we are currently living in Arizona, I can't even rationalize this with the inclement weather excuse. It's seventy five and sunny out people! Now if I had noticed one or two wayward carts, I can promise it would not have stirred my attention. But I stopped counting at fifty and started in thinking on what an infuriating statement this was about humanity. I know, I know, kind of heavy thinking for a Target parking lot. But I kept returning to my mental angst over the unmistakable and decidedly unpleasant statement this made. What is the statement? To put it, not so politely, it would appear that unless it is easy or convenient, most of us don't really give a shit. We're a bunch of slackers. Disturbingly lazy and unconcerned as a general rule.

While this might seem overly heavy on both assumptions and importance I would argue differently. Many of you have heard me profess my deep belief in the Truth that "what you are in anything, is what you are in everything." My kids have heard this declared so many times I am certain they roll their eyes in that charming beleaguered way when I'm not watching. But it is something I believe utterly and completely. You simply cannot convince me that this isn't profoundly true. Nobody has a house that belongs on an episode of Hoarders but runs a tidy, organized business. Nobody has a handshake agreement with honesty around friends and family but is rigidly ethical in the work place. Nobody can be void of compassion and caring for their fellow man but claim to offer this up with sincerity and abundance to their friends and family. No one can insist they are truly forgiving and genuinely accepting of others if they flog themselves with exacting judgment on a regular basis. Nobody can be a truly great guy at work and with his buddies, but go home and treat his spouse and kids with embarrassing indifference. You can't claim to be a loyal, listening girlfriend but not hear the heart your children need and want to share. If you are honest you are honest always. If you are compassionate, you offer it to all who are deserving. If you are principled, you abide by those ideals in all times and all spaces. And if you are too lazy to walk your shopping cart to its proper destination, I can guarantee you are universally lazy about your own life and generally selfish and unconcerned with others.

I would, in fact, go so far as to say that you could very nearly write a PhD thesis on this theory. If you were to interview those people who "returned" their carts and those who just left them sitting there in the adjacent parking spot, I would be willing to throw some money on the fact that strong patterns would indeed bear themselves out. Evidence would hold that those who went the "extra mile," or in this case the extra fifty feet to return a shopping cart, would be revealed to be the people that valued this effort and characteristic across the entirety of their life. They would prove to be more engaged, more considerate, more attentive, more aware and more financially successful by several fold.

I try valiantly to give a really wide and considerate berth to all kinds of people and personalities but I will unashamedly assert that two qualities that I simply cannot stomach under any circumstances are laziness and dishonesty. I readily admit those are two qualities I will never make allowances for in my life, or in those I surround myself with day in and day out. So I am convinced we should all live with great earnestness and regard for the fact that every single one of our choices reveal in both little and large ways something true and undeniable about each of us. The smallest actions on our part create perhaps unexpected, but undeniable ripples in our lives. None of us are perfect. But judging from the Target parking lot, many of us could try a whole lot harder.

The "Why" of it all…

Call it what you will. Your "Why," your Purpose, your Reason, your Calling. Regardless of the name you choose, what we all yearn for and relentlessly seek is the same. That essential connection to what we are meant to do and who we are meant to be and become. If there is one question, one quest, one search, frustration or excavation project that I most frequently encounter people in, it is that search for the part of themselves that feels "meant to be." It is our humanly desperate desire for a connection to Meaning that we know intuitively will deliver a certain sense of peace and purpose. The sensation that we have found our Why and that our lives, our time, our actions and activities all serve this inspired calling, is a craving that comes from our very essence…the soul of who we are and why we are here.

If this sounds overly metaphysical and is a little too woo-woo for you, then I contend that you have given up. That you have chosen to surrender to your circumstances and settle for a life that is good enough because you've stopped believing in the extraordinary. There is not a great thinker, leader, achiever or person of cause and consequence who does not know, with every fiber of their being, that in order to have a chance at an utterly spectacular life, you must first realize Why you are here and then go about passionately perusing that Reason. The knowing of our Purpose and a tireless commitment to it is an endlessly uplifting endeavor. We can accomplish other undertakings with excellence, but the effort will tax and drain us. Giving to and striving toward your Why can require unimaginable effort, but is wonderfully unique in that every ounce of effort you give, returns to your soul something of virtue and value. And this is a fuel, a power source that may require much but never takes. It fills and fires us with joy, intention, peace and immense satisfaction.

So what is a person to do if they know at the very seat of their soul that they are designed to live and contribute a very singular and unique purpose but struggle to find what, precisely that is? The truth of the matter is that most of us seem to be frantically trying to figure it out. I often come across people who live on the verge of near panic over the fact that in spite of all the seeking and searching, they don't know their Purpose. That this "Calling" this "Why" we speak of in such lofty, enlightened terms continues to endlessly elude them.

The answer is not to be found in the quest, but rather in the quiet. Each and every one of us owes it to ourselves, to our loved ones and to our Creator to earn an understanding of WHAT exactly we are here for. And in order to do that we must be still and quiet enough to listen. We must hear the "whispers" as our soul speaks to us. Many of us are so "busy" that the whispers must become a deafening roar before we hear what we are being called to do, to offer, to become. At times the "noise" goes beyond our perceived busyness. It is heard as overwhelm, responsibility, the judgment or expectations of others, self-doubt or lack of belief in what is truly possible. And what is possible is the deepest, most abiding sense of purpose, peace, drive, enthusiasm, connection, focus and ease imaginable. We cease to struggle with our time, our choices, and our emotions when we discover that which we are called to do.

To be sure this can be an evolution. When I was younger, I was consumed by all things equestrian. Horses were my life. They were everything I wanted to spend my time, my energy and my effort pursing. Your Purpose is that "thing" that delivers to you the greatest sense of joy and satisfaction. That effortless endeavor that you could labor at for endless hours and wonder where the time had gone. That work that for some perhaps undefinable, indescribable reason just feels right, worthwhile and simply makes you happy. After having kids my passions shifted. Being a wife and mother became, without a close second, the most important endeavors in my life. Not because they were supposed to be, or I felt obligated to them, but because THEY were now my most drawing, enticing, rewarding, and cherished commitments. I could have gotten stuck on the fact that my Purpose wasn't big enough, impressive enough, glamorous enough, or financially lucrative enough. But if I allow my mind to think on those concerns the consequence is that I no longer hear my heart. I know A LOT of people who accomplish simply for the sake of accomplishment. I have affectionately termed them the Mt Everest folks. When asked why they did that, accomplished this or achieved x, y, or z the answer amounts to some form of, "because it was there." Simply because the challenge and opportunity was in front of them, they took it on. To prove something? To be busy? To say, "Look what I did?" Perhaps all of the above, but these are all just reasons, they are not YOUR Reason.

There are MANY things that capture my interest and attention. Business and people intrigue me to no end. But I was recently reading a couple of books. The addendum to the classic, "Good to Great" by Jim Collins as well as Entreleadership by Dave

Ramsey. And while the content was fascinating for its own sake I found that most of what I was doing was drawing connections between the "business" principles they laid out and how exactly those notions would help me become a better wife, a better mother, a more focused and disciplined giver to what I absolutely know my Why to be. When we have found our path, EVERYTHING aligns to serve that undeniable cause.

Discovering your why is not easy. But it is the single most necessary job we have. Important and essential above all else. And when we relinquish the notions of what our Why SHOULD be, we will then hear, truly hear, what it IS. Then and only then can we give to the world the gift of our deliberate design for being here and our soul the unparalleled joy and satisfaction of knowing we have lived the life and the Purpose we were absolutely and undeniably intended for. Each and every one of us was made and meant to shine. Find your fire and with it, you will light the world.

Affluence and Influence...

While philosophically we could argue that Knowledge is Power, in this day and age it would seem more consistently true that Money is Power. And we could choose to wish and believe that the following chain of command is undeniable: Those who have Knowledge, earn the Money that garners the Power. But for better or worse, life and experiences have taught me that this would-be esteemed triumvirate of Knowledge, Money and Power is not the honored and impressive triad we would want and wish for. As often as not, those with money are dangerously reckless, and those with power tend to wield it either ruthlessly or foolishly and all too rarely, wisely. And while true Knowledge remains an admirable and untarnished asset, those with Money and Power often suffer from a precariously short supply of good sense. Case in point...Congress.

The fact of the matter is, I have struggled with this theme more than is sane, sensible or you could even remotely imagine. And if I am to offer a full and complete confession I believe that my inner turmoil around this entire topic stems from my Catholic upbringing. Now I want and need to make it abundantly clear that

44

this monkey on my back was not something taught or espoused by my loving parents. It was a message I absorbed from a little too much religious doctrine without the maturity, knowledge or good sense to pull it apart for the sake of understanding. Instead, I just heard and internalized a message that I have spent my entire adult life trying to shed and shake.

Many...too many of us, grew up erroneously internalizing thoughts such as "money is the root of all evil." Or that it is "easier for a camel to go through the eye of a needle than for a rich man to enter the Kingdom of God." (Mathew 19:23-26) or the generalized declaration that it is the "meek" who shall inherit the earth. The references could go on and on and these sentiments have reached beyond the pulpit into the general population as some warped way of either creating some false sense of virtue around the lack of material success or to allow insecurity to rule the day and vilify those who HAVE simply because you HAVE NOT. It has taken me a lot of years and a nearly rabid pursuit of knowledge and understanding to un-pack this nonsense and begin the tedious work of ridding my mind and my heart of this dangerously flawed dialog that has far too many of us in its burdensome and unrelenting grasp. My "Aha Moment" of sorts came when I discovered that in its origins the word "meek" meant "strength in service of something." It was applied initially to spirituality and religion as a call to those of Faith to throw their strength into the service of their belief. But like so many things, time and man's less than noble intentions have warped its meaning as well as our mindset.

Suffice it to say that I have done and will continue to do the work of internalizing a far different and infinitely more correct conviction and at the end of the day, what I know is this: Affluence undeniably creates Influence. Consider it as much a certainty as gravity or that chocolate is a food group. Now lest you get ahead of me, we will all agree that Influence does not REQUIRE Affluence. Beloved souls from Gandhi to Dr. Martin Luther King to Mother Theresa have led lives that testify to this truth. The pastor at our church has a wonderfully immense amount of influence but he would never claim to be affluent. Affluent or not, we each have a profound influence on our friends and families and those selfless souls who volunteer their time and energy to worthy causes also touch lives and hearts on a daily and enduring basis. However, everything from a church to the Red Cross needs funds to operate and do its good work so whether directly or in more subtle anonymous ways, we cannot deny that Affluence continues to have a hand in our ability to Influence. As we accept the undisputable truth that Affluence has always and will always create Influence, the dilemma becomes whether those who possess it are using it for good or more nefarious pursuits. Are those with Affluence creating The Gates Foundation or are they building the boiler room that defies every SPAM filter I can find and keeps finding ways to stuff my Inbox with everything from "Oprah's carb blocker" to Mail Order Brides to How to Have an Affair…and then get a good deal on windshield replacement. I often wonder where the world would be if these brilliant people applied themselves to something that uplifted humanity rather than offering…online…the quickest way to the gutter. So I view THIS as the single best argument for those ethical, principled, devout, strong and kind souls to shed any doctrine, fear or insecurity that has held them captive in order to achieve unbridled, unapologetic greatness so that THEY are the ones who will be sharing their light, their leadership, their voice, their insight and their Influence on the world.

I often listen to a radio program hosted by Dave Ramsey – a highly successful, hard-driving entrepreneur and also a devout Christian Man. And I had to laugh out loud as he railed about the sheer stupidity behind the vilification of success. To be sure, money is NOT the problem. The people who have it are the problem. As Greg so often astutely asserts, "if you were an a**hole before you had money you'll be an even bigger a**hole with money." Truer words never spoken and the solution lies within each and every one of us. The answer is not to shrink from success, but to aspire to it. The answer is not to malign wealth and privilege but to work your rear end off to acquire it. The answer lies in the fact that Affluence always has and always will create Influence. So at this point it is my firm belief that virtues of kindness, compassion, character, generosity and Faith will never cost a dime. But we all live in the same wondrous world where Affluence will continue to create opportunities for Influence so I can only hope and pray that the very best of you, that have the very most to offer, take on the challenge of becoming outrageously successful and use that gift to offer the world less of what it has and more of what it needs.

2 Corinthians 9:11

It's a fine line...

What's a fine line you ask? I well realize that many things are. But here I am speaking of that fine line between being Amazing and being an A**hole. Now these two ways of being sound like they should be worlds apart. As different as night from day, black from white or useless decaf from a full-octane cup of great coffee. But after much consideration I believe the truth is that they are so close to one another that aiming for awesome leaves one hovering precariously close to the alternative on a shockingly regular basis.

Interestingly, there is no grey area in our opinion about people. Most everyone we meet quite distinctly belongs in one camp or the other. They are either full-fledged awesome or a world class a**hole and we can't imagine one being within such easy striking distance of the other. But still I insist that in terms of personality, behavior, actions and expectations what separates the two is about as wide a chasm as a piece of dental floss.

How can one person be cocky and arrogant and another is admirably confident and self-assured? How is one warmly viewed as caring and concerned and another is a nosy busy-body? How can one person be appallingly devoid of any sort of tenderness or compassion but the other is our greatest advocate who pushes us relentlessly and uncomfortably toward becoming our best selves? How is one person possessed of immense wisdom while another is an impossibly annoying know-it-all? How does one person present as high and mighty and holier than thou while another has admirably high ethics and expectations? How is one parent a looming tyrant while another would classify as being principled and impressively involved? How can one person be lazy and unmotivated and another has reached the Zen state of living in the moment and realizing just how little they truly "need?" How can one person appear as polished, sophisticated and put together and another is shamelessly shallow and materialistic? How can one person possess the courage to share their heart, their struggles and their fears and another is experienced as being appallingly adept at manipulation and victimhood? How does one person advocate well and nobly for themselves and another is infuriatingly passive aggressive? How is one person loathsomely selfish but another is honoring their own unique spirit? As you see the list could be exhaustingly endless.

Are each of these things two sides of the same coin? No...not really. They are wildly different traits belonging to vastly different people so how and why do we come so solidly down on either one side or the other when it comes to our opinion of others? We don't consider someone to be primarily confident with a side order of arrogant. We somehow unequivocally decided and determine them to be one OR the other. So if there is indeed such a shockingly fine line separating one sort of person from another, is our estimation of those we meet or know mere whimsical folly? Or is there something else at play that allows us to determine just what our feeling about another is and should be? Is our assessment of each other fleeting and fickle or is there something more foundational guiding how we "feel" about those we encounter.

To be sure, a reasonable portion of how we experience and interpret another is based on our own personality and set of experiences. But that is merely a filter... I want the facts. WHO are you and WHAT are you made of? It is either woeful or wonderful...not both. So while I am certain that there have been many times where I myself have walked that razor's edge, I have knowingly risked being seen as one way for the hope of being experienced as another. I have thrown those dice time and time again in my life and I can only pray that on balance people have chosen to look most closely at and feel most deeply my Intentions. And therein lies the indisputable, unarguable difference. It is what makes us one sort of person or the offensive other when the difference between the two can seem a gnat's breath apart. The difference is Heart. I believe that we FEEL the heart space others are coming from. I believe we intuitively respond to our instinct around their INTENTIONS and it is from here that we view their ACTIONS. I believe we, on some unflinchingly gut level feel whether another is operating from a place of love, care and generosity or from some other distorted set of motivations.

So the infinitely more important element is not WHAT a person does, but WHO a person is. It is through the honest light of this lens that we may give ourselves permission to render a verdict. So while we should be exceedingly careful to avoid snap judgments and knee jerk reactions, I am convinced that if we listen to that still quiet voice within each of us...the language of one soul understanding another we will, so very rarely be wrong.

Keep your "Selfies" to yourself...

I feel quite certain that I am in a slightly sheepish minority on this subject, but I'm going to go out on a limb and simply say I don't get, "selfies." And as it was Greg's humor and similar curiosity that encouraged me to take this on, here I am, having a go at a phenomenon that, quite simply, escapes me. I realize that these informal, iPhone enabled pics are the calling card of any outrageously hip Facebook page, but I remain at a loss. With endlessly murmured concern over the rampant narcissism of upcoming generations, the dominance of the "selfie" would seem to suggest that perhaps our concern is well founded.

Now I well realize that on numerous fronts I would willingly and readily consider myself to be unapologetically "old fashioned." However, when even my fourteen year old daughter mentions that she just feels "weird" about taking them, I find some encouragement around the hope that perhaps I'm not as hopelessly counter-culture as I often feel. By way of acknowledging just how trend averse I am, I should mention that in 2012 Time Magazine considered the term "selfie" to be one of the "top ten buzzwords" of the year. As well, the term has gained entrance into the Oxford English Dictionary due to its undeniable place in our lives and culture. It is the undisputed darling of any reasonably with-it Facebook page or Instagram account. So the evidence would in fact suggest that my squeamishness around the proliferation of people taking pictures BY themselves and OF themselves is, indeed, ridiculous.

But here's the rub. I think that taking a picture OF YOURSELF, for purposes of relatively public comment and viewing is what's ridiculous. One cannot deny the somewhat absurd protocol of the Selfie. They all look relatively similar as the person IN the picture is taking the picture which leaves little room for anything that feels or looks elegant or uncontrived. Contrary to what devoted selfie takers would envision, studies have found that "posting photos of oneself (taken by oneself) correlates with lower levels of social support from and intimacy with...friends." Which one can only assume is the precise antithesis of what Selfie Masters are aiming to achieve. Allow me to go on record and say that snapping a picture of you AND A FRIEND, or with A GROUP where a moment in time and a memory is being logged in and savored...A-OK! I totally get it. Bravo for having the presence of mind to create a permanent record of something special, wonderful or just plain weird that can be both remembered by you and where the joy, laughter, spontaneity, beauty or wonder of a singular moment in time can be shared with others.

But still I wonder if the Selfie isn't just photographic evidence of being slightly self-absorbed. To my way of thinking a photograph should be something soulful and passionate. It is our singular way of capturing forever, a look, a moment, something we are seeing or experiencing that leaves us either slightly or immensely in awe. Photographs have always been a way to capture a fleeting glimpse of something romantic, inspired, humorous or just beautifully human. It has been something that tugs at our heart, moves our soul or captures our bliss. What of this is ever accomplished by holding a camera phone at arm's length and taking a shot of YOU, who knows where, for generally no good reason? Does a picture need to have a "reason?" Yes! It does! A photograph IS a reason. It is a reason to remember something of enduring value, importance or beauty. It is a reason to stop, to wonder, to experience and to share a moment of poignancy, worth and value. Any of us trying to take our own picture looking silly, sultry or anything in between is nothing short of over indulged nonsense. Are we needing applause and attention or are we simply doing it because everybody else is? Neither one resonates as a terribly impressive purpose. Now, one could rightly argue that I am taking something common and casual far too seriously and I could easily admit you are incredibly correct. But when I think on the way certain photos have captured my heart and made me FEEL, I cannot help but revere what I believe they can and should ever remain. A moment of life – perhaps anguish, or beauty, triumph, struggle or joy. It is hope, outrage, laugher or love captured in an eternal and tangible way. A photograph is a feeling…a memory, a part of our magical story, and I believe we are best to honor and esteem it as such.

A New Year...A New You...

While our house is still wearing the trappings of the Christmas Holiday (and will do so until the New Year), my thoughts, admittedly have already turned toward my hopes, wishes and grand intentions for the coming year.

I have never been one for New Year's Resolutions per se. More often than not they are far too capricious and lack the conviction that they so often deserve. Not a one of us is unaware of the monumental surge in the purchasing of gym memberships and Bow Flex machines only to have both collecting dust by mid-February. At that point your New Year's Resolution becomes a resolution to actually KEEP your resolutions. All nonsense aside, there is great value in a time which calls us to ponder, reflect and to give meaningful ATTENTION to our INTENTIONS.

All too often life feels more haphazard than it should. It becomes about our day to day reaction to situations and circumstances rather than a proactive plan that each day brings us closer to the life, the vision, the family, the business, the sense of Purpose and Meaning that we wish for each day to be filled with. I feel certain that every one of us is acquainted with the defeating frustration of having grand plans for any given day and before you know it, the clock is mocking you by late afternoon for the fact that you've gotten absolutely and utterly nothing done. But here's the deal; WISHING for our days and time to look and feel a certain way is as effective as trying to reason logically with a two year old. Much as I long for either one to work, neither of them do…ever.

So what is one to do? Stop wishing and start planning. Now I am not talking about planning for how to nurse the legendary hangover you are going to succumb to after your New Year's Eve festivities have regrettably gone too far. If we want to have our life FEEL a certain way, it is incumbent on us to decide and know what those ingredients are and then purposefully PLAN them into our day. If I realize that I think better and feel better if I've had some fresh air and exercise, it won't do me a damn bit of good to wish for that opportunity, I need to plan for it. I need to set my alarm, get dressed and to take that deep breath I desire. If I want my soulful connection with my spouse or significant other to thrive in deep and everlasting ways, that too requires a plan. Date nights, getting a sitter if need be, scheduling time to be together, to talk, to listen, to enjoy one another's company. None of this is wishing material. It is what is "given" to those who have created a sense of purpose and intention around claiming this for their life. If I want my family to reach for joy and adventure, this too takes a well-oiled plan. Any parent can vehemently attest to the fact that "we'll be right there," is a state of affairs that ceased to exist the minute you had kids. So if you want to be anywhere, participating in anything, you need a plan, extra diapers and a snack bag before even the smallest excursion has a chance of getting off the ground, or out of the driveway.

If you want your business to grow, to expand, to develop and to flourish, a detailed plan around precisely what you want and the meticulous steps you are going to take to get there are what you should be resolving to craft as your New Year's Resolution. What marketing materials do you need to create? What relationships do you need to seek out or continue to nurture? What innovative ideas are you going to at least try to have a go at? What do you need to spend time learning and mastering in order to build, evolve and create something of great value?

I have heard many times people take a pass on an opportunity because they "didn't have the money." Now this is not in any way trying to be disrespectful of all of us setting appropriate limits on what we can and should do. But time and time again, I see that what people are truly limiting is their own right to claim an experience, a memory, to foster a relationship or have a conversation that will return to them ten-fold the price they paid for such. Sometimes plans require a leap of faith on our part. A belief that what CAN be is the rightful dominion of those who understand the power of belief, determination and resolutely creating what you want, not wishing for it. Having any part of our life be extraordinary requires relentless intention and purpose. Wishing may get you a Barbie Doll or Lincoln Logs on your seventh birthday, but crafting a life of endlessly spectacular opportunities and experiences requires more than candles. It requires unwavering commitment.

So while I whole heartedly believe in and am in favor of spontaneous joys, a life well, and fully lived is anything but. It is the product of faith, belief, a sense of Purpose and a Plan to set you toward your heart's desire. This New Year's, resolve to be intentional about your life and what you want. The incredible journey you will then claim just may astonish you.

"The sooner you start planning your life, the sooner you will live the life you dream of."
Hans Glint

Speak Up or Shut Up

It can be a daunting question to say the least. When are we safely within our rights and within a realm that would warmly welcome our sage like insights and input? And when are we in that No Go Zone that should have caution tape and flashing red lights around even the notion that our thoughts or opinions might be welcomed? And to complicate matters further, under what circumstances do we throw caution to the wind and put our thoughts and feelings out there simply because it's important to do so and forego the mental wrestling match over whether or not our words and actions are invited, appreciated or appropriate?

While I can and will readily throw out a disclaimer that each and every situation is different, I do believe that some set of principles or guidelines around the matter are necessary for ourselves and our sanity. Analyzing every circumstance and situation is a dangerously flawed policy that could drive anybody's sanity to the harrowing point of either an explosion or a full scale meltdown. I'm a firm believer that both can and should be avoided at all cost.

So what is one to do? Create categories. I think that whether we realize it or not we put our diverse relationships into various and sundry classifications. We have mere acquaintances that we see very occasionally and sporadically. These are not people we proactively spend time with but occasionally stumble across at the company picnic or bump into at the grocery store. In this case, keep your opinions about their obnoxious kids you met at the picnic and the bad beer in their grocery cart to yourself. Your thoughts are neither warranted nor welcome so your only task in this instance is to be polite and move on allowing yourself to feel only slightly smug about your darling children and organic produce.

The only addendum that would apply here, whether someone is intimately familiar to you or an utter and complete stranger, is that if you see or are aware of something that flies in the face of decency, honesty and ethics, you have a moral imperative to "speak up." And speaking up doesn't mandate full scale fisticuffs. Neighbors of ours that are dear friends were sharing a story about being paired up on the golf course with another couple. The husband of this other couple was loudly and unabashedly insulting and berating his wife. In that instance, several options are open to you: you could take this guy out the woodshed, so to speak, and give him a full scale "come to Jesus," or you could make a more subtle, but infinitely powerful choice just as they did. They told this couple they couldn't play with them any longer and left the game and the golf course. I am reasonably certain their quiet yet obvious disgust spoke volumes to the caveman they had been paired up with. Regardless of your approach, in situations of unarguable wrongdoing, the world needs more courage than is commonly seen.

With a business partner, I believe the exact opposite is in order. While most partnerships go down in blinding flames, I am convinced that one of the ways to guard against the fate of most is an uncommon level of candor and transparency. As one of my favorite authors points out, "there is no such thing as a firewall between business and personal relationships." The two are inescapably woven together. And a partnership of this sort

58

counts so strongly on the performance of everyone involved that forcing yourself to believe that a business partner's personal life is "none of your business" is a declaration that will prove to be foolish at best and disastrous at worst. I believe that once you cross the threshold into this sort of relationship, nearly everything is fair game and your ideas, thoughts, opinions, concerns and suggestions, should be voiced with care and compassion and without risk of punishment or penalty. For example: If a business partner drinks to excess every time you get together with clients for a dinner meeting, this needs a discussion. If your business partner's SPOUSE over imbibes regularly, this too is beyond relevant and can and should be addressed. No such discussion should need to be tiptoed around for fear of being met with defensiveness or hostility. If this doesn't seem "fair" I would highly suggest a sole proprietorship.

Now where family and friends are concerned the situation becomes far more nuanced, tricky and riddled with unfortunate uncertainty. And so this is where laying claim to both the courage and the confidence in your convictions becomes absolutely, unequivocally necessary. If you see a family member once or twice a year they fall into the first category. They are a genetic "acquaintance" and those rules around holding your tongue, you must forcibly apply. If however you really and truly have a relationship with another, be it friend or family, your thoughts and opinions should come from a place of love and care and should be welcomed as such whether they are pleasant to hear or as difficult to swallow as that worm someone dared us to eat when we were eight. I believe that the highest calling of any relationship we hold dear is that it inspires us to our best selves and challenges us along the way to do so and be so. If you are afraid to disagree with someone for fear of it harming the relationship, you do not, in fact, have a relationship. By definition any true connection we share with another has essential elements of honesty, integrity and forthrightness. It is a place where our thoughts, our feelings, our imagination and exquisite ideas are welcomed with warmth and precious safety. It is also a place where we are called upon to welcome the wisdom of others for how it can shape us into far better people than we would otherwise become.

Now this is not license to tell your sister-in-law that her house resembles a disastrous drop zone for garage sale caliber crap. Nor is it permission to tell a friend that a Ford Pinto would have gotten better mileage than his latest business idea. Honesty is essential but so is tenderness and compassion. Offer to help your sister-in-law clean up the house or to host a strategy session with experienced business owners for your friend. . Having said that, we all know people who just need to put on their big boy pants, stop whining and complaining and just get about the business of doing and being better. Still, we all have a far easier time with change when suggestions are served up with encouragement rather than condemnation and our heart senses compassion rather than criticism.

So this Christmas, give yourself the gift of Freedom of Speech. The freedom to share your thoughts, your ideas, your inspirations and opinions. And give others the gift of your willingness to listen with an open heart, an open mind and a realization that there is great Wisdom every one of us has yet to unwrap.

Thanks for nothing!

For much as I am loathe to admit it, we all seem to fall into that state of mind so easily these days. Where notions of want, scarcity and a focus on everything we lack over all that we love seem to hold unreasonable sway over our hearts and minds. It's almost as though modern society with all of its relentless suggestions toward everything we need and simply MUST have, locks us in a covetous vice grip that only the most deeply soulful and self-aware people manage to avoid or escape.

It is so dreadfully easy to slip into thoughts and feelings of everything we lack and all we desire and feel we deserve that an ever present awareness and sense of abiding gratitude is as rare an occurrence as my children acting civilly in the grocery store. Both are alarmingly uncommon.

I was reading an article in a magazine the other day about teaching our over-indulged, entitled children to be grateful. While I cannot argue the need for gratitude, I most certainly do not believe that we should be pointing the finger solely at these unappreciative, spoiled brats we are all raising. As any child well knows, "it takes one to know one." I think as many adults share this affliction as children. And generally speaking, when I have the unmistakable pleasure of running across a less than charming child, their parents are more often than not equally delightful. To be sure, kids are almost instinctively self-absorbed. It's simply part of their learning curve. But the question is, if they are in the process of learning, what are we in the process of teaching? Do we readily and reflexively show, express and model gratitude? Do we speak of how blessed we are or do we whine about what we want? Do we outwardly resent what we don't have or very consciously speak of our good fortune? Do we realize that "good fortune" is not to be found in the stuff we have, but the people we love, the laughter we share, the memories we savor, the relationships we treasure as a wealth beyond riches?

I could not with a straight face or sound conscience insist that I am not personally as shamefully guilty as the next person of allowing my thoughts to be high-jacked into dwelling on how I "wish" things were. Constantly delaying my sense of happiness to some undetermined point in the future at which time all the stars will line up and I will, at long last, be content. But each and every day I go to battle against my own reflexes that insist I will be happy when… For all of us, "when" is now and gratitude is a state of mind not something we will at long last feel when we arrive at some life destination or find a Porsche in the driveway. Don't get me wrong, I don't think any of us would have our feelings hurt by a sports car in the driveway, but true Gratitude is, in every way, an inside job. It is a soulful awareness concerning what matters. What really, truly matters. Life, love, faith, health, joy, laughter, family and friends.

The pastor at church last Sunday had me laughing out loud as he recounted how he would have these moments where he would peek into his children's rooms when they were sleeping, and the awareness of just how impossibly blessed he was would literally overwhelm him. Then he acknowledged that we all experience that tidal wave of love and how infinitely precious our children are...when they are asleep. All kidding aside, gratitude isn't just what we experience when all is well. Gratitude isn't getting a screaming deal on a flat screen TV or the "It" Chanel handbag. It is a deep and soulful knowing that carries us through the storms of life without being doubted or diminished. It is what centers our heart, our soul and our joy. It is where we rest in the Grace that is ever and always ours for the taking.

So in the spirit of Thanksgiving, I will thank all of you who have taken the time to allow my wayward thoughts, opinions and notions to cross your mind. As "time is at once the most valuable and perishable of all our possessions," I feel humbled and honored that you would take the time to read my thoughts and to occasionally share yours. It is and always will be an honor and a privilege to hopefully reach your mind, touch your heart and share the stories of the journey we are all set upon.

Judgmental or Just Opinionated?

It can be hard to discern the difference really. And never more so than when trying to evaluate ourselves and our own generally above reproach behavior. We are all endowed with an expert ability to pass ready verdicts on how other people conduct themselves and deem them either amusingly opinionated or downright judgmental. The latter is most commonly paired with an ever so appealing heavy dose of hypocrisy. Lovely really. So how do we best cast on honest eye on our own performance while at the same time being mindful in a fair yet, unapologetic way about the conduct of others that we are related to, interact among or concern ourselves with? It is no easy task, but I do believe it's a worthy one.

In making the initial distinction, it is essential to go on record with the perhaps subtle, but ever so important difference between opinion and its nefarious relation, judgment. There can be no doubt that I have plentiful opinions. I have opinions on everything from topics that weigh in with an enormity of importance such as relationships and raising kids, to whether one should choose paper or plastic at the grocery store. But bear in mind that MY opinions are MY views. My thoughts, preferences and ideals based upon my experiences, my history, my desires and my values. They belong to me and I consider myself fully entitled to own and exercise them. We ALL have a right to our personal inclinations and opinions. Where we risk falling in with the Dark

Side is when we decide we have the implicit right to judge another person as being good or bad, righteous or wrong-minded, worthy or scorned based on our ever present opinions. By way of example I have VERY strong opinions about the best, most impacting and loving way to raise kids. And while every single day I come up short, my opinions about how it SHOULD be done rarely waver. HOWEVER, the minute I begin to judge another parent as being good or bad, devoted or displaying lack-luster commitment because they aren't approaching it MY way, I have made an awful and unwelcome leap. There are nearly as many "right" ways to parent as there are kids needing parenting. To be sure, there are some unarguable truths and principles that apply across all time and space. Unconditional Love, care, boundaries, affection and devotion are essentials. And yes, I will gladly go on record and say that certain things are not matters of opinion but just flat-out wrong. Any parent that drives in a car smoking a cigarette with a child held captive in the back seat is a complete moron. No if's and's or opinions about it. But I digress. Yet precisely how we go about implementing the "givens" is a path entirely of our own choosing. I have every right in the world to my opinions and I never have and never will be bashful about voicing them. But once I cross into that realm of believing in some sort of misguided entitlement to pass judgment on another for their behaviors, their choices, their way of doing things, I have made a grave mistake indeed.

Extended family relationships can be the stickiest and trickiest of all. As one of four kids I often marvel to the point of near disbelief over how all of us raised in the same household, with the same parents could evolve into such astonishingly different people. Without question I see the same baffling reality revealing itself in the dramatic but precious differences in each of our own kids. But still we can revel in and enjoy being decidedly different. We CANNOT however decide that because we are different, one is right and the other can be carelessly labeled as wrong. There are people in my life that I love deeply and have little to nothing in common with. My opinions on how to live, be, act, care and conduct myself couldn't be more at odds with their own. I can find them frustrating, disappointing and at times see little in them that I esteem or wish to emulate. But still Judgment is not my job. We could all, at many points along the way stand a hearty helping of humility; the awareness that we are allowed our thoughts, ideas and ideals, but we are not allowed to render a verdict about someone else's worthiness. It's quite a relief really to acknowledge that coming to endless conclusions about others simply is not our job. As our oldest daughter's science teacher, a former Navy Seal sagely shared in chapel the other day. "Everybody is fighting a battle you know nothing about." Having said that, we all are fated to know our share of people who are not of this mind. The ones who gossip, condemn and criticize and more often than not, they are blind to their own hypocrisy. In these situations, my best advice is steer clear. Love them from afar perhaps but drawing them close and allowing them meaningful access to your life is a wager that must be made with extreme caution. The irony here is that I am most drawn to people with strong and deeply convicted opinions. People who have lived life, taken their lumps, learned, laughed and purposed to love through it all. I don't need people around my dinner table who AGREE with me. I desire people who are bold enough to think, to share, to weigh in and take a stand, ever and always with a spirit of humility, fairness and open-minded endless discovery. I downright adore people who can share their thoughts as freely as they are willing to listen and consider the wisdom of others. This is opinion. Judgment is the person who storms out of the room declaring everybody else to be complete idiots; hopelessly lacking and offensively flawed. Hmmm...Don't let the door hit you on the way out.

I believe Jack Karouac said it most brilliantly: "the only people for me are the mad ones, the ones who are mad to live, mad to talk, mad to be saved, desirous of everything at the same time, the ones who never yawn or say a commonplace thing, but burn, burn, burn like fabulous yellow roman candles exploding like spiders across the stars."

Be full of life, full of opinions, full of compassion, mistakes and soulful experiences. But leave the judgment to the only One who ever has been, or ever will be, qualified for the job.

Ready or not, here it comes…!

I'm honestly not sure when Halloween became such a big damn deal. Now this isn't a miserly comment, but rather a truly curious one. When I was a kid we bought those Halloween costumes that came in a simple box. Character of choice with cheap plastic mask included. In the here and now, people dress their dogs in more elaborate costumes than we wore and I'm not even kinda kidding. These days it would seem that most parents contact the American Actors Guild and hire a wardrobe consultant in order to properly attire their offspring. And proper Halloween attire seems to imply a strange game of one-ups-manship with parents spending a paycheck on wildly elaborate costumes that could do a turn on Broadway without seeming amateur or out of place. Now I run the risk of sounding bitter because I simply can't compete (and have no desire to really). What really sends me into a tailspin is when I see these STUNNING costumes that some wildly gifted and creative mom actually MADE. With her own two hands! On something called a sewing machine! Coming from a woman who quite literally couldn't even sew on a button, my level of awe in these circumstances is immeasurable. So while I am insanely impressed with the creativity and dedication that these gifted mom's put in to create these works of Art for the Halloween festivities, I STILL don't know when this began. Clearly I missed the undeniable transition between the silly get-ups we ALL wore as kids and over the top wardrobes that now wander the streets on Halloween night.

Now I am all in for any Holiday. I adore tradition and celebration. And yes, I have an Anna from Frozen in the house. Toothless is also making an appearance and we found something really cute at a second hand store for the youngest. I've already played my hand and shared that I don't spend a mint on costumes and I couldn't hand-make a costume if one of my kids decided they wanted to be a paper bag for Halloween. BUT rest assured I do have standards. Our oldest, at thirteen is right on the cusp of wanting to participate in the festivities, but not wanting to approach it like a "kid" either. So she tells me that she is going trick-or-treating as "Pajama Girl." Excuse me? What or who exactly is that? "Well I'm going to wear my pajamas and just make a cape." Hmmm. How delightfully imaginative of you. And the answer is…not a chance. For as much as I'm not in the camp of astronaut costumes that actually include a space pack and princesses riding real, live horses for Halloween, my take is that if you're going to participate in the Holiday, you need to respect the Holiday.

I felt compelled to share with her the insider information that every adult passing out Halloween candy on that bewitching night who has some slouchy teen show up at their door in their football jersey calling it a costume wants to slam the door in their face. You aren't cool and you certainly aren't cute. I mean really. Why don't you just walk into Safeway on any given day and ask them for a Snickers bar? It's essentially the same thing. If you aren't willing to make the effort to partake in the Holiday as it was intended…don't bother. Trick or treating in your pajamas, jersey or gym shorts doesn't count. Long story short, she is feverishly trying to come up with Plan B.

That little rant aside, October seems to mark the beginning of an all-out Holiday Marathon. It begins in early October with our pilgrimage to the pumpkin farm of choice and doesn't let up until we find ourselves utterly exhausted, frazzled and flat broke by the time we crawl our way to the finish line known as New Year's Eve which mercifully brings the marathon to a drunken close. Every single year, I vow to discover the ways and means to do a better job. To prioritize better, to be more mindful and less frantic. To focus on intention, meaning and memories instead of merchandise. And every year I fail epically. BUT, I refuse to give up. There is a way and I am bound and determined to find it. But my point as we stare down Halloween night is that the Holidays are not about who can do the entire Season more brilliantly. Who can manage it all with seamless, and enviable panache? Who can make it all appear effortless and easy? Who can make it look like their house fell out of a Pottery Barn catalogue and their dinners would make the editors of Bon Appetit Magazine drool with culinary envy. Again, please don't misunderstand me. I am downright crazy for this stuff. It would literally be a dream come true to have the design team from Pottery Barn show up at my house and say, "don't worry, we got this." So what I am hoping we all, myself more than anyone, can keep in mind during this precious time is the heart of the matter. And the heart of the matter is Moments. Shared with those we love and care about. It is those things and only those things that will endure long after the candy has been eaten, the pies have been baked and the gifts have been unwrapped and outgrown. May the magic and wonder of the impending Season belong to you and yours and wish me good luck in finding the same. I'll need it.

You want MORE!???!

So Greg and I are recently returned home from a yearly event in Las Vegas that akin to last years' experience was inspiring, humbling, uplifting, demanding, enlightening, edifying and soulful. There is simply no possible way I could select a singular message expressed, story shared or challenge spoken that was more moving and impacting than the one which came before. Yet in the midst of it all I find myself dwelling on certain truths more than others. One presentation that will neither soon, nor ever be forgotten, came from an NFL football player who spoke in impassioned terms about our desperate need for gratitude. Deep, abiding, ever-present gratitude.

Through little fault of our own we have been conditioned to feel as though we exist in a perpetual state of scarcity. That we are always lacking that which somebody else is thoroughly enjoying and we most certainly need. Our house isn't big enough, our car isn't flashy enough, our job isn't impressive enough, our kids aren't Abercrombie enough, our dog isn't pure bred enough, our vacations aren't exotic enough, our hair isn't thick enough or blonde enough, our clothes aren't designer enough, our food isn't organic enough, our bodies aren't thin enough, our opportunities aren't abundant enough, our expectations aren't met enough, and our lives aren't Reality TV enough. So to hear someone with deep conviction and a humbling level of candor say, "ENOUGH!" To be taken to task in the most brilliant, earnest manner and asked to hear that voice that has given us SO much say, "You want MORE?!" is cause for some uncomfortable but essential reflection.

Interestingly this isn't a call to settle for your lot in life or to be content with the hand you were dealt. Rather it felt like a beautiful directive to work, to strive, to persevere, to overcome and to set your sights on achieving your God-given purpose. All the while realizing we need to spend FAR more time feeling blessed and FAR less time feeling slighted, deprived or wronged. A question of this utter, if uncomfortable importance has the unavoidable side-effect of insisting that I evaluate myself in this manner and take a true, unedited look at others in my life and wonder at how I work my way through the world and to weigh the level of giving and gratitude I both offer as well as surround myself with. Because I think that to some degree, a mind-set of scarcity and "what about me?" is woefully contagious. If we keep company with self-indulgent, entitled people, we tend to take on those charming characteristics. On the flip side, if we surround ourselves with generous, appreciative people how can we help but to try to rise to their impressive and enlightened standard?

Speaking personally it can be a tremendously unsettling realization to find that people we love are not necessarily loving. An odd and unnerving turn of events to be sure. It can be strangely difficult to acknowledge that those unexpected others, who come from a more giving spirit deserve the most lauded places in our lives. Why? Because they have earned it through gratitude, giving, selflessness, enduring appreciation and their powerful example and influence on our lives and hearts. We simply must surround ourselves with people who can be truly deeply happy for us in times of great joy. We should purpose to surround ourselves with those who are able to, regardless of situation or circumstance, "do the next loving thing." We need to plant the seeds of our potential among those who encourage our gratitude rather than our greed, and easy tendency toward being a bit too self-indulgent. We stand our best chance of our best selves if we are in the midst of those who refuse to pander to our shortcomings but rather insist that we are capable of MORE. Of wanting more? No. Of BEING more? Absolutely.

This is certainly not a call to expunge from our lives those who struggle with generosity and gratitude. The reality is we ALL struggle with it ALL the time. But let's just call a spade a spade. Some people we know and love are admirable examples of a life driven by the purpose and intention of whole hearted encouragement and giving. Others whom we also know and love will continue to vex us with their inability to see things from our own, recently acquired, Gandhi like level of enlightenment. But we stay the course. We continue, no matter what, to do the next loving thing. We work tirelessly to be the sort of person that doesn't constantly want MORE but tirelessly gives MORE. And yes, this could well be the most thankless job in the Universe. Giving in a world that takes. Loving in a world that looks out for itself. And finding our way toward a spirit of Gratitude rather than the endless chant of "what about me?" All too often I have been inwardly humiliated over reflexively indulging my own woes, struggles and troublesome "problems." Fortunately for us all, there are those stronger souls who continue to show us a better way.

I feel impossibly blessed to not just have heard the message but to have those beloved examples in my own life who remind me not to want more, but to become more than I could have been had they not been tenacious enough to let me learn from their unwavering example. They possessed both the courage and conviction to expect more of me than I was, or could ever have been without them.

Is your YES really a YES?

For reasons I cannot explain, I seem to be on a roll lately of experiences where people commit to something and then, generally at the eleventh hour, decide to take a pass. Having this happen occasionally is one thing but the frequency with which this seems to be happening lately leaves me wondering if we don't have some sort of odd epidemic on our hands.

Now I fully realize that life is dynamic. Emergencies arise. Plans change and shit happens. But it would seem of late that people will commit to something and then cancel not because of some unexpected emergency or semi-catastrophic act of nature, but simply because it is mildly inconvenient or something better came up. Please realize that this complaint coming from me is more than a bit surprising. Generally speaking I am bizarrely easy going about such things. For as much as honesty requires me to admit that nobody has ever described me as "easy going," I am, in these jurisdictions of life shockingly laid back. I couldn't care less if somebody is late as being late is, I believe, part of my personal genome. I am generally unperturbed by a cancellation, a change in plans or the need to accommodate things that invariably come up. So the fact that I, of all people, am looking at the alarming frequency of people bailing out on their commitments truly must mean that the situation has reached critical mass.

Now Greg is an absolute stickler around issues such as timeliness and follow-through. If he says he is going to be somewhere at 9:00 you can set your watch by his unwavering punctuality. Similarly I don't believe that I have EVER seen him cancel on a professional commitment of any sort. So his adamancy in such things and the way I have learned to count on him because of it, provides an exceedingly sharp contrast to the less than impressive level of commitment that people seem to have to their pledges of performance these days. Perhaps we are getting our language mixed up? If you were to say, "Yes," I'm going to do that, should that be more loosely interpreted as, "yes, I'm going to do that as long as I don't need to feed my goldfish instead that day?" I well realize this sounds sarcastic, but it really has gotten that bad. It would seem that the most minor obstacle, impediment or alternate interest is enough to have us completely bail on the people that, crazy as this sounds, are actually counting on us. And no, they probably aren't counting on us to donate a kidney, but that's not the point. These days, I'd take the unbreakable pinky promise of a child over the commitment of most adults.

As a devout believer in the philosophy that "what you are in anything is what you are in everything," you cannot convince me that if a person, a friend, a family member, a co-worker or any person in your life, is willing to bail on a small commitment, chances are that placing your confidence in them on the big stuff is a less than astute idea. Which kind of leaves me at times wondering with impassioned eloquence, WTF? When did yes stop being yes and actually become, "I'll pencil it in loosely. Very loosely." When did "I'll be there," begin to consistently carry the caveat, "unless something else… anything else, comes up." When did our pledges and promises become these watered down, subject to change without notice, placations that carry no weight, no meaning, and no substance? I'm not sure if it's just that we believe we're too busy or that it is somehow justifiable for us to change plans on a whim with little to no regard for the impact our lack of follow-through has on others. But the bottom line is that I believe we need to course correct. I think we all want to be able to count on others. To be able to truly lean on and put weight on their commitment and intentions. And if we want that in others we MUST give that which we desire. No excuses, no small print, no exceptions or exclusions apply. If you say YES...make it matter.

Life will continue to throw all of us the occasional curve ball and we are all obligated to allow for that. But day in and day out, our word needs to become our bond once more. It needs to take on the gravity of being something precious, important and sincere. As people we all need to surround ourselves with those we can count on and believe in. It is what we need to HAVE and so it is what we need to DO without fault, failure or compromise. When our word is compromised, so too is our integrity and I can think of few things more worthy or deep regard and respect than knowing that you are one of those rare and wonderful few that someone else can count on...no matter what. It may not be easy, free spirited or spontaneous but a devotion to, "no matter what," is something that should absolutely matter to us all.

Where have all the good men gone?

Now lest you think I am taking a bizarre foray into some commentary on the state of dating, match making and the like, allow me to assure you that I am leaving such things to the impressive panel of experts on reality TV. This query is around my occasionally desperate pursuit of true, noble, and effective leaders which seem to be as rare and illusive as black eyed tree frogs. (Yes, I had to look up the world's most endangered species.)

In truth, my interest is a universal one that applies to both men and women alike. I harbor a more than mild curiosity around what seems like an alarming lack of strong, determined, relentlessly principled leaders among us. This isn't a discussion about our general goodness as people or our collective or individual character. Leadership, is an entirely different, and infinitely more complicated proposition. Are leaders born or are they made? Are leaders situation dependent or are some people wired for the role across all times and spaces? Can we learn to be leaders or are those qualities innate? Is leadership based on a specific set of individual traits or rather on individual behaviors? This discussion could become highly academic, but we can set aside all of the various studies, approaches and models and return to the original question. Where HAVE all the good men gone? Have we just gone soft? Is there no longer a pressing need amidst our relative ease for powerful and passionate leaders? I personally believe our need is perhaps greater than it has ever been.

A pessimist I certainly am not, but our government is largely run by self-serving, less than idealistic individuals. Many of our companies our being run by a bunch of crooks with aspirations that rarely extend beyond wealth and power. Our media unashamedly serves its own self-interest. Our health-care system is a bureaucratic mess of unfathomable proportions. Problems are solved with law suits rather than level-headedness. Our schools have a habit of drumming out devoted and passionate teachers in favor of a system that serves a self-important administration first and the kids it is tasked to educate last. Divorce, dysfunction and distance seem to define our homes and families. Have we stopped caring? I don't believe so. But we most certainly have stopped leading.

I cannot claim to know the root causes of this dangerously pervasive apathy. Are we simply afraid? Are we indifferent? Have we forgotten how to do everything from taking a bullet to taking the blame? Are we so averse to conflict that we continue to nod politely or altogether ignore injustice? Are we afraid to take a stand for fear of judgment and ridicule or is it just too damn much work to be principled when we're already constantly overwhelmed? We could ask questions and argue the answers until I see a Unicorn in my back yard, but the fact remains. WE have stopped leading and because WE have stopped doing the work, our children don't stand a chance of learning how to take on a responsibility we have largely abdicated.

Many of you have suffered through my rants about phrases such as, "she doesn't work she stays home with the kids." But this is where empowerment begins. With mothers realizing they are, in fact, leading their family and their children's growth, development, self-esteem and sense of purpose. With fathers realizing they must be leaders in thought, in principles and ultimately in devoted action. We need to teach the lessons that life is about oh so much more than the bottom line, the cars in the garage, the titles you hold or the technology you have mastered. We are not defined by our "likes" on Facebook or our following on Twitter. We are all ultimately defined by WHO we are, HOW we act, and the COURAGEOUS choices we were brave enough to make.

All too often we confuse leadership with grand acts of extraordinary valor. But leadership is as simple and profound as how we treat our spouse, how we love our children, how we set an example, how we treat a stranger. Leadership is as simple as a spoken concern, a card, and an act of simple caring. Leadership is about the right choice not the easy choice. It is about honesty, integrity and unwavering compassion. Leadership is not about what we manage to do, it's about embracing what we're capable of. Leadership is simply standing in the gap and insisting that IT matters. That it ALL matters and every act of common courage is endowed with the power to change the world just a little bit. Leadership is about being responsible for the choices we make, the lives we touch and mark that each of us chooses to make every single day. Leadership is understanding that we don't live in a world where some things matter, we live in a world where EVERYTHING, oh so beautifully matters. Leadership doesn't mean, "I can," it means "I will." I will care. I will love. I will believe. I will endure. I will be strong. I will be tender. I will embrace with honor that fact that every day, I make a difference. And every day, without pause or excuse I will take on the beautiful burden of knowing it is within me to either linger in complacency or lead the way toward resolve and Purpose. If we dare to choose the latter, we aren't just leaders, we may very well be Heroes.

HELP is a four letter word…

I can't claim to know what percentage of people suffer from this affliction, but I know it isn't just me. The affliction that through some warped logic would have us bleed to death before asking for a single Band Aid, starve to death before asking for so much as a pack of Skittles, or exhaust ourselves physically, mentally or emotionally before we would utter a whimper for anything that even hints of help from others. The irony is that often times those who are most averse to asking for help find the greatest joy in offering it. Perhaps it is the fact that it has great meaning to them. Perhaps it is a nature that defines sharply around giving and "taking." Admiring the former and condemning the latter. Is our uneasy relationship with help just pride run amok? Perhaps. But I'd like to think it is more complicated than that. At this point I relatively, sort of, kind of firmly believe that personal temperament, upbringing and culture are all part of a somewhat sinister triad that leaves many of us with this ridiculous disorder. And yes, most of us who are plagued with an aversion to assistance can be solidly classified as ridiculous.

Why? Because the last time I checked I didn't have a red cape tucked away in a phone booth, a closet or anywhere else I might care to look. I don't have super powers, a magic wand, pixie dust, a bat mobile, bionic body parts or any other hocus pocus that might negate my need for help. In other words, I'm human. Frustratingly, humbly, wonderfully human. And that means that none of us were made or meant to go it alone. We are designed for connection and to care for one another, but our overall admirable, but occasionally errant culture has, I believe, led us a bit astray.

We place such regard on independence, self-sufficiency and the lingering frontier spirit which shaped us, that it is hard to separate these notions of strength, self-sufficiency and independence, from the qualities that nurture our spirit and connection to one another. Add to that a relatively modern ideal that equates help with weakness and we're more or less doomed. Doomed to suffer in some level of self-imposed isolation because of our refusal to reach out, and allow others in. As such, my self-defined virtue of being an exceedingly giving person was abruptly taken to task when I read in a Brene Brown book that we cannot GIVE without judgment of others if we cannot ASK without judgment of ourselves. What!?! Do you mean that I am judging others that I "help" because I would judge myself for "needing help?" Yep. And allow me to save you the time of refuting the claim or arguing its truth. I've tried…and failed.

To some degree I have passed on the burden of my wiring to those around me. Literally telling people, "you know I won't ask, so don't make me." Suggesting that they intuitively know what I need and respond of their own volition rather than require of me a nearly impossible to utter request. Now, I firmly believe that when we truly care for others, we instinctively know their need. But mind readers we are not. And I would love to arrive at a place where we ALL view care and compassion as a gift which is required to be both given AND received. As a result I have personally chosen to expunge the word HELP from my vocabulary. I don't HELP anybody. Instead, I am allowed the JOY of being part of their lives. If I am watching my little "granddaughters," I'm not helping their mom, I'm being allowed the spectacular gift of time spent with them. If I am allowed the opportunity to lean in and "help" a friend, I don't see this as anything I am doing for their sake, I embrace it as something they are allowing me to do for OUR sake. Because the more I am allowed to DO in the relationship, the more we receive FROM the relationship. Is this terminology ban necessary for all? No, but my condition is excruciatingly severe.

Personally I think this is especially problematic when it comes to raising children. Sociologically we were never meant to live in nuclear families. We were meant to be part of tribes, clans and extended support systems where work and responsibilities were shared. And without that framework we are fated to be exhausted, overwhelmed and miserable unless we allow other people to pitch in and be part of our world, our rhythm and our lives. We are all better for relationships being bound to our hearts and lives and true connection with others requires both the ability to give and the courage to need. As a person who has lived my entire life being fiercely independent, it is a tremendous but necessary leap for me to discard my view of needing "help" as revealing some weakness or shortcoming on my part, but to rather see it for what it is. A beautiful, vulnerable, and utterly necessary part of any true, deep and intimate relationship. Are there people on the other side of the spectrum? People who will ask you for everything from a loan to doing their laundry. You bet. There are givers and takers and the best of all are those who are at ease with and understand the essential nature of both the give AND the take.

In short, "help" is not a burden we heap upon people, it is an honor we unravel when we are allowed the blessing of being part of one another's lives. And I am forever grateful to those lovely souls who have "helped" me to understand the difference.

Is Blood thicker than Water?

Well…I think it depends. Witty and profound? Not hardly, but frustratingly true nonetheless. I believe there are but a few blessed individuals that don't struggle, at some point in their lives, with whether the ties to family are ones which bind or gag. Now I am a person who has built my entire life and being around the importance of family. It is, and always has been EVERYTHING to me. I place great reverence in the ties between us and I am a keeper of and believer in connection, history and tradition. And on the whole I have been unspeakably blessed by the family I call my own. Both by birth and the fact that my In-Laws are some of the finest people I know and have taught me untold volumes of what it means to be "family" and how to care for one another. But let's just say that life has thrown me a few curve balls that have caused me to question the wisdom of not just the energy we put toward, but to redefine my overarching belief in this thing we call Family. I have been witness to heart wrenching situations where parents can be mean, belittling and unloving. Situations where extended family use, take advantage of and judge with alarming hypocrisy one another yet never themselves. Situations where grown children seem to be inexplicably attached and beholden to family members that treat them unkindly, unfairly and without a seeming shred of faith, encouragement or belief. And it makes me wonder why? Why do people do this to themselves? Why is it so blindingly difficult for us to wash our hands of those who serve absolutely no positive, encouraging or supportive influence in our lives? And the answer is that I have absolutely no idea.

Now lest you think I've detached from prior passionate pleas to prioritize family above all else and gone completely rogue, allow me to clarify. Still and always my highest calling is to nurture, care for and love my immediate family. Where the waters begin to get murky for me is with extended family. I have participated in countless conversations that insist that I not just wonder but question the notion of an unevaluated loyalty and investment in "family." NOBODY would sign up for a business investment that was a sure fire guarantee to lose money. But time and time again I see people pour themselves into family relationships that do absolutely nothing to encourage, uplift or bring something to the table in terms of true care and investment in the relationship. With my whole heart I believe Family should be that unending ever enduring source of unconditional love which is the foundation which guards our hearts and that we build our world upon. And if this isn't that case, they aren't family, they are just an unfortunate biological coincidence. I believe that while Family should be a given, we earn the right to that relationship through consistent care and actions that tell one another, "You matter." So often we learn how to care FOR others as a wonderful result of how we have been cared about BY others. With that definition, I fervently believe that friends can be as much a part of our Family as anybody we happen to share DNA with.

I cannot imagine any parent not attesting vehemently to the fact that biology is the easiest part of parenting. A walk in the park compared to the heart effort of the years of wonder, amazement, struggle, effort and elation that follow. So I am hesitant to insist our actions, our relationships, our time and our energy, and ultimately our hearts should be loyal to something as random as biology. Would we, and ultimately our families not be better served if we invested ourselves in those who care most for us, regardless of whether they are family or instead friends? Mind you, caring for someone, truly caring for them, does not in any way obligate us to agree with them. These thoughts are not intended as a license to ban from your world family members for not agreeing with you, being like you, having the same spiritual or political alignments and beliefs systems or rooting for the same football team. (Go Hawks!) There is no question in my mind that having the courage and wherewithal to lovingly disagree with someone is a voice and a force we should all welcome into our lives. But the most essential and revealing question is not whether people in our lives agree or disagree with us, it is whether or not they truly and deeply want and wish the best for us. And I could easily make the case that family or not, if people don't want the best for you, you need to surround yourself with different people.

Time and time again I have ached inside as I watch good people throw effort after foolishness trying to please, persuade and live up to judgmental, self-serving and ridiculous expectations heaped on them by "family." Families are not torn apart by differences, distance or disagreement. But they struggle against the weight of one another. Relationships call upon us not to judge, criticize or condemn, but to lift, love, encourage and heal. Sometimes love is the strong but unwavering voice that says, "You messed up, but I believe in you. Get up, stand up and do better." And sometimes it is the gentle, soundlessness of arms that wrap you in a love and compassion so strong that when one heart may be broken, its beat is strong enough to sustain you both. How we care for and about one another isn't driven by DNA, it's driven by our desire to give, to care, to contribute to invest and to nourish one another.

At the end of the day, I think that for me, Family is still everything, whether I'm related to them or not.

A wise man once said…

Actually, I don't care who said it. If there is wisdom out there for the taking…sign me up. I'm always a buyer. Ever on the hunt for a pearl of advice. A story with a moral that hits you between the eyes. An opportunity someone offers to learn from their mistakes. A chance to forego reinventing the wheel. I don't care what you call it or what package it arrives in, a story, an experience, a book, a best friend, a CD, a website, a struggle, a triumph, a tale of great endeavor. I am a huntsman of wisdom. A determined, relentless, voracious, insatiably inquisitive seeker of not just knowledge, but its enlightened relation…Wisdom. Wisdom in its essence goes beyond knowledge and takes us to the bright realm of true and deep understanding. This is my ever enticing pursuit. My chase that hath no end. My Promised Land of Wisdom and its offspring Compassion await, if only I have the humility to need it and the patience to tenaciously pursue it. So for as much as I have long realized that Buddha-like enlightenment is my daily quest (which just as a heads up offers no point of completion, diploma or trophy for trying), this notion of the essential nature of Wisdom was brought into sharp and demanding focus by my husband's oldest daughter Amy when she called attention to the following:

"WISDOM cries aloud in the street, in the markets she raises her voice; at the head of the noisy streets she cries out, at the entrance of the city gates she speaks; "How long O simple ones, will you love being simple? How long will scoffers delight in their scoffing and fools hate knowledge...For the simple are killed by their turning away and the complacency of fools destroys them." Proverbs 1:20

Philosophical and heavy perhaps, but nothing is heavier than the burden of ignorance. And nothing is more deserving of ridicule than those who refuse to daily be sworn to the quest for deeper understanding, heightened awareness and true, compassionate Wisdom. Whether you are more apt to crack open a Bible or a beer doesn't really matter. The words are true for us all. Wisdom does indeed cry out for our notice, our attention, and our dauntless efforts toward discovery. And never will there exist any acceptable explanation for being simple in our thoughts and understanding. Simple in our needs, sure! Simple in our focus and direction, you bet! But simple in our hearts and minds...inexcusable.

"How long will scoffers delight in their scoffing?" How long will people sit on the sidelines of life calling out, criticizing and condemning those who are earning, through blood sweat and tears their knowledge and wisdom? I heard a great quote recently that said, "Be so busy improving yourself that you don't have time to criticize others." This isn't a directive to forego your moral compass and no longer believe in right or wrong. It is rather a statement that those who spend their time scoffing, disparaging and disapproving of others when they have no stories to share or battle scars to show have earned nothing but disinterest and disregard. But there will always be some moron sitting in the cheap seats waiting for you to stumble, to err, to falter or fail. Keep in mind that THEIR affliction is fear and the only cure for the fear that persuades us to criticize, complain and condemn is Courage.

Yet "how long will fools hate knowledge?" Answer: For as long as they are too lazy and ignorant to work for it. I can listen to and learn from anybody who is earnest and sincere in their desire to know better and do better. But ever present fools who think they have it all figured out while never having earned an opinion or realized their need for humility will at best be ignored and at worse will lose the best that life has to offer. Joy will elude them because they have never realized the awe and wonder of searching for the stories, the surprises and the sagacity of an ever curious and well examined life. Their complacency will be the thief that comes in the night and steels their dreams because they never earned the right to rejoice in the bright light of promise and possibility.

Our second child for some reason asks me often why adults don't go to school. It baffles her. She seems stupefied enough to keep inquiring about it and regularly I tell her that the best people are the ones who are ALWAYS learning. Always stretching, trying, growing, learning, failing, apologizing, applauding and achieving. And while learning doesn't need to arrive in a diploma or doctoral degree, it needs an exalted place in all our lives. It can happen…it must happen every single day. We must open both our hearts and our minds to what we need to know and understand in the hopes of realizing the person we are capable of becoming. Knowledge is like the cocoon that wraps our ignorance in understanding long enough for us to emerge with the beauty of Wisdom that allows our most spectacular selves to take flight.

Or perhaps we should set aside the weighty philosophy and acknowledge that perhaps Jim Rohn simplified and said it best, "there's nothing worse than being stupid." Actually, let's just boil this down to brass tacks with a shout out to Forest Gump. "Stupid is as stupid does." Or maybe a football analogy sums it up; "the best defense is a good offense." Nothing will ever equip you better to win in the game of life than the tireless, no excuses pursuit of Wisdom and Understanding. So hear the cry, answer the call and seek Understanding. You won't just be a wicked competitor at Trivial Pursuit, you'll be the most able competitor in the race of a life well, wisely, compassionately and abundantly lived.

What's your worth?

An intriguing question for many of us and quite likely the first things which come to mind are notions of income, equity, balance sheets, bonuses, investments and a rock solid 401k. But in honor of Father's Day, I would love to brave a bit of a discussion on embracing a worth, more true, more noble, more satisfying and infinitely more essential than our financial fortunes. A man's greatest worth will never lie anywhere more precious or meaningful than with his family. The woman he loves, the children he is an example to, and the priorities he sets his mind and his heart toward. These are where a man's worth will always and forever be most dearly and especially valued. I have certainly monopolized enough time to voice my ever emphatic opinions on my deep love, respect, honor and esteem of motherhood. Not rare are my attitudes voiced about the irreplaceable and beloved role mothers are given upon receiving the blessing of their children. But one can hardly speak to one role without an equal and opposite acknowledgment of the other. I often wonder on how our lives and world would look if we were to esteem men with as strong a voice of approval and admiration for their roles as fathers as we do their roles in being

"successful," competitive, goal oriented and tough.
Men can achieve wealth, status, influence and power. But if they have not altered the lives of others in meaningful and enduring ways their accomplishments are both empty and unimpressive. I can think of no other role in life that carries as much loathing and disdain when done poorly and as much reverence and regard when done well, as Fatherhood. An interesting, but inspired set of extremes. Few would disagree with the wise words that:
"It is easier for a father to have children than for children to have a real father." Pope John XXIII

For a world that values fortitude and determination, it is an unwelcome irony that we don't offer up these qualities to our children and families with as much concern and commitment as perhaps we should. I know plenty of parents, myself, at times included, that consider themselves good parents while setting a less than exceptional example. If I was to look at all of my actions and intentions through the lens of my children's' eyes, oh how humbled I would be and how altered I would rightly become! That we love is not enough. How we LIVE is of equal importance and dare I say greater esteem.

So this is nothing more than a moment to honor those men who consistently pursue both…love and living it. Here's to those men who are adoring and respectful husbands. To those men who are tender, patient and devoted fathers. To those men who would do whatever it took to provide for and protect their families. To those men who can wipe a child's tears and hug their hurts away. To those men who don't need to be right, but always feel a need to be better. To those men who make their families feel safe. That their home is safe, their hearts are safe and that someone strong is guarding the door of their childhood such that nothing and no one can do them harm. To those men who know that their greatest treasure lies in the embrace of child's trusting arms and feel themselves wealthy men in the riches of their memories of laughter, discovery, learning and growing. To those men who are certain enough to set boundaries, but realize that their greatest leverage is love. To those men who are persistent, consistent and unwavering in their commitment to those who desperately need to believe in them. To those men who do not TELL their children, but SHOW their children. To those men who have never sacrificed a single thing for their family but are ever and always aware that anything they "forego," is returned a thousand fold because they know where their treasure lies. To those men who are as able to comfort a child as are able to confront a threat to their wellbeing. To men who realize that how much time they spend reading to their children will have a direct impact on how much time the police spend reading your wayward teen their rights. To men who realize that pride is the enemy of compassion and have the strength and wisdom to choose the latter. To those men who value the approval of their family over the applause of others. To those men who are endlessly enchanted with the awe and wonder they are able to both watch and inspire in their children. To those men who give selflessly, live courageously and love with tenacity and tenderness. To those men who can stand in the face of a teenager yelling, "I hate you!" and reply calmly with, "and I still love you to the moon and back." To those men who stay up with a sick child or comfort a frightened one. To those men who have taught a child how to ride a bicycle, hit a baseball, catch a pass or catch a frog. To those men who love and honor their wives and are deeply aware of the fact that they are not only setting an example but offering their children the priceless gift of peace, security and unconditional belonging. To those men who are strong when they need to be, and tender when they ought to be. To those men who live with unwavering principles regardless of circumstance. To those men who would choose to be exceptional rather than make excuses. To those men who would fight for their country, fight for their family and defend tirelessly the greatest riches in their kingdom...the hearts that belong to them. To those men who accept with pride, devotion and honor all they have because of who and how they love. To those men who realize that they are in EVERY way the real life hero of their precious children and accept that challenge with both responsibility and imagination. To those men, who every day do all this and so much more. You are changing lives, changing the world and writing a story which shall never be forgotten.

*To those men whom I love. My heroes, my inspiration and my EVERYTHING.

"For where your treasure is there will your heart be also." Luke 12:34

What's happened to our manners!?!

Now this in not intended as a rant espousing Emily Post style etiquette on society at large. But the disturbing reality that I seem to be bumping up against with alarming frequency is that we no longer even have a handle on the basics. For as much as we could all use some awareness around dilemmas such as which fork to use or which bread plate exactly is ours, it would seem our civilities have eroded to a level as remedial as "please" and "thank you."

To be sure the absence of please and thank you is most noticeable in children. Yes, it's a monstrous inconvenience to remind them four hundred and fifty two million times to say "thank you," but do it anyway. It always provides me with some amusement when I hear kids make a demand or a request, then their parents follow with a leading, "what do you say..." and the child responds with "please." So what structure are we teaching them exactly? I'll tell you exactly. We are teaching them that they make a demand, then we follow with our scripted line of, "what do you say...," then they finish the statement with the appropriate and constantly prompted "please." I have to remind my kids of this as much as the next exasperated parent, but the correction ALWAYS involves them stating the ENTIRE request over again with the unprompted "please" at the end. Eventually they realize it is on THEM to make the "please" a part of their request and that it is a lot less work for them to make it a habit than it is for them to have to repeat everything. Eventually I get to the point where if they make a request that lacks the prized please at the end I simply ignore them. Flat out act as though they don't even exist. I'm not going to prompt, correct or cajole. If you want something, I highly suggest you learn how to ask.

On a similar and equally simple note, I'm one of those silly girls that still believes in chivalry. And for as cute as it is to hear or say that "chivalry is not dead," it is most certainly on the endangered species list. Our older two children are girls and when we found out that we were expecting a boy with the third I broke out in a cold sweat. My concern was born out of the fact that I believe it is an increasingly difficult task to raise boys to be good men. How do you define "good men" you say? I'm so very glad you asked. A good man knows how to treat women with gentleness and respect. A good man knows how to break a sweat, work hard and knows what he is working for. A good man believes that his word is his bond and wouldn't dream of making a promise he wouldn't keep. A good man commits with a handshake, not a legal document. A good man looks people in the eye and can look himself in the mirror. A good man honors God, loves his family and is loyal to his friends. A good man doesn't care what's trendy he cares about what's right and has the courage to seek integrity over approval. With this intimidating task in mind, I do simple things as consistently as humanly possible. When I am serving dinner I make a point of serving the girls before the boys and saying, "ladies first." When we are walking into a store I have our five year old son run ahead to open the door for myself and his sisters. My hope is that these small things, over time, will become part the men, my sweet boys choose to be.

In the interest of fairness I shall point out at least one of my own various and sundry shortcomings. When our first son was a toddler my in-laws were over at the house for dinner. And let's say that while I would very much enjoy describing my son's behavior as playful and rambunctious, the fact of the matter is he was unabashedly out of control. My father-in-law made a comment on his less than endearing level of discipline and while I must admit to bristling at his input as it called out my own, umm…oversights as a mom, the reality of the situation was twofold;

1. Their heart was, is, and always will be in the right place. Care is speaking up, not staying quiet.

2. He was right.

It is neither amusing nor cute when little Johnny is swinging from the drapes and jumping on the furniture. No one is impressed with his athletic prowess. They simply think that HE is a pain in the ass and YOU are a fool. The moral of that story is to listen to the people who truly care for you. Even if you're not over the moon about what they have to say, their wisdom is a gift not a nuisance. While it is easy and somewhat charming to talk about teaching our kids good manners, there is little charm in their alarming scarcity in both children and adults alike. So considering the fact that brevity is perhaps best here, a highlight film will hopefully suffice:

If someone gives you a gift, write a thank you note. Not an email, a text, or a Facebook message; a WRITTEN note. Real pen, real paper, real stamp. If someone gives you their time, energy or hospitality send a thank you GIFT. Acknowledge the fact that what THEY have given you is a gift and reciprocate in your own, but meaningful way. One of the best "thank you" gifts I ever received was from a friend whose family had come to stay with us for a few days. To be sure time together with great friends is its own reward, but beyond this, she sent a thank you card to every single one of us including our kids. With each card she recounted a memory, an experience or a laugh she had shared with each of our kids and in doing so, her words were a gift that made them feel deeply valued and special in ways that they truly will never forget. Nor will I.

If you are invited to a party, RSVP. If however, you are one of those fine folks who cannot be bothered with this simple courtesy, all will be well as within relatively short order you won't be invited to anything and you will be duly relieved of this burdensome task. If on the other hand you RSVP and therefore have the pleasure of attending a get together or a dinner...BRING SOMETHING. And no, I don't care if they cheerfully chirp, "Just bring yourself." Bring something anyway! If your kids are invited to a birthday party and the hosting family generously allows you to bring your entire brood, either bring a gift from EACH of your kids or get an especially nice gift for the guest of honor in thanks for the fact that they are entertaining (and likely feeding) your entire clan. Don't leave a mess...ever. Clean up after yourself and your little darlings. ASK people for their time, don't take it. Do more than your share, give more than you're asked, and work harder than expected. DO NOT show up to any experience with your kids armed with their Game Boys or any other gadget in tow. All our children are embarrassingly bound to their isolated worlds because of these bewitching devices. Do they have their place? You bet! Like on an airplane, during a painfully long car ride or in the midst of a power point presentation on how to use Excel. Otherwise, these digital mind melters shouldn't be seen OR heard. Thanks in part to these electronic gremlins, it seems to be the norm that children, instead of looking adults in the eye and speaking to them with ease and regard, look down, mumble, and want to get any such experience over with as quickly as possible. Kids need to learn how to be with, engage with and have conversations with adults. This skill will serve them FAR better than their expert abilities at Angry Birds.

Be thoughtful, attentive and aware of OTHERS. See a need and attend to it. Don't ever steal somebody else's thunder. Let them have their moment before you claim yours. "If you borrow something return it BETTER than you found it." My husband was raised with parents who insisted on this impressive directive and I was so smitten with the notion that I apply the philosophy to nearly every aspect of my life. Give credit where credit was due. If the thought, the inspiration or the experience wasn't yours, acknowledge who and how it was brought to your attention. And speaking of attention, whether you are in line at the grocery store, grabbing a latte or ordering a meal at a restaurant, get off your f***ing phone and acknowledge that there is a human being in front of you. Look them in the eye, and speak to them with dignity and respect. Being on your Bluetooth while ordering a four shot Americano doesn't make you important or impressive it makes you an idiot.

So for the duration of this post I have sacrificed verbal dexterity for sheer volume of thoughts and still we have only scratched the surface. The reality is that we are becoming detached, disinterested, unconcerned and generally unimpressive when it comes to how we weave our way through the world. The mark we make is a function of how we treat others. Part of that mark is inevitably our manners. Have I mastered this craft? Not even kind of. But because it matters, I will continue to try...every single day, I will show up and try. Are these ideals outdated, old fashioned and unnecessary? I can assure you, they never have been and they never will be.

"Take your time, hurry up…"

The choice is yours, don't be late." For those of you who grew up with the same musical influences as I did you will quickly recognize these contradiction filled words as belonging to Kurt Cobain. Whether grunge rock was your thing or not, music…real music, is present day poetry. Music tends to be where we find the words that resonate with something restless or wondering in our soul. And at times we need to hear the music, the poetry before we even realize that THAT song, is our song.

For some reason we all seem to be taking our time sorting life out. Tomorrow we will tackle that problem. Next week maybe we'll start to work on our relationship. Down the line I'll be in a better frame of mind to work it through or work it out. After I get on top of my bills, then I'll start to think about passion and creativity. Once I master this skill, then I'll be ready to take on something else. For so many parts of our life we seem to be waiting for the "Right Time" which always has been and always will be a WASTE of time. So perhaps we should "hurry up." Maybe some urgency is in order so that we can engage in our best life, our best self, our best business, our best relationships…right now.

I remember before I was even married my sister saying to our mom that she and her husband were talking about starting a family but they just weren't sure if it was the right time. And my mom looked at her with compassion and understanding and said "honey, there will never be a right time." Words of great wisdom which shall never be forgotten. Yet with nauseating repetition I hear my own inner dialog working to talk me out of something because next week would be better. Or once I've finished THIS project then I can take THAT one on. Or it really isn't a good time to be diving into a challenge or experience because I'm just too "busy." When I finally acknowledged that "busy" is bullshit, I was left without my laundry list of excuses for why I wasn't or couldn't get more done. How ironic that time and time again, the "busiest" people I know are often the least effective. Those who conduct themselves with purpose, intention and resolve rarely feel busy. They feel as though their lives are full and they are being productive in directions and endeavors that are meaningful and important to them.

Yet because so many of us have yet to identify or understand our Purpose we lean on being busy in order to feel important and worthy in the world. If we are overloaded, overwhelmed, in demand, at the end of our rope, and simply have NO time, then have your people call my people and we'll pencil in a time to have a conference call about our busyness. Busy has become some misguided merit badge that immerses us in a false sense of significance. Speaking personally, my co-dependent relationship with being busy was more about the fact that I didn't want to allow for the time and space to tackle the things in my life that made me feel deeply uncomfortable, scared or uncertain. It was much easier for me to embrace being busy, than it was to do the work…the REAL work. It got to the point that I was nearly addicted to the adrenaline of being busy because I was without the sustainable energy source of deep inspiration and soulful motivation. It was far less challenging for me to be inundated with an endless to-do list than it was for me to get about the business of owning and embracing my WHY and becoming purposeful and determined in that direction.

Most busy people lead messy lives of struggling at work, being frustrated with their relationships and as a general rule are irritated and baffled with their own discontent. By contrast, those who have chosen to embrace their Why are rarely lost in a flurry of useless activity. Instead their lives are full, on task and determined and while they seem to enjoy being insanely productive their lives lack the manic, grasping, frazzled nature of those who are endlessly, obsessively busy. It's as though the fact that they have found their Purpose allows them to live life with the rhythmic, resolute beauty that comes when one is living their Purpose, their Poem, their Song. There is an absolutely profound and undeniable difference between those who are living with deep, great Urgency around delivering their Verse to the world and the work that goes along with that spectacular calling, and those who are too busy running from their Reason. So what if we were to stop living a life of conflict and contradiction? What if we were to stop being busy and to begin instead to be Purposeful? What if we were to take our time to find our Why, and to Hurry Up about the business of living and loving that passion day in and day out? What if we were to trade in Busy for our Belief in who we are and what we are called to do? What if we searched for and honored Why we are here and were fearlessly determined on behalf of this noble cause? This quest is our right and should belong to and concern us all. Yet at the end of the day, "the choice is yours, don't be late."

"There is nothing the busy man is less busied with than living, and there is nothing harder to learn."

Seneca

When Good Enough is Enough...

So for the hordes of you who read the last post this one will, at first blush, strike as odd. You may ask, "How does she get on her verbal podium one week talking about Excellence and within mere days she is spouting off about "Good Enough?" I'm honestly not just trying to mess with your smartness. Allow me to explain myself. I remain steadfastly committed to ideals of Excellence and Achievement. I believe these principles are the yardsticks we measure our life by. Have we engaged, invested and endeavored earnestly in what is precious, prized and deeply important to us? And this is as it should be. But excellence is a finite resource. It asks much of us and so needs to be reserved for that which matters most. We need to define our lives, our actions and put our energies toward that which we hold most dear. Somewhere along the line we need to choose those parts of our life that are non-negotiable. We need to arrive at a reasonably concise list of what we most cherish in life and offer up the lion's share of our heart and soul in this direction. What we choose as precious deserves, in every way, our commitment to relentless Excellence. The rest however ummm...not so much. Once we have arrived with heartfelt conviction at what is utterly essential and unwaveringly important in our life, our obligation to anything and everything else needs to take on a very Jimmy Buffet like level of concern. "It's all good. Not a big deal. Maybe tomorrow. I'll get to it later. It's good enough."

Understand that if they were to hand out awards for those people who consistently get their knickers in a twist over absolutely NOTHING, I am loathe to admit that for much of my life I would have been obligated to acknowledge my professional level of skill in obsessing over the irrelevant. I would have a trophy case jam-packed with unwanted but embarrassingly earned statues acknowledging my uncanny ability to get wrapped around the axel over utterly ridiculous concerns. So as the uncontested poster child of those who have spent enormous amounts of energy fretting over the frivolous, I can, with great certainty, attest to how exhausting and useless this practice is and always will be.

So at this point there are but a few things I know for sure. We can begin with the obvious, that we all have the same number of hours in the day. "The great equalizer" as Greg so aptly asserts. But beyond the ticking of time, our energy is, as well, a limited resource. There is only so much of ourselves, our emotions, and our oomph to go around. And that precious energy MUST be spent on what really and truly matters. Speaking for myself, the sacred circle includes Faith, Family, Work and Relationships. Real relationships I might ad. If something in my life falls into one of these crucial categories it deserves my wholehearted focus, energy and resolute commitment to Excellence. If not, good enough will do.

I used to get wound up about how the kids were dressed for school. Not so much anymore. Case in point, if you have a five year old that insists on wearing rubber lady bug boots and a pink tutu out the door, nobody, but NOBODY is going to think you dressed her, so don't worry about it. When the kid's schools sent out notices that if you were sending in "treats" for your child's birthday, they needed to be store bought versus homemade due to allergies I let out an exalted Halleluiah! Now the box of Nilla Wafers I sent in aren't just my expression of "good enough," underachieving has become mandatory! If I get emails or voicemails that don't relate to one of my pillars of importance then I do NOT feel obligated to stay up late responding and replying. If I get to it within a few days...good enough. If people are coming over for dinner I promise to pull out the nicest paper plates and plastic forks I can find. In my world, that's good enough. While I admire Martha Stuart, I lack her panache for parties. I LOVE having friends in my home, but do not hand-stitch quilts with their initials on them prior to their arrival and hope to have them depart with lasting memories but rarely have they left with impressive door prizes. The time spent together is priceless. Everything else can be...good enough. I recently got my haircut and the gal asked me what I "usually do with my hair." "Put it under a baseball cap," was my immediate and honest response. That's good enough.

For so many of us, life can feel like we are damn near compulsively drawn to agonizing over the expectations and obligations that quite likely exist more in our own mind than anywhere else. So choose purposefully and carefully what matters. Give these concerns your most passionate effort and soulful commitment. For everything else, good enough is sure to suffice. I am convinced that this is an essential step in our efforts to belly up to the bar of a balanced, purpose driven life. And once you are extraordinarily clear about what only needs to be good enough, be sure to toast your intentional mediocrity in Margaretville.

The Perfect Punch

Okay, so I should admit right off the bat that this post is really an exercise of trying to sweat it out with conflicting philosophies. It's like I'm about to air my battling beliefs and survival of the fittest will determine which set of principles will come away victorious.

Let the games begin...

On the far side of the arena is the part of me that holds fast to being a recovering perfectionist. I am sold out to the belief that perfectionism is at best a fools' errand and at worst, is a precipice that dangles us over the jagged rocks of judgment, anger, depression and every other nasty, unforgiving snare we can waltz our way into. Perfectionism is, and always has been, more of a way to conceal our flaws than to showcase just how wildly remarkable we are.

Yet, in the same breath, I would consider myself to be a tenacious advocate for holding ourselves and those around us to ideals of excellence and achievement. With every fiber of my being I believe that, "what we are in anything is what we are in everything." That our smallest actions are vital ripples of our most profound truths. That if we believe in something, stand for something, and embrace chosen ideals as our own, then we must do this always. Not when it is convenient. Not when somebody is going to notice and be in spellbound awe of our sheer awesomeness. We don't get to choose one set of values when in the company of our conservative republican friends only to abandon it for a like-minded alliance with our unfettered pot-smoking friends from college who concern themselves with dime bags and donuts more than and fiscal policy and fund-raisers. Excellence is, and always has been, a stand-alone product. It must exist for its own sake. It must be given a lofty place in our lives based solely on the merit of how deeply it matters, not because of any accolades or applause we consider our due for being so enviably impressive.

And achievement. Actually, not just any achievement, extraordinary achievement. To be sure there are as many ways to achieve epically as there are people endeavoring to do so. I can confidently bet the bank that what I would consider high achievement is something that other far more accomplished folks would sprinkle on their breakfast cereal in the morning. But if it is something that I have to push and reach and stretch for then it is my precious own, and I am allowed to end the day with a satisfied, "job well done." The other day I wrote a letter to an extraordinarily accomplished women. In THIS endeavor my odds fall soundly in the opposite direction and there is a greater chance of Kim Kardashian and Kanye celebrating 20 years of blissful marriage than there is that she will ever come in contact with my communication. But I did it. I thought about it. I wrote it. I put an actual, real live stamp on it (paper square of approximately an inch in size with various pictures on it, which is sticky on the back and meant to be applied to something commonly referred to as a "Letter"). And for as much as it is our responsibility to strive toward exalted achievement I also believe it is our obligation to encourage others to do so as well. I am loathe to admit that I know FAR too many couples that either don't bother to encourage one another or they themselves become the soul-sucking cynics draining the life out of those who are trying. Quite wicked really...when you think about it. So now I'm really going to hit you below the belt and share with you that a couple weeks ago our thirteen year old daughter said to us, "if your goals don't scare you, they aren't big enough." Oh for the love of all things holy! I need to get busy! At least she announced her position so I know I need to step it up if I want to do that whole parental, "set a good example" thing.

Okay, so over the course of dragging you through this post, I am needing to come to some sort of epiphany about how Perfectionism and Excellence and Achievement are absolutely and unequivocally NOT the same thing. Not even so much as second cousins three times removed. Am I being duplicitous to not just advocate, but INSIST on Excellence whist resolutely shunning the plague of Perfectionism? In a word...no. Excellence demands that we push. It expects us to be afraid and to do it anyhow. It REQUIRES failure where perfectionism would have us avoid that messy, unsavory experience at all costs. Excellence and Achievement are things which beg us beyond the limits of what we are comfortably confident about toward that which scares the hell out of us. Perfection fights for us to expend enormous amounts of energy impressing others. Excellences wages its war on behalf of our very selves, our soul and our brilliant potential. Perfectionism is the sentry at the gates, barring us from the victory of becoming all and everything God intended us to be. Make no mistake about it, these two philosophies are NOT on the same team. I suggest you pick your side carefully because if you have the guts to choose the virtues of Excellence and Achievement, your road is destined to be paved with trials and triumphs. But the after party is guaranteed to be AWESOME.

Overworked, Overwhelmed…Overjoyed!

I often feel as though life these days for not just some of us, but dare I say nearly all of us, is a tormented tug between our work and our life. What we must do versus what we would love to do. Our obligations and responsibilities versus our passion and giftedness. Hope and desire versus practical needs. Having it all versus wanting it all. A stellar career versus a thriving family. Living the dream versus the occasional daydream. Our job versus our joy. Our compassion for ourselves versus pleasing others. Our unique soul versus performing for the approval and accolades temperamentally bestowed upon us. Punching a time clock versus where did the time go? Faith and spirituality versus doubt and cynicism. Exhaustion versus elation. "If only" versus "I can and I will." "I wish" versus "I deserve." I could go on and on and on. In other words, we are CONSTANTLY duking it out within our own lives. It's so real and impacting it's a wonder we aren't sporting tell-tale bumps and bruises. And weary though we may be, we are day-in and day-out wrestling with a relentless tug-of-war between what is and what could be. Trying desperately to find that Promised Land of a serene balance between work, and life where everything feels well and right and ever so pleasantly designed.

So for as much as our life of This VERSUS That feels like a

never ending slug-fest, we can begin to win our way back to experiencing hope, joy, gratitude, belief, belonging, passion, soul, and blissful centeredness with the slightest and simplest tactical move. We need to let go of our death grip on the daily grind and our frazzled, strained juggling act to let the balls drop and realize that it isn't about the circus act we are performing, it's about being part of the laughter going on in the stands. We need to approach our life not from the perspective of getting our life FIGURED out, but FINDING it out. I've mentioned Steve Nys in a previous blog and another impacting statement he made is worth a mention here. In his words, "I believe that everything happens in perfect order, even though I do not fully understand." But instead of trusting and believing in the perfect order, we are draining ourselves trying to figure out our life; "Do I like my job? Can we afford a bigger house? How am I going to pay the bills? Will I get the promotion? Should I go back to "work?" What if this relationship doesn't work out? Private school or public school? Nanny or daycare? Starting a business or being an employee? Paper or plastic?" Uugh! It's nothing short of exhausting. So instead, let's FIND out. Let's find out each day what we have the opportunity to discover. Let's find out who we are supposed to meet and where an unexpected opportunity or surprise acquaintance may lead. Let's find out how we feel about our day and what parts of it feel good and true and then drift in that direction. Let's believe in and trust the perfect order of things. Let's stop forcing ourselves and our lives toward being FIGURED out and instead perhaps we can enjoy and embrace FINDING out what wonders await an open heart and mind.

By the way; this is not intended as some passive, "let's just see what happens" naïve approach to life. FINDING out about your lives is not a suggestion to be a spectator waiting for your show to start. Rather it is the most active, purposeful role I can espouse. When we are FIGURING out our life and trying to cram our experience into predictable boxes with predetermined expectations we are going to miss the moment. We are going to miss the road signs on our journey that point us in the direction of what is possible not necessarily what is practical. We are going to pass on an opportunity, or forego an encounter that are both intended and necessary to bring us where we belong. If we are consistently pulling in that tug-of-war trying to figure it all out, the ONLY outcome of spending our time and energy on such a thankless task is that we will be overworked and overwhelmed...constantly. We are day in and day out writing away trying to determine our story. What is it about? How does it go? It's akin to taking notes during an amazing lecture. The more time you spend scribbling things down, the less you actually hear the wisdom being shared. Or perhaps it's like trying to video tape your child's second grade acting debut. Being busy recording it, means you aren't actually watching it and let me tell you, the replay on your iPad is NOTHING like the original masterpiece of a performance. But you've missed it. The true moment has come and gone without you. And if you are fixated on figuring your life out, what you truly need to find will go unnoticed and undiscovered.

All of your writing on the script of your life about what you have figured out will amount to a lot of effort and numerous chapters of pure nonsense. Drivel that no one wants to read...honestly. I have etched MANY chapters of the appalling stuff. If instead you spend your precious energy finding out how your story will go...allowing the perfect order and all of its unannounced opportunities to pen your pages, the story will be written as it was intended and your experience will not be one of overwork or overwhelm. It will be a tale of wonder, belief and intention. And you and anyone fortunate enough to read your work will experience the Joy that lies within.

Target Practice

For better or for worse, I'm not talking about a bull's eye. I'm not speaking of darts, BB's, bullets, firing ranges or bales of hay with those familiar red circles pinned to them. I'm talking about YOU. I'm going to go out on an insanely precarious limb here and suggest that you allow yourself to become a target of sorts. For what? For the rest of your life. Allow me to explain: Some of you reading this had a chance to hear Greg interview a friend of his, Steve Nys on a recent teleseminar. If you had a chance to hear the interview, super! If not, here is a bit of what has been on my mind of late and was brought into brilliant, though uncomfortable focus during a conversation I got to have with Steve who is by all counts one of the most interesting, infuriating, challenging, inspiring, generous people I have ever met.

Of late, I have been on a personal crusade of sorts to lasso my own issues and take on, as relentlessly as possible, areas of my life that are needing a rehab. I've always been pretty squared away, but finally decided to face the fact that I keep things very SQUARE – regimented, controlled and predictable so that I can keep other things AWAY. In other words, I am the proud owner of a strangely evolved sort of compensation technique. "If I really excel at these things, it will make-up for the fact that I'm completely ignoring other areas of my life that are wildly uncomfortable for me." And it is certainly no stretch to suggest that if something makes us uncomfortable, we avoid it, and things we avoid we don't stand a chance of being good at. And I am no good at Target Practice. In fact, it is no exaggeration to say that I world class suck at opening myself up to criticism, it's more sophisticated cousin "critique," and until relatively recently I have lived a life where failure was simply not an option. I have spent inordinate amounts of time and energy being really good at certain things so that nobody could take a shot at me. Everything on display was pretty polished, and all for the express purpose of avoiding having anybody take aim at my flaws or failures.

So this friend of Greg's, Steve, has experienced some of the most unimaginable, take you out at the knees, life experiences ANYBODY could imagine. A brutal divorce, a failed business and being dead broke, and the most devastating of all sufferings, the loss of a child. But in the course of our conversation he kept using the word "vulnerable." And I kept pushing him to explain this to me. How could someone who has endured such crushing hardships actually DESIRE vulnerability? And for as much as I poked and prodded and tried to pull apart his motivations and HOW he thought, he would look at me like, "what else is there Shauna?" Here I am completely vexed by his ability to continually allow the world to take its best shot and his response was akin to, "how could I not?" He shared and explained that hurt, hardship, failure and vulnerability were the ONLY path where he could experience learning, growth and deep, abiding joy. Steve is willing to be wrong as earnestly as he wishes to be right. He accepts who he uniquely is yet works harder than any person I have ever met at becoming better. He didn't just sign up for Target Practice...he welcomed it! Now as a recovering perfectionist, I find his openness and vulnerability utterly terrifying, but he honestly was perplexed over the notion of entertaining any other option. He was completely and utterly sold out to the belief that his best life is intrinsically bound to his willingness to wear the red circles.

So while I have, for some time now, been wrestling with finding ways to be open, imperfect and embrace failure, I couldn't quite figure out how Steve didn't struggle and fight and wince at the inevitable slings and arrows that come with this way of being. As human beings we are both cursed and gifted with our heart, our emotions, our joy, and our fear. They are the essence of what makes us human. They are also the essence of what makes us vulnerable. But the reality is that it is because we ARE vulnerable that we must BE vulnerable. It is because we are capable of feeling joy, sorrow, achievement, failure, hope, longing, grief, exuberance and delight that we simply cannot afford to dumb down our lives and our hearts in favor of avoiding hurt and disappointment. The very REASON we have to sign up for Target Practice is the fact that we will hurt and bleed. Our beautiful battle scars are inescapably what earn us the right to living life in all its messy, wonderful glory. A paradox that is a world class pain in the ass but undeniably true nonetheless. Our ability to experience Joy is only as great as our ability to experience sorrow. Our ability to immerse ourselves in the satisfaction of success is never greater than our ability to embrace the failure that taught us how to get there. Our ability to be courageous depends on our ability to endure unwelcome judgment and cheap disdain. Our only chance at the best that life has to offer is to know that we can endure the worst. Our ability to love and be loved is never greater than our ability to accept ourselves and others with unconditional embrace. In other words, only by being open to the sting of a kill shot, will we know, experience and deserve high achievement...in all things. Life does not willingly reward the faint of heart, so sign up for some Target Practice and it's a pretty safe bet that YOU will be the one taking aim on the most amazing life you could imagine.

Stop messing with my smartness!

So when my sister's son was a little boy his dad was messing around with him in one of those ways all parents oddly enjoy and my nephew looked him dead in the eye and said, "Dad! Stop messing with my smartness!" And it got me wondering, at what point do we all allow society and all its influences to do such a bang up job of messing with our smartness? When did we surrender our instinct in favor of other people's ideas, influence or opinions? I am a die-hard believer in instinct and intuition. I believe our gut reaction is there for a reason so why do we consistently forfeit how something feels in favor of going with the flow, giving someone the benefit of the doubt, or just flat out ignoring the fact that something rubs us the wrong way? Are these behaviors innately bad? Definitely not. But when giving someone the "benefit of the doubt" is offered at the expense of ignoring a gut feeling or sixth sense about that person we're placing our trust in the wrong direction. We're choosing to trust a stranger over our own inner voice. Or perhaps we are choosing to not say or do something in a given situation because: "it's really none of my business. What would people think? Nobody else is saying or doing anything. I don't want to make a scene. His business card seemed professional so this must be legit." We've begun to think our way through life and stopped feeling our way through it.

I've had a couple of interactions and discussions lately that got me to wondering: "Why have we stopped trusting our animal instincts in favor of our intellect or worse still outside influences?" Are we really so evolved that we no longer need to take a radar sweep of how something sets with us? Are we better for leaning on our intelligence rather than committing to our intuition? Why have we accepted so many things as truth, or that's just the way it is. Says who? When is the last time we sourced something out or better yet, when is the last time we trusted our gut and allowed the sound of our inner bullshit meter to lead the way. I recently had an experience with a vet who came out to suture up a wound on a horse and within short order we received what I would consider to be an outrageously ridiculous invoice from him. Now I could look at the itemization and not be able to launch an argument on any single line item since I wasn't actually there when he looked at the horse. Or I could pay attention to the fact that aside from the ludicrously high charges, something about this just felt funny. Like we were being taken advantage of. What the vet didn't know is that for better or for worse I've paid more vet bills for equine accidents in my life than I care to count and therefore have perhaps too many past experiences to draw from. Yet what I found myself mostly drawing from was the fact that something about this just didn't feel right. It had an opportunistic vibe to it. Something like, let's just throw this out there and see if they pay it. So at that point I have a dilemma in front of me. Pay the bill and move on, or say that I think this is horseshit, pun fully intended, and we need to talk. But option B runs the risk of involving some sort of confrontation which we are understandably loathe to engage in. Going against the grain. Standing on principle. Trusting your instinct rather than submissively going with the program takes an enormous amount of time and energy that we can ill afford to waste.

117

We are constantly being bombarded by situations, scenarios and encounters that call for good judgment and what precisely is the origin of this thing we call judgment? I contend it is that inner sense of right and wrong. Not the knowledge of it...the sense of it. Greg recently called my attention to a speech that was written by a professor but delivered publicly many years later by Matt Damon. Within the speech the accusation is made that our problem isn't civil disobedience, its civil obedience. We've waived our instincts in favor of being well behaved. We've allowed society, government, a peer group, a boyfriend, a girlfriend, and the media, to mess with our smartness. And the disturbing thing is we aren't putting up much of a fight. It kind of just happens either so incrementally that we don't notice it, or we do, in fact notice it, but lack the wherewithal to react to our inner Jiminy Cricket.

So the challenge we all need to consider is disobedience. Stepping away from the flow of traffic to listen to what your gut is telling you about a person, a situation, a business, a transaction, a politician or a policy. Maybe it's time we all risked being called a smartass in order to rescue our smartness.

Go BIG or go home…!

Okay, so we've all heard it. And either it has challenged us on some level or we have summarily dismissed it as unleashed, overzealous locker room talk. I have two strong thoughts on this topic and while at first blush they may sound at odds with one another, I will attempt to argue that they are not. GO BIG. You bet! Bravo! And if I could high five everyone who embraces throwing down this gauntlet in their life I would. I am resolutely a believer in Daniel Burnham's quote, Make no little plans; they have no magic to stir men's blood." Small plans are for small people. Mediocrity is an entirely intolerable state of existence. There is little regard and even less esteem given in life those who settle for that which is typical, average or "good enough." I don't hesitate to insist that nobody was ever moved, inspired or learned anything of profound importance from ordinary influences. Yet that which is commonplace it all too common and excuses for our lackluster performance in life are never in short supply.

I think that in our heart of hearts, we all want to GO BIG. We all long to be fearless, brave and able to not just bring something to the table of life but to leave it there because it's just that damned cool, important or meaningful. I think we all long to leave a mark and make a difference. So why have more than most of us given up? Why is it that our once lofty notions and ideals have been replaced by our laundry list of justifications for our lack of willingness to day in and day out, GO BIG? I don't have enough time. I don't have enough money. I'm not smart enough. Somebody else will do it better...so why bother. They wouldn't be interested. It's too complicated. I have too many other things to worry about. The list is far from complete, but certainly something here looks familiar to each and every one of us. Yet some people seem immune or just oblivious to the chatter that has unwelcome power over the rest of us and they consistently GO BIG. And have you noticed that this seems to be an across the board, no holds barred, life choice for "those" people? It seems that those who GO BIG in life do it all the time! They do it in everything. It's somehow at the core not just of what they do but WHO they are. Rarely does a person do one grand thing then spend the rest of their life eeking out a mundane, average existence. So it would seem we all have a choice in front of us that isn't so much a matter of GO BIG, but rather a matter of BE BIG. Can we set aside our fear, worry and endless excuses to step into our own? Can we boldly embrace the belief that ordinary simply isn't enough and we were meant for so much more? Can we GO BIG with our life, our purpose and our actions or do we wander aimlessly home lugging the unbearable burden of why we couldn't, didn't or won't? We all have it in us, so what's the problem? And here is the answer that may seem odd, but I hope is not AT odds with this notion. GOING BIG isn't about doing big things. It's about doing extraordinary things. It's about being exceptional in some way...your way. You get to decide what your own kind of amazing is and how you will live it. We avoid going BIG because we don't feel capable of being big, but somewhere along the line we forgot that our contribution needs to be grand, not grandiose.

I recently had the distinct privilege of talking to an incredible, world-renowned photographer who is an inspired artist and visionary. He was commissioned by the ESPY awards to create a series of pictures of world famous athletes. Athletes that for most of us seem larger than life, who have accomplished and achieved at nearly unimaginable levels. And I believe that Rick, the photographer, would tell you that what made these pictures extraordinary, what made them soul-stirring and inspiring was that he took all the BIGNESS away. He didn't make a photo of an athlete in all their muscle bound glory, wrapped in medals or surrounded by trophies. He took pictures of the people they are. Rick captured what makes them human not what makes them heroes and in doing so gave us all permission to believe that we too could be great.

Similarly, Greg had, on a climbing expedition, once flown into a country stricken with extreme poverty and he had the compassion and desire to ask and wonder, "If you were in charge, where would you even start to try to fix this?" And my answer, my belief is that you start with one. Believing that a single life changed or made better because we are here is enough. A single life, a single soul, a single circumstance altered in a meaningful way because of you isn't just BIG, it's HUGE. And it alone is more than enough. Going BIG is not, and never has been a matter of who can make the loudest noise, the biggest splash or land themselves on the cover of the most magazines. Going BIG is as small and as simple, as words of encouragement. Playing with a child. Comforting a friend. Sharing a meal. Hearing the wisdom of an elder. A single mother who struggles, but day in and day out gives it everything she's got. The recovering alcoholic that every day makes the choice to stay sober. A man who grew up with an abusive father but has chosen to never raise a hand to his own children. The ability to forgive, to believe, to endure and to overcome. Standing up to what's wrong. Standing up for what's right. Fighting for your marriage instead of filing for divorce. Believing…truly believing that your worthiness is not a conditional gift but an irrevocable right. Being afraid but doing it anyhow. Choosing compassion over anger. Telling a woman she is beautiful, a man he is able, and a child that they are indescribably precious.

Life simply doesn't get any BIGGER or better than this…

Don't worry! I've got your back.

Most frequently this phrase is associated with some sort of male bonding ritual or code. Due to the phrase having its origins in the seedy realm of bar fights and parking lot brawls, this is entirely understandable. Guys want to know that their buddies, "have their back," and this is now true and expected everywhere from the bar to the boardroom.

At some point we all get to grow up and hopefully our need for a backup at the bar is replaced by our need for the same, perhaps nobler, defense in other areas of life. I believe that regardless of our age or stage, we never stop appreciating the feeling of having someone there to support us, encourage us, and keep an eye out for a life-blow that might blindside us. But here's the deal boys…we want in. While women rarely, slap each other's shoulders, helmets or backsides, we still want someone to "have our back." Namely YOU. And what a win-win! You guys are already good at it. You've practiced since puberty! You know how to be loyal, supportive, brave and ready to take or throw a punch if the need arises.

Truth be told I long to see men do more of this in their relationships with women. Ask yourself, does your wife or girlfriend, feel like you, "have her back," in the same fearless, committed way that your buddies do? If not something is wrong. Does your wife, girlfriend or significant other feel as though you are ready and willing to jump in and support them no matter what? This is not an academic discussion of right and wrong. This is a suggestion that while it is important to source out right and wrong at some point, your partner in life needs to know that you will react on their behalf automatically and even impulsively. No buddies in a bar fight have ever said, "hey look, dude, before I get involved in this did you say something insensitive to piss this guy off because if so, you're on your own." No way! You react. You support. You defend instinctively and perhaps ask questions later while licking your wounds.

So if you could throw a little of this bravado our way that would be super. If somebody is critical of us, be as willing to rush to our defense. If we are being undercut, undermined, underpaid or underappreciated, it would be really great if we could count on you to support, defend or encourage us, no questions asked. Or at least asked later. I will gladly lay claim to being REALLY fortunate in this regard. Greg is my greatest source of support and encouragement in ALL things. If I have a business idea, he encourages it. If I have a heart desire, he will take it on as his own. My thoughts, my dreams, my hopes, my endeavors – I have always felt his strong and unwavering support. Even if the idea eventually goes down in flames he'll just help me put the fire out - not stand there warming himself with the heat of a smug, "I told you so."

As parents, we try to be very much on the same page but right or wrong Greg ALWAYS supports me in those inevitable moments of conflict. He is quick to say things like, "don't argue with your mother that way," or "do what your mom told you to do," or "if you ever speak to your mother like that again, you'll wish you hadn't." He doesn't stop to assess the situation, he reacts in the moment with an "I've got your back," attitude and I think this is so meaningful in a life partnership.

On the flip side I think women need to be ready to go to proverbial blows too. There have been instances in our life where someone has said something critical about Greg and I nearly lose my mind. Does this mean that occasionally a child doesn't have a reason for acting out or that a business contact doesn't have a valid complaint? No. But it does mean that come hell or high water we all need to know that we have somebody that will love and support us NO MATTER WHAT. This isn't about setting good judgment aside, as at times your necessary role will be lending wisdom to your partner's less than prudent choices. It's about knowing that in spite of our sensibilities or lack thereof we have a source of unwavering belief in us.

Bottom line: We all need a wingman. Someone that is willingly and courageously in the dogfight with us. Somebody ready to "go to guns" on our behalf. Life is an undulating series of victories and defeats. Are you brave enough to be there for both? Whether you're a guy or a gal, a husband or a wife, we ALL want and need to know that win, lose or draw you've got the guts to "have our back," and to be there fearlessly loving us every step of the way.

My life is AMAZING! Just not yet.

To give credit where credit is due, I owe this line of thinking to my husband's oldest son. Long have I heard the tale of Joel as a very young boy perched longingly on a fence railing waiting with the sort of awe and anticipation that only the unencumbered minds of childhood allow, for his turn to ride a horse! And as he is trying his hardest to wait patiently for his turn at something he has been imagining and dreaming about for so very long, he turns to his dad and says, "Dad, this riding horses sure is fun. Just not yet."

Every time I think on this story I get tears in my eyes thinking about that pure, untainted belief and wonder that is part of childhood. That Joel, as a young boy could so vividly feel the experience before ever touching the saddle is a testament to the sort of vision and imagination and the certainty about both that seems reserved for children who have yet to be altered in their beliefs by the weight of the world. And each time I hear this story, it makes me wonder with admitted sadness, where has our imagination gone? Our vision for our amazing lives that is so real

126

we can wholeheartedly declare, without pause or hesitation, it to be AMAZING.

Well, much to our collective chagrin, AMAZING has been put on hold. We're apparently all participating in the life lay-away plan. My life will be amazing when I graduate from college. When I get married. When I land that job. When I quit my job. When I finish grad school. When I get that contract. When I close that deal. When I lose 10 pounds. When I have kids. When I get a boob job. When I buy a first house. A better house. A better car. When I finally go on that vacation. When I have money in the bank. When I retire. When I meet "the One." Problem is, our delayed life is completely and utterly useless to us. Now I am not talking about the exuberant anticipation of some special moment or event. I am talking about our endless ability to put joy on hold in favor of some imagined check point where and when we will finally give ourselves permission to be happy.

Anybody who has ever been on a regimen or diet knows that this constant deprivation does nothing but make us downright surly. As it should. I can only hope that we are all irritable over the fact that we keep telling ourselves that happiness is just one job, one date, one deal, one dream away. The reality is that this sort of thinking ensures only one thing. That the beauty, the joy, the wonder, the magic of life will always be out of arms reach. Why? Because we need to taste it now. We need to be present with every win, lose or draw in the game of life as it is playing itself out. We need to allow our moments to be so warm with the pulse of life that we cannot help but be drawn to their enticing rhythm. The more that is on our to-do list, the less we will have on our "look what I did!" list. Because life isn't about grinding, it's about grabbing. Grabbing onto the here and now with your whole heart.

Simple case in point; during the holidays I get a bit wrapped around the axel shall we say. Focused with rigid, obsessed anxiety on orchestrating every detail of the Season. What it must look like, feel like and how, above all else, it, and everyone involved, must submit to my Plan. All of my intense and concentrated efforts are aimed at creating a ridiculously specific type of experience for my family. So to cut to the moral of my story I was making myself and everybody around me crazy trying to engineer an experience for the payoff of some incredible ensemble of memories. But contrary to all my intense efforts toward overachievement, do you know what my best moment of the entire Season was? Doing a puzzle with my five year old son in the early pre-dawn hours one morning. The house was quiet. The morning was peaceful and I had not yet begun my relentless assault on manufacturing our memories. This wasn't planned. I just let it happen. I just enjoyed it. I allowed myself to settle into the wonder of the moment and in doing so I can confess that amidst all the flashiness and expectation of my willful determination, it was the single best moment of the entire Season. For a brief pause it wasn't about clawing my way toward a desired result, it was simply and blissfully about a moment so humbly spectacular that I will never forget the memory or the lesson it taught me. It is BECAUSE I wasn't focused on the next thing that I, oh so briefly, enjoyed something AMAZING.
So stand on the fence of your life for just a moment and watch what is happening around you. Allow every hope and dream you have to be so real, undeniable and vivid in that moment that you can taste the experience of it. Allow yourself to dream, wish, hope and to create with all the brilliance you can imagine, but while doing so realize that right here, right now, even though IT hasn't happened yet…your Life is amazing and waiting for you to notice it.

Let it go…

Let what go? Oh, pretty much everything. I'm not sure how many of you have kids, but kids or no I'm recommending you go see the movie "Frozen." It's been in theatres for months…yes months. And why months when most movies have an active, "in theatres" shelf life of about 3 weeks does this one continue to draw us in? Because people are going to see it not just once but four or five times. Most I've heard of so far was from an employee at Barnes and Noble who said she and her roommate had seen it six times. Ridiculous? Perhaps, but I too was struck by the message.

To be honest the first time I saw the movie was during an escapade with the kids in the throes of the busy, oh so hectic and therefore distracted, Holiday Season. And I enjoyed it, but will admit it didn't knock the wind out of me. But the kids were begging to go see it again and so a couple weeks ago, we did. And when I allowed my mind to not just enjoy the entertainment factor, but to dwell on the message I was more than a bit enthralled. The reason for my perhaps delayed, but assuredly sincere enchantment was that it struck at the heart of a struggle I believe we all endure. How to let it all go and simply and oh so wonderfully, be WHO we are.

Disney has always done a bang up job of entertaining us with the age old battle of dark against light. Good vs. Evil. A war that rages within us all. How do we let our light shine when the darkness of self- doubt and the less noble aspirations of ourselves or others are always there to challenge our character and ask what we're made of? Disney always delivers the goods, and the noble, the heroic and brave always wins out over those dark and threatening forces. But our battles never seem to wrap up in tidy and inspiring ways after approximately 90 minutes of chivalry. Day in, day out, we face our demons and wonder why we are battle worn and weary. Until now. Until as I sat and watched "Frozen," (on the second go around) with my kids, and said to myself, "this is it!" "This is the message we all need to not just hear but to live and breathe." We need to just "let it go!" The battle? The struggle? Oh hell no! We need to let go of every worry, every sense of self-doubt and insecurity that weighs down our ability to fight for what we deserve. Every question of our worthiness, our competence or adequacy, our lovability, our right to succeed needs to be dropped like a bad habit. Because what gets in the way of our success is not our desire to fight for it, it's the legions of worries, concerns and fears that relentlessly assault our soul. What will people think? What right do I have? That's never going to happen, I have responsibilities. What if it doesn't work? I SHOULD do this or I'm EXPECTED to do that. I'm not smart enough. I'm not thin enough. I don't earn enough, I'm not pretty enough, I'm not successful enough. F**k it! LET IT GO!

At first blush it could sound like I'm advocating rash irresponsibility and inner anarchy but quite the opposite in fact. What I'm advocating is letting go of everything the world is telling us to be so that we stand a chance of becoming everything we were meant to be. So really it's an argument for loyalty rather than rebellion. Loyalty to your WHY, that purpose, that sense of meaning, that undeniable reality that each and every one of us is here for a Reason. And if you keep listening to the chatter that the world surrounds you with what chance do any of us stand of hearing the whispers of our soul? The real and ironic tragedy is that our truest self is exactly what this world is counting on us to be. Not some never ending circus act performing to and for someone else's expectations. I realize that in entertaining this discussion I run the risk of sounding like some gauzy, dreamy charlatan, peddling intangible, unrealistic notions. But here's the deal; unless you've already mastered the craft of being you, some unspoken part of you aches desperately to try this challenge on for size. Go ahead. Give it a shot…your best shot. Disney has hit the nail on the head with this message and then some. Let it go.

If we were all to let go of the exhausting burden of acting like a bunch of dancing ponies performing for other people's expectations and trying to be what they need vs who we are, I am convinced that true and meaningful success would reveal itself to us in ways so abundant and overwhelming that it would blow our minds, but fill our hearts. And truth be told that is the emptiest part of us these days. It's not that our bank accounts are empty and it's certainly not that our lives are empty. But our lives are cluttered like some unruly garage full of nothing but junk and what's empty is us. And the best way, the only way, to fill that void is to find the courage to LET IT GO and once you do, your joy will unfold before you in such spectacular fashion as you have never known before.

New Year's Revolutions
...I mean resolutions.

Or do I? No actually I'm in favor of fewer resolutions and more revolutions. Making New Year's Resolutions has, for some, become as meaningful as roses on Valentine's Day. We do it because we think we should, but it isn't really our idea and our heart is rarely invested in this annual declaration of grand intention. But a Revolution! Now THAT by its very name and nature has some weight, some substance, some fiery grit and determination to it! Now Resolutions are all well and good, but tend to be quite cliché when they arrive on New Year's. As a result, our hearts and therefore any true resolve rarely hold their ground for the long term. To be sure people do occasionally use this time a year to launch into real, deep and true change. But more often than not, New Year's resolutions result in rarely used gym memberships and a juicer that collects dust before finding its way to a garage sale. So it occurred to me that the answer to these take-it-or-leave-it resolutions was to entirely forego them in favor of something infinitely more deep, meaningful and enduring. A Revolution.

Now once you start a revolt, it more or less implies that there is no going back. No shrugging your shoulders and saying, "next year perhaps." No one from your local gym is going to come knocking on your door when you've gone for over a week without grunting, or groaning, your way through your latest resolution. But a revolt, is a far more powerful personal performance. To stage a revolt requires an entirely different level of determination and commitment. Now when the colonists made the rebellious move to toss a bunch of tea into Boston Harbor, I'm pretty convinced they knew the fallout would be dire. Yet none of those brave souls showed up on the dock the next day apologizing for their hasty actions and blaming their defiant behavior on one too many pints at the pub. They didn't merely resolve to file a complaint about tyranny, they led a revolution to rid themselves of it forevermore. They didn't just agree with the notion of freedom they went to war to win it as their own.

So what freedom do you have yet to claim? What part of yourself and all you could become are you holding prisoner with your fear, your uncertainty and your excuses? What mediocrity have you settled for in your life rather than the inevitable, heartache, struggle, and battle scars that are part of any true transformation? Is your internal upheaval a force to be reckoned with or is it a vague and weak notion of what would be nice if it weren't for the battalion of excuses that thwart your efforts with little to no resistance from you. Greg has spoken often of the "anti-you" as he calls it. That voice of fear and uncertainty that keeps us from realizing the absolute splendor of who we might become. That dialog of anxiety and procrastination that convinces us that we can't, we shouldn't, we are undeserving or unable. Call it what you will, the "anti-you", the alter-ego, the devil, or just a nasty boss or unsupportive family that you allow to plant the seeds of worry and self-doubt. Are you willing to go to battle? Are you willing to be beaten up by that phalanx of forces that will try to keep you from your God-given purpose? Are you willing to leverage your heart and mind against legions of naysayers, with yourself being perhaps the most formidable opponent of your potential? Yes or no? It's only the essence of who you are and all that could be that hangs in the balance. Now lest I paint an errant picture that glorifies this struggle as needing to resemble dire and dramatic combat zones of sweeping martyrdom, such is not always the case. Perhaps the battle is the successful CEO who in his heart of hearts wants to coach high school football, but succumbs the pressures of society that suggests that we value status, wealth and influence. Perhaps it is the mother with years invested in her education and career that has the courage to decide that the job of being a mom is where her heart truly lies. Or perhaps it is found in a daily willingness to confront that which keeps you from the bright light of possibility and purpose.

So I am suggesting that we can the cliché in favor of a crusade. An all-out, unapologetic Revolution for the life, the joy, the passion that is our right if we are willing to not just want it, but to fight for it. Do we retreat to the trenches of ease and acceptability or do we rise to the challenge of deserving more and dare to inspire others along the way. Personally I'd rather be wearied and wounded by the battle than wonder what might have been…

***In loving memory of Marci Millican who taught me how to be brave.

"She doesn't work...she stays home with the kids..."

Every time I hear this phrase I'm not sure if I want to scream or just weep uncontrollably. So let's evaluate which of the two responses I should employ to properly express my exasperation. Screaming...or as Robin Williams would say from one of the greatest movies of all time; giving it my best "barbaric yelp." There are few things that leave me more crazed than hearing men AND WOMEN use this impossibly ignorant expression. Am I overreacting? Is it just a harmless saying? I think not. If we are willing to get up in arms over calling a football team the Washington Redskins, because the term is insensitive and politically incorrect, how we continue to get away with an expression that renders valueless the greatest endeavor known to human kind is beyond me.

Since when did raising human beings begin to carry the same effort equivalent of going on a Royal Caribbean Cruise? Admittedly, I have railed about this unpleasant phenomena before. But as the adage has yet to be expunged from the human lexicon, my crusade is far from over. It is literally impossible to imagine a wife saying, "my husband doesn't work, he just manages projects, oversees employees, organizes corporate finances and expenses, controls inventory, specializes in product development, moonlights as a janitor, a chef, a tutor, a coach and an EMT, and in his spare time seeks to discover and nurture the human potential." And while he "isn't working" he puts in approximately 97 hours a week, gets no time off or paid vacation (because after all, he isn't working), is on-call 24/7 three hundred and sixty five days a year. His retirement plan is non-existent and his "lunch break" consists of four minutes at the counter and the crust of a slobbered on peanut butter and jelly sandwich. The MOST CONSERVATIVE number I found for the estimated pay of a stay-at-home mom based on hours worked, expertise required etc. was a Forbes magazine article which placed the extrapolated annual salary at $115,000. John Medina, the author of one of my favorite books, and a well-respected researcher and professor, puts the number at somewhat higher than that. So in the face of some rock solid comparisons to other "jobs," I struggle to understand why this offensive phrase persists.

And to be sure, this isn't about taking men out to the woodshed, women are some of the worst offenders when it comes to perhaps mindlessly employing this expression. Women, can you even imagine having a conversation with another woman at a cocktail party, and she tells you that she's a NASA astronaut and you nod agreeably and say, "That's sweet. But what's your day job?" If we are so careful to honor other occupations, why do we so quickly surrender the inestimable value of motherhood? And please do not register my hearty complaint as an argument over the virtues of women who work outside the home vs. those who stay home. Mine is a comprehensive plea that no matter who we are and what we do, we offer as much respect and reverence for the occupation of raising kids as we do anything and everything else.

Now lest you think that as a mother of four WHO LOVES HER JOB I am overly sensitive to the esteem my efforts receive, I will argue that my opinion on the offending phrase is unrelated. I've never been an accountant, but I don't envision myself saying, "They don't work, they goof around with numbers all day." I've never gone to medical school, yet the time will never come when I view their exhaustive efforts at school, residency, internship and a medical practice as a mere prelude to an impressively low handicap on the golf course. I've never been a general on the field of battle but does that mean I view them as running around in the desert playing army? Sir! No sir! The moral of the story is that we don't need to DO something to value the heart, the soul, the dedication, the proficiency and the passion involved in that effort.

So here's the deal. Families are the very heartbeat of our human condition. They are our connection, our motivation our beloved concern. Children are the most precious, fragile, magical parts of this framework and putting the role of raising them on par with soap operas and pedicures is a thoughtlessness that requires adjusting. Why do we admire the role of a corporate CEO, but fail to realize that a household is quite literally a business that needs to be run with not just expertise and efficiency but with heart, soul and tireless devotion?. The skill set of a mom is more complex and demanding than nearly any job I can think of. As well, I am hard pressed to think of another profession where the cost of failure is so unimaginably high. Why? Because of the priceless nature of your product...people...little ones.

So to go back to the beginning of my rant, the second option on the table was weeping uncontrollably. Well, perhaps I'll just take a pass on that and continue to offer a subdued correction each time I hear this unwelcome phrase. But I will say that every hug, every kiss, every peel of delighted laughter, brings me such joy that not a day goes by that I don't have tears in my eyes. Why? Because six figures or not, I have the best JOB in the world.

Mean people suck...

Eloquent? No. True? Undeniably.

I think we have all had the displeasure of being forced to deal with nasty, unpleasant people. Let's face it, there are times when nasty people seem to pop up in our lives more abundantly than scorpions in the desert. And they are just as revolting and painful. Can you tell by the analogy that I'm still smarting from a recent encounter? But the seriously unpleasant visual is, I hope, serving my point. Mean people, like scorpions, are flat out disgusting creatures and both inflict a kind of sting that is terribly hard to forget.

But what do we do about them? These vile creatures that invade our life, our experience and mess with our shazam? Despise them? Plot a revenge assault worthy of a CIA text book? Ignore them? Forgive them? It's hard to say because often times the appropriate response can only be determined on a case by case basis. Are there relevant circumstances? Did they feel provoked? Or are they just the flat out vicious sort and merely being within striking distance puts you in harm's way? While I do believe that context is critical, I am also loathe to admit that I am convinced there are people in this world who thrive on creating discord. They search for ways to create struggle, strife and difficulty for others. Their purpose is unpleasantness and they have honed their skills to an utterly alarming degree of proficiency. They seek out opportunities to hurt, harm and create chaos. When I have come across these spiteful creatures one of my first reactions is always, "where do they find the time?!" I swear that even if I had to admit to the self-demeaning state of despising someone I wouldn't have time to actually DO anything about it.

I am writing this on Halloween and as I dropped the kids off for school this morning and I see all these little people dressed up as Super Hero's I can't help but think, "what if these people put that same energy into saving the world?" Or if that's asking a bit much, imagine if they spent their energy on something positive or at least productive? But alas, we don't live within the pages of a Marvel comic book and the villains in life seem to outnumber the heroes in vexing proportions. A particularly frustrating characteristic of mean people is that more often than not they are self-righteous fools who teeter precariously on the precipice of their own hypocrisy. SO annoying. And speaking of heroes, if you were to look at the top 20 movies of all time you would find a powerfully consistent theme. Nearly every one of these movies takes on the epic battle of good versus evil, dark vs. light, courage vs. cruelty. Now does that stuff just make for cinematic magic or is there an undeniable connection in the cord that is struck by this unending battle? While we may not be Luke Skywalker, Iron Man, Aragorn, a humble Hobbit or an awkward boy named Harry Potter, we too wage this war every single day of our lives. Personally I have found consistent answers when I endeavor to always choose actions that I can be proud of. Not reacting. Not responding. Not getting back at someone who has wronged me. It is choosing to act as the person I want to be rather than the person unwelcome people or circumstances would have me become. All I have to say is thank God there's no

Nasgul involved or bravery be damned I'd just run for the nearest Elf.

Now I will be the first to admit that there was a stretch of time in my life where encounters with nasty people would get me hotter than a Texas A&M bonfire. My instinct was to fight back and more often than not, I did. But I have arrived at a point in my life where I have realized that every single moment I allow myself to be dragged into the world of someone else's bitterness and ill-content is a moment that is being robbed from something infinitely more precious. And it is all my fault. No one but me is to blame when I allow this cynical soup to boil. We are the gate-keepers of our life, our moments, our meaning and our purpose. Resentment and hostility dim our own light and life and what an unforgivable shame that is. And when I fail and falter along the way, I feel so very blessed to have inspiring role models who recalibrate my compass when bitterness begins to get the better of me. If someone choses for their Purpose to be spitefulness, anger and retribution my new philosophy is to kill 'em with kindness. And if those efforts are in vain, then I need to let it go. Judgment isn't my job. It never has been and I will leave that role to the ultimate Authority on the topic. Now to be sure, there are times when the best defense is a good offense and we are morally bound to protect our family and our livelihood. Okay. So establish a perimeter and be done with it. Build your fences, but don't get sucked into the thorny no man's land of petty actions and small thinking. There's a reason this enlightened path is called, "taking the high road." The view is much better from here than it will ever be from the gutters of anger and resentment. The world, and those you love need you to stay true to what matters and to continue to pursue your light as it was intended to shine.

To this end, it was not the lights on the Las Vegas strip that caught my heart and my attention a few weeks ago. It was being in a room filled with amazing, noble, giving, inspiring people. It is moments shared with such astonishing souls, the laughter of my kids, the love of family, or the blessings in my life that humble me every single day that deserve my time, my energy, my attentions. So when mean people darken your life, focus on the brightest light you can find and run fast and hard in that direction. It will never let you down.

Show up! It's your life!

Having just returned from one of the most encouraging, challenging, intriguing and inspiring gatherings I have ever experienced, I can't help but dwell on the Heart of the Matter. I am speaking of course of the All Star Weekend in Las Vegas presented by the Cor Company two weeks ago. We came to learn about real estate and grow somewhat wiser in our chosen line of work. What we ended up learning wasn't nearly so much how to be better investors, we learned how to be better people. What we thought would be education was ultimately inspiration. And what we hoped would be motivation became a glimpse of our astonishing promise and, not to be denied potential. We came looking for the professional "take away," and ultimately we were swept away by the undeniable truth that aligning our intentions toward what we can give, is infinitely more powerful than searching for what we would hope to get. I personally had my sights set on creating an impacting, dynamic, educational experience that aspired to offer people the energy and expertise to go out and achieve. How to buy, sell, expand, acquire, and invest. What this experience ended up being surprises and confounds me still. What made this event so extraordinary? What made it so enchanting? Why was I laughing, crying and literally gasping in awe over what was happening? Why did I feel so inspired? Why do I feel so humble and full of promise all in the same breath? And why do the challenges of it all excite rather than fear me? It's because over the course of four days, I had the unique and unforgettable experience of being surrounded by people who were showing up for their life in a BIG way. They weren't hoping for good things. None of them were wishing for success. No body there was kind of in. EVERY SINGLE PERSON there came with the whole of who they are. And better still, they gave everything they had. To the event, to one another, to the experience that none of us could describe, but all of us shared.

By way of confession, I am not AT ALL a woo woo kind of person. No group hugs, pat your neighbor on the back or kum bay ya encounters for this gal thank you very much. So the LAST thing I want to do is cast this event in that hazy, intangible, ungraspable light. My lack of ability to adequately describe the experience is solely the fault of my own limited ability and imagination. But the inescapable reality is that this event blew my mind, so in truth it is not my fault that I have none of it left with which to write this post. Once something has blown your imagination, I think it takes a while for it to grow back.

So maybe I'm asking you to just trust me. But really we'd all be better served if you trusted "Them." Ask someone who was there. Someone who took it in. Someone who knew this would be a valuable experience and so came, but I can absolutely PROMISE you that nobody there expected all of what came our way, myself included. I think Facebook has taken us all from six degrees of separation to about two and a half, so chances are, if you're reading this post, a friend of a friend was in Vegas. While I am hard pressed to describe what happened exactly, it is less of a challenge for me to share a few of the most profound Truths that were abundant and ever present. To begin,

EVERYBODY at the event was showing up for their life...in a huge way. They weren't just on a journey they were forging a path. Determining what they want and passionately pursuing it. They were committed, devoted and steadfast in their vision, their beliefs and their whole hearted involvement in their own lives and with whom and what they love. They were making choices, and not easy ones, that purposefully drove them towards that which stirs their soul. And as likely we all know, passion is a magical flame that cannot be resisted. Simply being near one whose fire burns so brightly cannot help but warm those lucky enough to be near. Some Presenters were scared to death of speaking, but their message was so captivating and occasionally jaw dropping that we were all riveted. And we were all rewarded. Rewarded by the overwhelming generosity of hearts and minds. Rewarded by the gift of being in a room full of people who understand what REALLY matters. This was not an experience solely built for the purpose of how to get better at what we wish to achieve, it became an experience about how to be better at who we are. Giving, sharing, belief, faith, passion, education, expertise and across the board a shared expectation that we are better people not because of what we do, but because of who we can become.

They say that "what happens in Vegas stays in Vegas" and I have personally been beating the drum of "oh no it will not!" Feeling compelled to the point of near obsession with expressing to anybody who would listen just what they missed. But perhaps I am on the wrong track. I think that to some degree, what happened in Vegas WILL stay in Vegas and you'll just have to join us next year to understand, first hand just what all the fuss is about.

I absolutely cannot wait...

Au Natural...

In honor of the fact that the ACA (Affordable Care Act) is upon us, I thought it might be an appropeaux time to posit a few thoughts on an empowered alternative to government run "health care." Like broccoli for instance.

Hopefully there is not a one of us that would argue the virtues of personal responsibility so at a time when the government is aiming to get involved in some of the most intimate aspects of our lives I think a healthy dose of independence is in order. Understand, my suspicious opinion of the upcoming overtake of healthcare and insurance is not related to the huge hearted providers in this field who serve their patients and their profession with commitment and compassion. It is related to the fact that our government possesses not just a lack luster performance record, but has proven itself as whole to be thoroughly inept when it comes to creating or applying any sort of true common sense based reform.

Admittedly I have not endeavored to become an authority on the upcoming changes or their implementation. I will also readily concede that Insurance and the Health Care business are ailing entities, but to put your wellness in the hands of Uncle Sam feels akin to asking my five year old to take care of the baby. At best unwise and at worse...a disaster of epic proportions. As laughable as this anecdote may seem, bear with me. Greg, myself and the kids made a stop at Whole Foods the other day and there happened to be a wildly entertaining gentleman at the store doing a Vitamix demo. This guy was whipping up everything from smoothies to Frappuccino's to tortilla soup in a REALLY expensive blender. He had all four of my kids drinking some bright green concoction and ravenously reaching for more. What sort of magic machine is this I ask!?

So as I'm standing in Whole Foods surrounded by green goop drinking kids it occurs to me that I am far more concerned about their health and well-being than Obama Care will ever be. In fact I am far more invested than any doctor, specialist, pediatrician or any other professional I may want to lean on. While it may be their job to care for their patients, it is my life to care for mine. To be sure this is not a criticism, but rather an acceptance of the fact that if I CARE the most I need to DO the most. I need to educate myself on what is going to keep my family well and healthy and going strong. And it could be as simple as opting for peas rather than a prescription. I may just need to look into muesli rather than medicine.

I was recently talking with a friend who mentioned that in the rural areas of China, each village tends to have a doctor. And if you get sick, the doctor doesn't get paid. Why? Because his job is to keep you well. What a concept! As well, I have recently learned that the United States has 5% of the world's population and consumes 95% if the world's supply of pain pills. So while we may be able to conjure images of haze filled opium dens in the Far East the alarming reality is that Americans are the ones

146

who can't get enough of the stuff. Apparently we pop pain pills like they were M&M's and wonder why we are unwell. On a personal note, I was talking to my doctor about a particular procedure and her response was, "insurance doesn't prevent, it just treats." Okie dokie. So bottom line; prevention is my job and your job, and we all better get on board and learn how to make a killer smoothie.

I am certainly no expert on this topic, but I think I may need to become one. I may need to get my own personal PhD in how to partner with nature and knowledge in order to keep myself and my family as healthy as possible. While I wouldn't shun modern medicine for a nanosecond in an emergent situation, perhaps day in and day out I need to do better. I need to step up to the plate, literally, and make sure most of it has something green and leafy on it. I need to really dwell on the reality that each and every one our bodies are miraculous machines and we need to equip this wondrous organism with the tools to help, heal and be vibrant.

Now that I've arrived at accepting responsibility for educating myself and the work that comes along with wellness, I would like for someone to lock all the "experts" in a room and have them hash out one true Wisdom on this topic. Should we all be vegans or is eating like a cave man the healthier approach? Are eggs good for us or should we steer clear? Is raw food the fountain of youth or is it found in a shot of vodka every day? Are whole grains the golden ticket to feeling like a million bucks or is there a darn good reason why Atkins has made millions? Should we be eating carbs or cutting them, and is there a solid reason why we're avoiding gluten like the plague? How exactly is grass-fed beef different from other beef and why is the price per pound for this stuff higher than the going rate on gold? Does milk really do a body good or is the dairy industry the Evil Empire? Should we be obsessing about non-fat, low fat or "good fat?" Call me crazy, but I don't think our bodies are nearly as trendy as the most recent best seller on how to lose 15 pounds in 15 minutes. I think there is one truth and I'd really love to know it and get on the fast track. I don't have the answers, but I do desire the wisdom, so I will continue to take to heart the notion that wellness isn't just a choice, it's a job and I'm the one responsible for doing it.

So I guess that leaves me with one true option. Realizing that wellness is a choice we make, not a policy we buy and I'd rather see a naturopath than navigate co-pays. It isn't just about the quantity of our time, but the quality of our lives.

The infant prince...

I am speaking of course of the newly born son of the Cambridge clan. It has been nearly two months since the wee one's heralded birth and as I was standing in line at the grocery store the other day I realized that the frenzy over this tiny poppet has yet to die down. I well realize that this country's birth was a choice to rend ourselves from sovereign rule but is it awful of me to say that I think having a Royal Family is an utterly delightful proposition? Our once noble Democracy is, in the here and now, run by nothing more than a comedic hypocrisy. As so the allure of something that still feels noble and more importantly, hopeful, tends to draw our eyes and our hearts with an interesting longing.

In late July the tireless media answered the anticipation of not just a country, but the entire world in announcing that Will and Kate had a beautiful baby boy. Now we are hungry for every delicious detail from whether or not they will hire a nanny, what they will be like as parents, how they will usher in a far more modern monarchy with warmth and real world charm. How did Kate lose the baby weight so quickly? What is she eating? What is she wearing? Is she breastfeeding? Even her boobs are our business. When will they return to their royal duties? As if caring for and being parents to the future king of England isn't considered a Royal Duty? At any rate, it got me thinking on why, precisely are we so obsessed with this family? To be sure this royal obsession lends itself to women far more than men but I contend that you should all hear me out. Men if you want to make the women in your life ecstatically happy you may do well to read this rubbish. And in exchange maybe my next post will be something that falls squarely in your camp. Madden Football perhaps?

So what is it, truly, that draws millions of us to the endless magazine covers, the news stories, and the delightful drama that continues to unfold around this new babe? And I believe what it boils down to is that this is a real life fairy tale and every single one of us wants desperately to believe in such magical things. We became learned in such fantasies as children, but none of us remembers when exactly we surrendered our belief in fairy tales, but we do know even the whisper of something that brings us back to that magical frame of mind where anything was possible, good always overcame evil and love conquered all is a terribly hard notion to forgo or outgrow. And apparently, on some often unspoken level, we never do. We, as women, never entirely let go of wanting a Prince Charming to charge into our life. We always want to feel swept off our feet in some romantic and wonderful way and then find ourselves wrapped safely in the arms of our beloved forevermore. We never stop believing in love, joy, happiness and grand adventure.

So now you take that childhood bliss whose enchanted notions we drifted off to sleep with and you bring that to life with this modern day fairy tale and it is hard to resist picking up People Magazine for a quick peek and wistful sigh. But here is where I believe the story becomes thoroughly enchanting. You have the son of a tragic but much beloved figure Princess Diana. Clearly she made some very progressive decisions about how she would raise her boys, but I think her true gift to them was that she was a woman who found her voice, her strength, her own self and in doing so she gave her sons permission, not to be pampered princes, but to be strong, loyal, independent, loving, young men. As such the elder Prince picks a lovely young woman who he falls in love with. And here is where we need to allow our often denied intuition to have a voice. Because what we all FEEL about William and Kate is that they truly, deeply love each other. These two are in every possible way one another's best and truest friend. We see that in the midst of throngs of thousands upon thousands of people William only has eyes for Kate and what Kate sees is not a prince and his stately trappings but the man that she loves and if he was William the gardener it wouldn't make a bloody bit of difference . These two are perfect partners that they lean on one another, through the mayhem it all must be. And they honor tradition while forging their own path keeping each other and their new family at the center of all things.

The next element that I believe lures us all is the notion of significance. Whether you consider it a blessing or a curse, this young price will grow up within a life where everything he does will be of profound importance and such power must be wielded well and rightly. As a Royal Family they have an incredible resource of influence and I think many of us are desirous of such power and persuasion. Some for the right reasons and others for less noble pursuits and desires. But in truth, I think most of us long for a life that "matters." That feels purposeful and rich in meaning and intent. We have a need to know what we are doing, why we are doing it and who we are doing it for. And that all of those Reasons count for not just something but everything. We long to feel that our efforts upon each other's lives make a difference. We wish to lead lives that feel noble and sophisticated yet deeply compassionate and impossibly tender. Some would contend that the relentless interest in the Windsor's is about an obsession with fame. I think people are obsessed not so much with "fame," but rather with feeling important. Hopefully our longing for significance is not for its own sake but again for the sake of feeling as though what we do with our moments and minutes matters. Really, truly matters.

So let us consider perhaps that we have the best of both worlds. While we may not have the Windsor resources at our disposal each and every one of us has the ability to create our own fairy tale. We can find a Prince Charming…they do exist. We can conduct ourselves with grace, dignity and sophistication. And we can, above all, make sure that our lives and actions are significant, impactful and of deep importance. We can love, and laugh and live with enthusiasms because fairytales don't have to end just because the lights go out or we outgrow such childish hopes and dreams. But our own story must be seized with a passionate grip that never lets go. So really the fairy tale is up to you, Happily Ever After is there for the taking and the magic lives on for those who believe in it most.

She's such a B**ch !

Well, as we learned somewhere around third grade, the best response to this assessment is, "it takes one to know one." I am loath to admit that these unpleasant tendencies begin at seemingly tender ages. Our oldest daughter is twelve years old and truth be told I have been literally astonished at how vicious these young vipers can be. I realize this sounds severe but the reality is that these sweet, young things can be flat out wicked. And unfortunately some of them never outgrow it, they just get better and better at it over time. They become near professionals at being spiteful and cutting. They dive into gossip and innuendo like it was a swimming pool in the desert. They occupy absolutely inordinate amounts of time judging others without so much as a passing assessment of themselves. An additional disturbing reality is that they tend to work in packs. Evil needs an audience and women seem inordinately predisposed to joint participation in this kind of carnage. Most will recognize the covert title of these group lynchings as "girl's night out." In fact, I would go so far as to say that the vast majority of the time, flat out jealousy and petty nastiness are the undisputed realm of women.

The utter insanity of it all is that we do it to each other! No man has ever been as malicious as an insecure woman. As I've mentioned before, it usually goes something like this: If she has a better job than you, she slept her way there. If her boobs are better than yours she had them done. If she's smarter than you she's showing off. If she throws a better party, she must have hired someone to do it. If she's a stay-at-home mom, she's selling herself short. If she has a rewarding career she's neglecting her family and her children are paying the price. If she's on the PTO she's a busy body and if that's not on her resume, she is uninvolved and unconcerned. If her children are well dressed she's preoccupied with appearances, if not she's lazy and inappropriately indifferent. If she occasionally swears, she's a bad influence and if she avoids expletives she's a phony. If she wears a low cut top she's immodest and if not she's uptight. If she's religious she's high and mighty and if Sunday service isn't on the agenda she's morally bankrupt. If her house is bigger and better than yours it's criticized for being gaudy and tasteless. If her hair is better it's extensions. If her wardrobe is better she's materialistic. If her circle of friends are intelligent and sophisticated she's a snob. And God help her if she's "prettier" than you. Then the gloves REALLY come off.

I have a relative of mine and what the world sees is that she has what they seemingly desire. A large, lovely home that is spotless and beautifully appointed. She has an adoring husband, four impossibly beautiful children, a second home for weekend getaways and to top it all off is just as pretty as a girl can be. What many would rather not acknowledge is that she is one of the most thoughtful, kind and utterly lovely people I know. But I can absolutely guarantee that BECAUSE of all this, most women at best avoid her and more likely criticize and condemn her. Why? Because she's committed the unforgivable crime of being spectacular and so for that, surely she needs to be punished or at least kept at a very safe distance.

So why do we develop the defense of keeping other women at arms length? Allow me to offer an example of where the problem lies: I remember talking with a gal I met who by way of conversation went into reasonably colorful detail about being at some airport lounge area and how a married man was hitting on her. As she went on and on about their conversation all I could think of is, "why the hell did this conversation last more than 30 seconds? It can't possibly take any longer than that to tell him he's an idiot." But SHE is one of the reasons why women so often succumb to the ugliness of jealousy. We don't believe in each other, we don't trust each other and we therefore have a tremendously difficult time supporting each other.

Is this always the tragic state of affairs? Of course not. I feel beyond blessed to know some utterly astonishing, inspiring, confident, encouraging women. If you are one of those lovely creatures, God Bless and keep up the good work. We are all made better by your ability to show us the kind of character and confidence we are capable of not just possessing, but inspiring in others. We can't all be Oprah, but let's aim for the stars anyhow. We try valiantly to rise above our selfish ways and consistently declare that we want the best for those we know. But generally the unspoken caveat is that we want the best for them as long as that best isn't better than what we can lay claim to or consider ourselves capable of. There is a gal I have recently come to know well enough to call and consider a friend. In getting to know her a bit I learned that she throws elaborate and terribly impressive birthday parties for her children. She creates a theme, sews costumes, creates hand tooled invitations and tends to every exacting detail of these extraordinary events. Many women would listen politely about the effort that she puts into these soirees but silently scoff and claim some sort of moral high ground because they are too busy for such concerns. But here is the reality of the situation. Other women can criticize these domestic persuits or acknowledge that her loving efforts take them to task. The truth of the matter is we admire the fact that she has given herself permission to be passionate about such things. This is relevant because I, personally, happen to be a complete lame ass when it comes to my children's birthdays. So I could offset my own shortcomings by being snide and judgmental about the inordinate amount of time she puts into these unnecessary events or I can deeply admire the fact that with every stitch she is creating the fabric of a lifelong memory for her children and I can learn much from her devotion. (I still stand by my philosophy on 1st birthday's but that is another matter entirely.)

Imagine for just a moment what would happen if we all spent our energy encouraging and uplifting one another rather than finding ways to take your imagined opponent out at the knees. Imagine if our assessments relied on WHO a person is rather than what they have or how they look. Imagine if we trusted one another's character and intentions. Imagine if we acknowledged that we are all mortally flawed and are deeply in need one another's encouragement rather than condemnation. Imagine if we recognized that the only one who's "judgment" we should concern ourselves with is that of our Creator and that His divine opinion of us would be impressively improved if we spent our mortal moments inciting the best in others vs. allowing the worst in ourselves. If this is not an argument you believe in or are compelled by, try this on for size. The most becoming aspect of another human being is not what they LOOK like, it's what they LIVE like. Confidence is far more fetching than appearances will ever be. Said a different way, insecurity is an ugliness that will reveal itself much more boldly than the car you drive or the labels you wear. So the next time you find yourself amidst a pack of she-wolves remember that bitch…I mean beauty is in the eye of the Beholder.

Envy vs. Encouragement

The Battle Royale. I think that at times even the best among us struggle with this tug of war. A tug of war that insists that we rise above our occasionally petty instincts to want what others have. Their life, their means, their adventures, their mindset, their overwhelming number of Facebook friends. So much to need, and so little time.

It is so easy to wander onto the green, green grass of vicariously living someone else's life or to wantingly eye their situation or circumstances. But as with so many things in life this is always a cautionary tale. I think that for many if not most people there is a "storefront." An image or impression that we are willing to readily share with the world and then there is the "boiler room." The reality zone where it all happens. Where we laugh and cry and struggle and do dishes and pull weeds and worry about finances and what's for dinner. "Reality" TV has worked wonders on our ability to live a simulated life or to desire that which seems so entertaining and alluring when it's streaming live onto our laptop. But at what point do we stop living and wanting someone else's experience and instead savor our own? I think society has done a bang up job of getting us to buy into the notion that if it's successful and flashy and fabulous, it is worth wanting. But in reality, it is a fool's errand to spend your time pining over somebody else's experience. I can absolutely guarantee that the more time you spend greedily eying the life you imagine somebody else to be leading, the less time you are spending purposefully seeking out ways to create your own kind of amazing.

To be certain, we all succumb, at times, to our more base and covetous nature. But experience says, be careful what you wish for. Science has shown that once very basic needs are met, money and happiness part ways and for as many episodes of Million Dollar Listing as you may want to watch, the truth of the matter has never changed and it never will. Happiness is an inside job. And you can't hire it out by the way. It will always be a function of YOU. Your energy, your efforts and what you choose to value and hold dear.

My youngest brother, as we speak, is in Italy. Yesterday, I got the pictures of Positano and his next stop was diving at the Blue Grotto. So here is where Envy vs. Encouragement becomes the choice. To be fair, I love my brother so much that it is instinctive to be happy for him. Scratch that, not just happy, literally overjoyed for the experience he is having, the memories he is making and the fact that he is the sort of person that seeks out that which is extraordinary. That he insists on it in his life. A few months ago he was in Thailand doing the very same thing. Capturing life and LIVING it. Not watching it, not hoping for it, but living it. If I was being texted similar pictures from a friend or an acquaintance, would these pictures sting just a little bit? Would there be a small, begrudging part of me that would envy the fact that these were their pictures of paradise and not mine? Not if I choose encouragement over envy.

The most impressive people I know absolutely take notes from others. They look around at people they know and admire and make a mental shopping list of what they want. They borrow inspiration from watching others and use this to identify what, for THEM is not just important, but necessary. Interestingly, they are rarely choosing what is necessary to HAVE, they are always choosing what is necessary to FEEL. A sense of love and connection with a spouse or significant other. The joy of a strong family that laughs and lives and shares. The ability to feel a sense of pride and accomplishment in what it is they "do." A daily experience of that which motivates and inspires them...a commitment to that which draws their passion and stirs their soul. An undeniable link to faith and a belief system. If they see this in others and it drives them toward their own journey, these are the people who have chosen to be encouraged, rather than envious. We can look at another's life and circumstances and want what we imagine them to have, or we can see that which ignites our own inner fires and use this to inspire our own enthusiasm and passion.

The good news is that the outcome is entirely of our own choosing. We can live enviously through cable TV and the impressive litany of lives it displays that are far more interesting or impressive than our own. Or we can take really good notes on what we see in those we respect and admire and allow how those priorities FEEL to encourage us to find our way to the Blue Grotto, a quiet campfire or any other vision that resonates with who you are and what you want. Choose encouragement and these moments, memories and feelings will belong to YOU. Choose envy and those spaces, places and feelings will always belong to someone else. So for as much as I can tell my brother that if I see one more picture of him frolicking in his Mediterranean playground, I'm going begin sobbing uncontrollably, the fact of the matter is, I'm smiling from ear to ear and couldn't possibly be happier for him. But at the same time his joy is inspiring me toward my own. And one day I WILL be touching that water and taking those pictures myself. So let us be grateful to those who are taking on life's adventure, as they are the best encouragement imaginable for us to create our own.

Illegal contact!

Though it's still a bit early, I have to say that I couldn't be more excited to have another football season upon us. I couldn't describe myself as a sports nut, but without question, I am crazy for football. With that in mind, we were on an outing with the kids the other weekend, which always sounds like a better idea in theory than the chaos that generally plays itself out. During the mayhem in the car Greg got me laughing so hard I nearly peed my pants and it all had to do with all the refereeing that goes on as parents. It makes managing a bunch of 200+ pound grown men amped up on game day adrenaline seem as simple as finding porn on the Internet.

Nearly immediately, this sporting event, otherwise known as a Saturday afternoon with the family is marred by a DELAY OF GAME penalty. For the HUNDREDS of times we have reminded the kids to go potty before getting in the car I can still absolutely count on some little person forgetting (clearly I have failed epically in my hopes of training these stubborn critters). As we all know with young ones tending to the need to go is not optional because they ALWAYS insist on waiting until it's an emergency. There is never a buffer zone of time to respond. By the time they say, "I have to go potty," the holding tank is maxed out. Count on it. So right out of the shoot our Disney-like day is marred by a FALSE START and whether we've even left the driveway or not at that point is largely irrelevant. It's the same cumbersome process whether you're in your comfy cul-de-sac or screaming into some random rest stop…it's an all hands on deck hassle. Once everyone is duly drained, count on the fact that upon re-entry into the vehicle chaos will nearly instantly erupt with a PERSONAL FOUL or ILLEGAL CONTACT of some sort. Cries of "He's touching me!" or "She hit me!" are usually the first sign that some sort of infraction has taken place. I wish I could penalize them with yardage, but the Family Vehicle doesn't allow for the luxury of such a thing. So alas, with such limited space, ENCROACHMENT penalties are some of the most frequent offenses; so much so that they tend to be flat out ignored by the officials in the front seat. Yet the refereeing must continue. In that same vein and nearly as frequent, ILLEGAL USE OF HANDS is also a common complaint and I assure them that if they don't act nicely I'm going to enforce a HOLDING penalty on them and nobody is in the mood for that. "Hug it out" is a threat that strikes fear into the hearts of most siblings and I regularly use this to my own frequent game day advantage.

As any parent knows, trying to keep your little darlings in their seats and if not acting nicely, at least minding their own business, often feels like an accomplishment worthy of the Nobel Peace Prize yet success is fleeting and illusive at best. More often than not, they end up OFFSIDES and the bedlam begins again. With nauseating repetition we need to address the nonstop issue of UNSPORTSMANLIKE CONDUCT and this state of affairs is nearly always preceded by an ILLEGAL MOTION of some terrible and offensive sort. Forget UNNECESSARY ROUGHNESS, merely touching one another is consistently cause for inexplicable outbursts. In fact, it isn't even remotely uncommon to have a breach of event etiquette that involves no contact at all! One of the most unforgivable transgressions I've ever heard of is the "mom, she's looking out my window," protest. Certainly somebody needs a suspension for that heinous rules violation. To be sure, looking out the window is cause for unimaginable alarm, but eye contact only adds to the hands-free offense and should be avoided at all cost.

When they are not in the midst of whining, wailing or pinching each other, they are plotting the INTERCEPTION of some treasured toy or trinket. Any defensive line would do well to take a page from the toddler playbook when it comes to the ruthlessness with which they will seek to STRIP a much beloved toy from a brother or sister. Keep in mind that said child only fell in love with the toy 20 minutes ago and their darling sibling couldn't have cared less about the object of their affection until the opposing team had possession.

I will personally go on record and say that what makes me most insane is having to continually call them for TAUNTING. Most parents will readily recognize this as the "He's copying me!" complaint. This behavior in children is more durable than a cockroach in the midst of nuclear winter. NOTHING I do has ever eradicated this particularly irritating infringement. To make matters worse, once the taunting has begun, other kids tend to smell blood in the water and are then hit with a PILING ON penalty as they begin to mimic the maligned child's cries of despair.

Truly, the mayhem is enough to make even the most seasoned referee hang up the whistle, and walk off the field, or out of the car...whatever the case may be. So all I can say is thank you to my husband for helping me laugh through the lunacy of it all. At the end of the day, or the drive, it's just a game, and rules, especially where children are concerned, were made to be broken.

I Believe...

Better still, a question. What do you believe? At the risk of sounding overly esoteric I find myself hard pressed these days to see and perhaps, more importantly, feel, what people believe in. I'm not talking about whether or not you believe in Santa Claus (if you don't you're a fool by the way), I'm talking about that soul stirring, singular, passionate, impenetrable belief in something...or someone. Is it just me or does this intense inner certainty about something...anything, seem to be going the way of the dinosaurs. Extinct.

I was thinking on the Tom Brokaw book, "The Greatest Generation," the other day. Actually, I wasn't thinking about the book, I was thinking about the title. And to be sure it begs the question, "what made them great?" At the risk of sounding plagiaristic since I have yet to read the book, I think what made them great is that they believed in something. They shared a common conviction. An idea, a principle was present among them that was so strong and so unwavering that it gave them the ability to endure unimaginable hardship. There are times when I feel as though I have gone for so long without seeing something inspiring much less heroic that I begin to wonder what we're made of anymore. Are we courageous? Not really. Are we strong? Seldom. Do we have a personal creed that guides us at all times and through all things? Um...no. I realize the tone here is not particularly optimistic, but that's kind of the point. I think that if you asked a lot of teenagers and young adults what they believe in, they would reply, "Being happy." Happy? Correct me if I'm wrong, but happy is a state of mind not a belief system. Yet for too many people, this simple state of being does seem to be their religion of sorts these days. They worship at the alter of self-satisfaction and material success. Since when did how you feel become more important than who you are? Now I am ALL in favor of an absolute abundance of joy, exuberance, wealth and high achievement in life. But this is NOT a belief system. It is a feeling, a state of being and a wonderful consequence, but it is not a Code of Honor.

There is a cable TV show called "Whale Wars," that I have yet to see a complete episode of, but the tag line is one that hit me like a freight train and it went like this; "You haven't lived until you've found something worth dying for." I remember hearing that and feeling it to be so true and so profound that it nearly knocked the wind out of me. And I dare you to deny it. In the same moment, as struck as I was by how profound this felt, I also felt immediately relieved by the awareness that I knew for me, what that something was. I knew, and had always known, what in my life, was worth dying for.

By way of a confession, I had a pretty unique growing up experience. I was born at West Point, the Military Academy and we lived there through my most formative growing up years. To be sure, I was surrounded by a larger than life belief system. Everywhere I looked throughout my childhood, I was reminded of something far greater and more important than myself. I lived and learned and grew amidst the words Duty, Honor, Country. I believed in it then and I believe in it now. And to this day, I believe that this belief is more important than me. If you have never read General MacArthur's speech, you should. Now let me head some of you off at the path of protestation by stating that my core and convicted belief in this triad is not related to politicians or their policies. It is connected to the essence of what those three words mean to me and how noble and right they will always feel and be. Still, for as deep and real and true as these words ring for me, I am not suggesting that we, on any level, need to share the same belief system. But I AM insisting that everybody should have an ethic embedded in their lives and hearts, that is so strong, so unwavering and so true that it is tied to the very essence of who and what they are. I am suggesting that everyone should know their something worth dying for.

In addition to the granite engravings I grew up with, I will also say with fearless certainty that the beliefs most present in my day to day life are faith and family. These things are my everything. Day in and day out I can honestly say that I am not just concerned with these enthusiasms, I am not merely devoted to what and who I love. They are, without question, things in my life worth dying for. So I will continue to choose to define my life along these lines. I hope for happiness, but I NEED Purpose, Reason and a Why. And in order to make our magical spin on planet Earth passionate, profound and meaningful, we need to find that which feeds our very soul. And if our soul is the very essence of who and all we are then it only stands to reason that that which sustains it must be of equal weight and worth.

So find what it is that you believe with limitless strength and conviction. Find and know what for you, is worth dying for. Believe in it, tend to it, and fight for it. I can guarantee that if you find that something to devote yourself to so wholly and completely, then and only then will you encounter the soul filling bliss of true joy.

The Ugly American?

As the summer months are upon us, many fortunate souls set their sights on exotic destinations, historic pilgrimages, romantic retreats or global exploration of some marvelous adventurous sort. We dust off our backpacks and suitcases then pull out our passports with giddy excitement thinking on the sights, smells and wonders that await us.

But then apparently some of us take that next step of devising a fairly convincing backstory that mutes our American roots and conjures up some story of how we are actually Canadian, but my mom's second cousin three times removed got me a job in the states….blah, blah, blah. Canadian? I absolutely LOVE spending time in Canada and we are fortunate enough to live within fairly short driving distance, but since when was that the go-to nationality eh? Now I'm not sure what I missed and when I missed it, but why exactly did Americans begin to feel the need to alter their nationality when traveling abroad? Now I fully understand that traveling in certain parts of the world is akin to bungee jumping tied to a rubber band…not a well thought out escapade. But when exactly did we decide it was okay to forgo our heritage and homeland in favor of an alternate identity of sorts?

I am well aware of the stigma of the "Ugly American," but the reality is that rude, obnoxious, unpleasant people abound and not one country can claim to be idiot free. Do some countries, due to cultural differences, have more than their fair share of morons? I think not. Differences are just that, differences. If a French waiter gets all in a huff because an American traveler has the audacity to ask for ice in his drink who's got the attitude…really? If an Italian man makes remarks when he sees a fair haired, pretty tourist is he a leach or just a wonderfully affectionate, gregarious lover of life and beauty? I don't think there is any thinking person that couldn't argue both sides of this coin. At the end of the day we're all just people. Different people and having a croissant at a café for breakfast isn't any worse or better than grabbing a scone and latte at the Starbuck's drive through. Though the thought of an unhurried café au lait along a sunny sidewalk in Paris is enough to make me weak in the knees.

However, for as much as we need to drop the attitudes on a global scale, I DO whole heartedly believe that travel is a nearly essential way to broaden our perspective and allow us a love and appreciation for just how magnificent our differences can be. I spent my first year of college at the University of Hawaii (long story) and I was in a program with very small class sizes for college. During one class we were having a discussion about I don't remember what but I DO remember a girl in the class commenting in casual fashion that she had never been off the island. Excuse me? Did I hear this right? You're a college age student and for your entire life thus far you have never been off the island of Oahu? I was dumbfounded. How can this happen? How can this be? It's a big world out there! To be fair, as an Army brat we had, out of necessity, been bounced around to various and sundry cities, states and continents. And for as unsettling a life as that may sound, I have ALWAYS appreciated the treasure chest of sights, sounds and experiences that came along with this somewhat gypsy-like upbringing. Not for a single moment did I ever resent my lot in life. Quite the opposite in fact. Even as a very young child I remember taking it all in with a sense of awe, wonder and appreciative intrigue.

Fast forward numerous years and I am in graduate school working on a psychology degree. As the professor begins the dialog on heritage and how people identify themselves along those lines this gal in the class pipes up and says, "Well, whenever I travel, I'm embarrassed to say that I'm American." I remember looking over at her with stunned disgust. All I could think in that moment was, "you stupid, stupid girl." Let's just start with how many young women around the world have the opportunity to get an education. Not just learning basic literacy skills mind you, but working on a professional graduate degree. Then let's think on the fact that you can actually say something so foolish with impunity and without consequence. You have the right and the freedom to say any idiotic, ignorant thing you like and you are using that liberty to its full advantage. I won't bore you with the rest of my internal dialog, but it was mindboggling to me that as she's sitting there bitching and moaning about the utter embarrassment of being American, she is taking full, flagrant and unappreciative advantage of the fact that she IS American!

So the Ugly American? I think not. Who we are and how others experience us is a function of walking through the world with both dignity and humility. Perhaps if we were all more mindful of whom we ARE regardless of where we're from, life and living it would get a whole lot easier. So throw on the back pack or stuff the suitcase. Take a train, a plane or an automobile to somewhere you've never been. Just make sure that when you get there you arrive with an open and curious mind, pour in a sense of awe and wonder, to be sure the rest will take care of itself.

The Blind Side...

I'm not sure what first comes to mind for people. Is it an incredible movie they saw about four years ago? Is it a coaching term they are familiar with or is it that spot in their car where they can't see what's coming or close? Regardless of what first comes to mind I think the reality is that we all have one and it takes a concerted effort at times to improve our field of vision. But improving our field of vision requires that first we know where our blind spot lies. What part of ourselves and our personalities do we not necessarily see for what they are? I heard this funny conversation on the radio last Holiday season and the hosts were talking about how every family has that one person that tends to create chaos and throw angst in every family gathering and if you think your family doesn't have this person...it's you. And it occurred to me that I know a fair number of people like this; People who are chronically involved in some sort of drama or controversy, but never seem to realize that THEY are the common denominator. So aside from the fact that this little quip made me laugh out loud, it does beg the question; how clearly and truly do you see yourself and perhaps more importantly, what parts of yourself and how others experience you are you blind to?

For some reason I seem to see this most consistently with parents and their children. There is this drop dead hysterical

Carlos Mencia comedy bit where he talks about getting in trouble because he came home from school late and he whines to his mother that it's because the bus driver kicked him off the bus a mile away. And for as much as he tries to whimper and complain about what has happened to him, his mom keeps asking him, "what did you do?!" I don't see many parents these days that tune out their children's tales of woe and ask, "what did you do?!" If I have learned anything in life it is that 99.9% of the time there are two sides to every story. Seeing one side of a dilemma or situation while being uninformed of the other is like backing your car out the driveway without so much as a glance in the rear view mirror. Neither is sensible or safe. I'd like to make the case that we can only benefit from taking a good glance at that which isn't necessarily right in front of us. Finding a way to look at the blind spot as it were. I remember when our oldest started preschool the teacher met with all the parents and said, "Let's make a deal, I promise to only believe half of what I hear if you only believe half of what you hear." In other words, kids, regardless of age tend to tell their story. Not THE story, THEIR story. They tend to be blind to what is the hard core truth because they are wee little balls of emotion that have terrible trouble sorting out fact from fiction. While this tendency can be looked at as an endearing aspect of childhood, when parents confirm the blind spot rather than interjecting wisdom, it makes me just this side of crazy. Our six year old got busted last year for putting sand in the hood of a boy in her class. Now per her story, he was teasing her therefore, the sand in the hood maneuver. Okay...at least she wasn't just being malicious. But the fact remains, SHE did something wrong and needs to be responsible for her actions. And far better that she learns the lesson of personal responsibility at six than at sixteen when the stakes are going to be much higher. Any parent that maintains a blind side insisting their precious offspring can do no wrong is in the process of creating a less than endearing human being.
On a different, but related note, I had an experience where I had

a problematic relationship in my life. The dynamic was strained and the relationship was not in a good place. But this person sent a birthday gift and a letter to my oldest daughter that was one of the most touching, thoughtful, loving expressions of care she has ever received. Shame on me if I allow my damaged relationship with this person to blind me to their incredible gesture. So I, in turn, wrote them a letter, saying that regardless of anything that has transpired between us I need to not just acknowledge, but appreciate with depth and sincerity the profound impact of their kindness.

Being aware of our blindside means that we look at our own shortcomings. That we see what is real and act accordingly. That we honor fairness over favoritism. That if a critique is voiced it is met with a listening ear rather than a defensive digging in. I'm not suggesting you accept all input and opinions, but I am insisting that we all have a blind side. A part of ourselves, our lives or our family that we may not see for what it really is. And the only way to illuminate the darkness of our blind side is to shine a light on it.

It's none of my business...

Says who? I got an email recently that placed this odd and somewhat unwelcome dilemma squarely at my doorstep. And it got me wondering exactly where does the virtue lie? Are we better people for not getting involved in other people's lives and their business or conversely, would we all be better off if we cared to get involved in the lives of our fellow man (woman and child)?

To be sure there is no one right answer but I found myself leaning in the direction of choosing involvement over intentional ignorance. Now it is necessary to differentiate as passionately as possible the contrast between genuine concern for a situation or an individual and its evil offspring...gossip. It would be hard for me to express my utter loathing and disgust of the latter. Gossip is for small people who lead small lives. It is the mental playground for those who don't have the intellectual ability to contribute in positive and meaningful ways. It is petty, hurtful, cowardly and often vindictive and those who entertain themselves with this banal chatter should be muzzled like an overzealous Chihuahua.

Okay, now that I've drawn that distinction, I still find myself believing that the hands-off nature of humanity these days isn't necessarily a good thing. There is this show on TV I have seen a couple of times called, "What Would You Do?" It basically films a fabricated, but dramatic situation and then chronicles how people act and react. Truth be told, my take away from this and numerous personal experiences is that we've become either cowardly or unconcerned and neither one of these traits is terribly impressive. It is stunning to me to see how people shun bravery in favor of, "it's none of my business." There is a quote I love from one of the best known stories of all time and it reads like this, "Mankind was my business. The common welfare was my business; charity, mercy, forbearance, benevolence, were all my business. The dealings of my trade were but a drop of water in the comprehensive ocean of my business! "From Dickens, "A Christmas Carol."

And the timeless point remains. Mankind should be our business. Not just the well-being of ourselves, but the well-being of others should be a shared affair. Do we only concern ourselves with doing the right thing in our own lives or do we resolutely expect it from others as well? Do we just try to do what is right or are we willing to speak up for what is right?" Several experiences come to mind… I remember one time being at the playground with our oldest daughter when she was just a toddler. Another family shows up with a small child and an infant in a car seat. Mom and Dad proceed to sit on a bench while little Johnny goes off to play and the infant in this car seat is absolutely screaming his lungs out. Not fussing, not crying…screaming. After about twenty minutes of this I just couldn't take it anymore and I went up and asked his parents, "Do you mind if I just hold him?" Not surprisingly their response was "go ahead," along with a dismissive shrug. So I did just that…I held him. He still cried, but I remember thinking to myself at least he knows that even if he's upset he'll still feel held, and safe and cared for.

Another instance I will never forget is being at my brother's wedding and hearing the priest declare to everybody in the church that we were ALL part of this marriage. He insisted that every one of us witnessing and participating in this ceremony had a responsibility in and to this relationship. I have never heard that before nor have I ever forgotten it. I admit that at times I have struggled to know how to be true to that directive. How to do my part and what precisely my part should be. But regardless, the words ring true. Would half of marriages fail if a support system was truly and actively involved in their success? I've mentioned this before, but I remember being out at dinner one time and there was a foursome of guys sitting next to us that had recently gotten off the golf course. As they were celebrating with more than a few beers, the conversation turns into them all bitching and moaning about their wives. And I remember thinking to myself how impressive it would be if one of these guys grew a set and said, "Hey guys, golf was great, but I didn't sign up for this. If you have an issue with your wife after spending the day relaxing and drinking you might want to take it up with her. I don't want to hear about it." How sad is it that not only did this not happen, but I would have been floored if it did. It takes guts to go against the grain, and mettle seems to be around in meager amounts these days.

I have also found myself on the receiving end of the "get involved" camp. One time my sister-in-law came to me with a pretty strong critique or concern about something I was involved in. And while I didn't and don't agree with her, I HIGHLY respect the fact that she had the guts to say something to me. I might not have liked what she had to say, but I absolutely LOVE the fact that she cared and had the admirable audacity to say it.

So, are you one that would get involved, stand up or speak up, or do you lean more to the "live and let live" life philosophy? I can't claim to know the right answer, but I do know that I have witnessed how getting "in the game" can be a game changer for people. Personally, I don't think that courage and valor should be antiquated notions from a bygone era. I'd like to think they are alive and well. But seeing is believing and I admit to feeling like I'm wanting to believe what I rarely see. Perhaps I just need to keep wistfully watching The Gladiator and Braveheart.

The Microwave Test

In life we seem to be quite fond of tests. Measures that assess value, worth, intellectual or athletic prowess and everything in between. There's the IQ test, the SAT test, the personality test, the DNA test, the drug test, the test run, the test drive, the white glove test, the litmus test and every conceivable form of measurement you can imagine. And to be sure I am not opposed to having some sort of standard by which to evaluate everything from a physician to an SUV. But there is one test that somehow is largely underutilized and often goes entirely unnoticed. Quite alarming really when you consider the copious amounts of evidence, intelligence and inferences that are potentially gleaned from this underutilized evaluation.

I am, of course, referring to the microwave test. Yes, that most common of household appliances offers a wealth of untapped information. How so you ask? Well for years people have secretly snooped inside medicine cabinets for reasons I honestly have yet to understand. Are they hopping to gossip about the Viagra prescription or "borrow" some of the left over oxycodone from your knee surgery? I will admit to the fact that our "medicine cabinet" is a seldom purged accumulation of wayward elixers. I have literally on occasion tossed out prescriptions over 5 years passed their expiration where I had absolutely NO idea what their original purpose or potential usefulness was. So in terms of relevant and current information I think the microwave tells us far more about a given individual than the medicine cabinet ever could.

Have you ever had the experience of being at somebody's home that you don't know terribly well and from outward appearances everything seems tidy and presentable? You wander into the kitchen not wanting to bother or inconvenience anybody hoping to microwave some hot water for an innocent cup of tea. You pop open the door of the microwave and think, "Good God what the hell happened in here!" It's like some horrific hazmat zone is being concealed behind that unassuming appliance door. You are literally frozen not knowing what your next move should be. Do you try to shut the door as quietly as possible knowing that if your gracious hosts realized you had just seen their Little Shop of Horrors they would be utterly mortified? Or do you bravely place your mug in the gruesome mess as if to say that the walls plastered with beans, BBQ sauce and cemented spaghetti is no big deal. Yet all the while you are thinking to yourself that if you get this water to a good rolling boil it will kill whatever microscopic creatures are growing in this fetid petri dish? It's a hard call.

But what is truly important is not whether you persevere in claiming your cup of tea, but your take away from the entire experience. You see I would be very wary of someone who offered a seemingly orderly and attended appearance, but behind closed doors (literally) their life was a mess. I would personally feel more at ease walking into someone's home that was an inviting disaster, knowing that if I go to use the microwave, it will at least be consistent to find it caked with every conceivable leftover since the dawn of time. I am infinitely more comfortable with the person that tells me to go microwave myself a Hot Pocket if I get hungry without caring what I might have to scrape out of the way in order to do so, than I am with someone who would sell me some sort of mirage where what you see isn't necessarily what you get. So next time you are looking to evaluate a person, a business or a situation, might I suggest a peek at that most unassuming and humble of appliances. The microwave. In a world of weights, measures, tests and evaluations, it can offer infinitely valuable insights into precisely who and what you are dealing with. And when not providing valuable covert information, it makes insanely good popcorn.

Except when they don't because Sometimes they won't...

That exceptional phrase from the book of all books, "Oh the Places You'll Go." While life is full of wonderful color and grand adventures we all on occasion have to wrestle with the fact that things don't always go in the sunniest of directions. The lousy reality is that shit happens and people WILL disappoint you. Not a one of us goes through life untouched by struggle or difficulty so the trick in it all is just how do you move on from it? How do you bounce back after being hurt, disappointed, let down, betrayed or just plain frustrated and fed up with things not going right? How do you avoid allowing the ugliness of bitterness and cynicism to set in when at times those two views feel and seem to be the only logical conclusion about life and the people who are a part of yours?

The answer in short is Wisdom. Consider the notion that every experience in life is simply a lesson hoping to be learned; an example, a moral, a message awaiting your discovery. To be sure there are times when all we need to draw on is sheer persistence and will power. A deal falls through, a remodel doesn't go as planned or a tenant trashes a unit. Truly these setbacks are of the simplest sort. We acknowledge what has happened, learn our lesson and move on. We become better at understanding and envisioning a remodel, we run that background check or call the references on every tenant where perhaps we were a bit lax and unconcerned before. These are truly trifling setbacks in this fabulous journey called life. The ones that can really take us out at the knees are those experiences where people close to us are the cause of some hurt, heartache, disappointment, or betrayal. These are the experiences that are agonizing, heartrending, disillusioning and especially devastating. These are the incidents that can shatter our hearts, our belief and leave our very soul shaken, doubting and damaged. That wonderland in our minds called our memory can store the most magical moments of life. Laughter, joy, spontaneity, success, achievement and bliss. But the mental vault doesn't discriminate. It stores equally well the hurts, the hardships, the failures and the frustrations. But the good news is that while these memories exist perhaps in equal parts wonder and horror, YOU get to decide how you internalize them. While all experiences in life AFFECT us, their EFFECT on us is wholly and completely our own choosing.

If we are affected by a hurtful family experience, what effect do we allow for this to have on our lives? We choose for the effect to be wisdom. We choose to learn from each and every circumstance. We may want to stand our ground and insist that WE are not the ones that need to learn a lesson; it's THAT son-of-a-bitch over there. But seeing as how that SOB doesn't seem fazed by their maliciousness or moral shortcomings, it is incumbent on US to draw something other than resentment from the circumstance. And again I say wisdom. What did this person, this encounter, this betrayal, this trial teach us? How to be bitter and disappointed? Or did it teach us how to be wise? Did it teach us anger and resentment or did it heighten our appreciation of what is good and right and lovely in our world? Did we learn to be afraid or did we discover how to evaluate people in careful and meaningful ways? Did we decide that people suck or simply acknowledge that indeed some of them do and here is how I will steer clear of their sort forevermore? Did we decide to insist that this is MY journey and I get to choose not so much what happens, but what I've learned and how I've grown? We can choose to be wronged or we can choose to be wise. And while it's often hard as hell, I pick the latter. And when you make this choice of determination, "will you succeed? Yes! You will, indeed! (98 and ¾ percent guaranteed) Kid, you'll move mountains!"

The Potty Dance...

I was recently talking with a dear friend of mine whose two year old daughter is in the throes of potty training. And apparently the wakeup call comes at 5:30 every morning and only mom will do. The sweet little tot won't have anything to do with dad during this morning ritual...lucky devil. And so bright and early every morning the girls are off to celebrate this momentous accomplishment. It got me thinking on how when our four year old was at the same stage that I vividly remember looking at my husband and asking, "how much longer do we need to keep this up?" How much longer do we need to squeal with joy, high five and dance around like complete buffoons celebrating the fact that he just went potty? How much longer with the hugs, the kisses and the over the top enthusiasm before the behavior is rock solid and happens without this excessive encouragement. I mean what's next? Do we need to hire the Dallas Cowboys Cheerleaders to perform the next time he pees in the toilet? It occurred to me in the course of our conversation that I know an awful lot of adults who have never outgrown the need for some sort of hurrah every time they do something of merit. With my kids I have always followed and spoken of the virtues of encouragement vs. praise. When we praise our children for everything from coloring inside the lines to getting an A on their algebra test we are wiring them to need the feedback and approval of others in order to feel satisfied and accomplished. If we encourage them, their motivation tends to be internal. They do and act in productive ways because it is simply the right thing to do versus an action that will bring them the admiration and attention of others. Children need an internal compass; a guidance system where they give and achieve because it is simply the right thing rather than what is likely to make them seem most impressive to others.

As is so often the case, the downstream of kids that need endless feedback for good behavior is the impossibly annoying circumstance of adults who look for applause for every effort or achievement. Now I'm all in favor of being appreciative of good deeds, but it seems as though time and time again, I see adults waiting with near baited breath for applause to follow their every effort or accomplishment. And truth be told I don't just find this bothersome, I find it concerning on a far deeper level. It worries me that in so many people it would seem that the moral compass was never installed. I worry that people aren't wired to do the right thing for its own sake, but for the sake of what they will "get" in exchange. What is it with adults who still need the proverbial gold star for doing what's right?

I remember Greg being a bit taken aback when becoming aware of my seemingly hard ass philosophy that I don't give brownie points for good behavior. I believe that giving every endeavor your best effort is the base line expectation that we should all have of both ourselves and one another. I certainly don't want or need recognition for working hard, trying to be a great mom, a good friend or any other such thing. Now I'm all in favor of freely flowing acknowledgement of grand deeds and appreciation of the kindness, thoughtfulness or generosity shown to us by others. Both should be doled out with sincerity and generosity. But when adults need or expect constant kudos for extreme effort or good behavior there is something truly amiss. So I'm happy to give my kids endless encouragement. But any adult in your life that seeks constant praise is badly in need of a time out.

He is mine!

Something about a
Turbo Porsche

My #1 four legged guy!

Why should they have
all the fun?

Disney kind of fun!   Cool in the desert

My brother and Seahawk Ring of Honor
Member Dave Kreig

I bought the firemen!

My son Cor McRae

An appreciative moment

Doing my best to educate, motivate and inspire!

He stares off into tomorrow a lot!

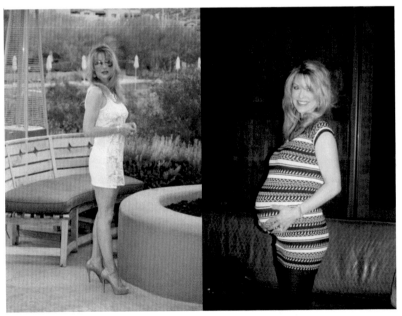

Date night with my husband   Baby number 5 on the way!

Kids & Grandkids

Certain as a Blue Moon

The Playground of Life

Loving Comfort   Through good times and bad

I'm bored!?

There isn't a parent alive that hasn't wanted to just howl when they hear their children whine and lament about being bored. Truth be told there are few things that rile me more than the notion that any of us spend time suffering in this state of ennui. As far as children go I am fully invested in parent led activities and spending great time with our kids. I work at being creative even though I can't claim it as my strong suit. I can only play "Go Fish" so many times before I want to lose my mind. So while I will occasionally spend some time honoring their requests, more often than not, I lead the way with something that I enjoy. A hike in the woods, a trip to the zoo, a walk on the beach, being out at the barn, or a trip to the local nursery just because it's alive, green and fragrant and I find that captivating. Some parents would lean toward building things, sports teams, craft projects or baking. And while I claim no talent for or desire to do the aforementioned activities, if it is what the parents enjoy, go for it. We can only endure so many Legos and Lincoln logs on any given day.

But beyond that, kids should be able to entertain themselves. I'm not talking about the TV or video games, those are a no brainer that can hold any child's attention and I am not begrudging the occasional respite that mindless entertainment can offer us all. But if your kids can't play by themselves or entertain themselves with something independent and imaginative I think this needs to be addressed. The fact of the matter is that if you turn off the TV and the Xbox occasionally they aren't going to stare at a blank wall. They WILL find something to do and that's a good thing (usually). We have had some "artwork" done on a wall, and other such calamities, so leaving your kids to entertain themselves does still require subtle supervision.

I feel fortunate in that two of our kids have always been innately really good at this. One of them not so much so it is a more proactive endeavor to make sure she does so on occasion. Our youngest's inclination remains to be seen. While I could lament the fact that children have lost their imaginations in favor of being entertained by ever willing technology the reality is that ALL kids have an imagination but not all kids are given the opportunity to use it or have someone who insists that they do. And as a result they suffer the affliction of boredom rather than the wonder of their own minds and imagination. The tragedy here is twofold. On the one hand we have children who will have little but fleeting brushes with the magic that can unfold within their own minds. The creativity, ingenuity and resourcefulness that this nurtures are precious and irreplaceable. The delayed aspect of bored kids is the unforgivable reality of bored adults. For this, I simply see no excuse. Why any adult would ever complain of boredom is at best a mystery but more honestly, is offensive. Life is such a brilliant, magical and fleeting journey that spending a single moment of it being "bored" is nothing short of tragic. Whether you fill your time with travel, adventure, creativity, books, gardening or with any one of a million causes that could benefit from your surplus time and attention, you are responsible for filling your moments with meaning. And if this isn't the case it is not simply a shame, but shame on you. Shame on those of us that spend five minutes being bored rather than volunteering at an animal shelter, stocking shelves at Goodwill, or simply reading an amazing book or planting a garden for someone who

186

doesn't have the time or money to do so for themselves. This Saturday we are going to watch a baseball game for disabled children that my father-in-law is spending a season coaching. My mother-in-law too is an inspiration in this regard. At 78 years old they are both some of the most active, engaging, involved people I know. I can guarantee that not one of them has ever looked at the other and said, "I'm bored." There is so much living and giving to be done in life that wasting a moment of it leaves me breaking out in a cold sweat. So start with making sure that your children's imaginations and resourcefulness are cultivated and encouraged. This will serve them throughout their lives. And the good news is that our window of opportunity to exercise our imagination is never ending. The spark can always be ignited and if a philosophical appeal is falling on deaf ears, simply put, bored people are boring. So live life with enthusiasm and imagination and you will be rewarded with meaningful days, magical memories and inspiring tales to tell.

Self-Respect

I'd like to make a case for a little self-respect. Not too long ago I was with our four year old at the nearby Children's Museum. Quite a magical place really. Full of a wonderful array of activities to stimulate your tots curious little mind and delight parents as they watch their budding Rhodes Scholar stimulate their impossibly impressive intellect. So here I am enjoying watching Race enjoy himself and I see this kid running around in his pajamas. This is not an 18 month old that just woke from a nap in the stroller and needed to toddle around. This kid was AT LEAST five years old and was bedecked in his overnight attire. Now I bristle at the idea of being judgmental but come on! Mind you, if mom had been there with four kids under the age of five, I would have given kudos for just getting out the door. But when you are there with one child and the notion of dressing him is just too much of a hassle something has gone horribly wrong. Call me critical but I couldn't help but think to myself, "At what point did you completely surrender your dignity?" I realize this sounds a bit harsh over something so relatively meaningless, but you just knew in an instant that this indifference didn't just apply to a morning at the Museum, it applied to life in general.

To be sure, I am all in favor of kids spending an occasional Saturday lounging around in their PJ's and not being rushed, loaded and trundled around for a day. But only occasionally. Life needs to have its pauses, but it certainly isn't lived there. And when you can't muster the energy to dress yourself or your children before heading out the door, your pause button is stuck. Now lest you think I am given to excessive concern over appearances such is not the case. On a day in, day out basis, I don't dress up, I don't bother with much of anything in the way of makeup and I am prone to wearing baseball caps because I don't have time or inclination to dry my hair on any sort of a regular basis. BUT I will be damned if you're ever going to catch me doing my grocery shopping in flannel pajama bottoms and slippers. Why? Because at that point I've given up. I've stopped caring and I simply can't allow that apathy to settle in. If you've decided that there's no point in making the beds in the morning because what's the point, you're just going to mess them up again at night, then you are on a very slippery slope indeed my friend. If I ever send my kids off to school looking like street urchins badly in need of a brush and some breakfast you will know I have officially abandoned my self-respect. One caveat here is that I have, on occasion, when my kids are dragging their feet about getting ready for school, threatened that if they don't get dressed they will just be going to school in their pajamas and to be sure this is no idle threat. In fact, there is this slightly wicked part of me that looks forward to the day that this actually transpires; the pictures would be priceless. Still my exasperation with this morning mayhem is not to be confused with indifference. I vividly remember one time telling my then teenage brother, "you can say anything you want to me as long as you never say…whatever." Whatever means I don't care. Whatever means I am indifferent. Whatever means I don't have the self-respect to bother or be bothered with anything. I propose living a life where "whatever" is entirely unacceptable.

There are a few truisms I believe wholly and completely and one of them is that what you are in anything is What You Are in Everything. So if you've thrown up your hands and ceased caring in one aspect of your life, my money is on the fact that all aspects of your life reflect this indifference. If I drive by the home of someone I am thinking of doing business with, and it looks like a wayward cross between a garage sale and a junk yard, am I feeling good about that person's professionalism and attention to detail? Not so much. Would you show up to a friend's birthday party with spaghettios stains on your t-shirt? Hardly, so why is it okay at the playground? So the moral of this story is give a damn. Self-respect isn't something you pick and choose; it is your way of being so I would suggest that if this is an issue, start small by creating positive habits. Eventually the mindset will follow and the PJ's will stay at home where they belong.

Cruel Kids

How can kids be so cruel? I honestly have no idea. It is one of the most alarming phenomenons I think I have ever experienced. Certainly I've known my share of adults that can be punishing and vindictive, but when did children become so merciless with one another's feelings? To be sure, part of it is in their upbringing. I will never forget one time driving by this less than luxurious apartment building along a very busy street and I saw a little girl who I would guess to be about four or five years old standing on the sidewalk. I remember looking at her out of concern for the fact that this was a busy street and I didn't see an adult anywhere in site. She notices me looking at her and promptly flips me off. A four year old! In that moment I remember thinking to myself, "this kid doesn't stand a chance." In a moment you knew she was on the fast track to tattoos, body piercing and teenage pregnancy.

But what about the kids that for all intents and purposes are being brought up well and right? I think it is their dark side that shocks and disturbs me most. Our oldest daughter got a cell phone for her twelfth birthday and without a doubt it is both a blessing and a curse. To find your child in tears over a hurtful text message or an Instragram picture that simply announces how they are, in real time, being left out and excluded from the latest and greatest social activity just makes my heart ache.

When did we allow kids to start living without compassion or consequences? One of the first things we told my oldest was that we would be monitoring her text messages and if she ever sent anything hurtful or inappropriate the phone was gone. Is there any good reason why ALL parents don't supervise cyberspace? I could say shame on these kids. But really shame on any parent that is too lazy or unconcerned with their kid's karma to get in the game. I actually know parents that are more concerned with their children's popularity than they are their principles. Enough already. Parents need to step up and put on their big boy pants when it comes to raising their kids. If you don't watch what they are posting on their Facebook page now, you can just post bail for your wayward teen later. Trust me, they have enough friends. What they need are parents.

The Do-Over...

I think that in life we all deserve at least one Do Over. A chance to hit the reset button and begin again. To be sure, we all know that life is a journey and that all that we are is a reflection of all that has been. We are a product of our experiences and hopefully the wisdom gleaned from them. And for as much as we are wondrously able to learn and change and grow, it goes without saying that more often than not we learn our lessons the hard way. Inevitably we are forced into our wisdom through trial and error and often the greatest lessons are learned more by error than trial if we are honest with ourselves.

To be sure, some of us seem to have giftedness at the crash and burn. Others of us tread more cautiously and try to feel our way in the occasional dark rather than just jumping off the precipice and hoping that the impact doesn't leave us too battered and bruised. I personally fall on the careful side of the equation and for as many virtues as this approach may seem to have, I cannot claim that its net results are any more impressive in the long run. In fact, I will admit that there is part of reckless abandon that I admire from afar. That freedom to risk and reap those rewards of a life lived with a certain amount of haste. Now I am not suggesting carelessness with what is precious and nonnegotiable in life, but to some degree the rest of our experiences seem to benefit from an affectionate embrace of risk tolerance. And let's just face it, being careful all the time and avoiding failure at every turn is downright exhausting. To be sure, I am not espousing a philosophy that suggests we live life without apology. I am suggesting a life where we are really good at apologizing. I propose we dare to choose a life that embraces our humanity and its inevitable failures and moves on from them with a sense of dignity rather than defeat.

As simple as it sounds, I have made a habit of apologizing to my children. If I am needlessly impatient or overly irritable for some reason, I will always come back and apologize to them for it. This serves several purposes. It calls out the fact that the behavior, whatever it may be, is wrong. But perhaps more importantly, my shortcomings allow them to be comfortable with their own. If I put out some standard that said I'm a parent and therefore I'm always right, I don't ever want them to feel compelled to grasp at such a ridiculous standard. And guess what, they ALWAYS say, "it's okay Mom."

So what this all comes back to is the Do Over. That freedom that says we are better for our humanity and the messiness that comes along with it. And if we are willing to have the courage to embrace our mistakes in ways that allow us to learn and change and grow, then we all deserve a new page. A chance to say this is what I did, this is what I learned and now this is who I have become. I think we give this more easily to others than we give it to ourselves. So I would suggest that we offer ourselves the amazing gift of the freedom to fail. Because as simple as it sounds, when we know better, we do better. So always be on the quest to Do Better and sometimes what we need is to be allowed a Do Over and a chance to begin again. There is an entirely different life that awaits us when we aren't just willing to make mistakes but we welcome them as part of our journey knowing that we can give ourselves and one another the gift of starting anew.

Do unto others...

Easier said than done. I don't think a single one of us has escaped the challenge of this mandate. I've talked often about how kids seem to be hardwired at birth to demand fairness. Any parent knows the tug-o-war that goes on over "he got more than me!" "She got more turns than I did!" "He went first last time!" And as frustrating as it is, it is hard to blame them for demanding an equal distribution of everything from kisses to cookies. We all want fairness so this call to forego that instinctive need is no easy task. The notion of "Do unto others as you would have them do unto you," is a moral, ethical and philosophical challenge of monumental proportions. It is a dictum that is spoken of in all of the world's major religions and has been espoused by all great thinkers and philosophers. Still it's as though our DNA tells us to do one thing, but our soul pleads with us to be better than these base instincts. If we have been hurt or wronged it is terribly hard to not lash out, and retaliate for pain or suffering that has been caused by another. But if we have ever caved to the attitude of "don't get mad, get even," we know just how shallow and meaningless those victories are. And if they don't feel that way then it's a safe bet that YOU are shallow and meaningless.

Without boring you with the sordid details of it all, life has put this challenge in front of me so many times you'd think I'd have the hang of it by now. But it remains a struggle that takes every ounce of my spiritual self to keep overcoming the assaults. I ran out of cheeks to turn a LONG time ago. So now I'm turning to belief and sheer will power. Belief that NO MATTER WHAT someone else does, I will not succumb to vindictiveness and retribution. And will power that says, I won't just ignore the person that is responsible for hurting me, I'm going to reach out to them in positive and loving ways. And at times this a most bitter pill to swallow. But do it anyway. On a somewhat lighter note we have this neighbor that is probably the most surly and cantankerous person I've ever met. So my strategy is "kill 'em with kindness." The nastier you are to me the more cookies and homemade jam I'm going to leave on your doorstep. I dare you to throw rocks in my driveway when I just offered to walk your dogs for you. To be sure this is child's play when compared to how unbearably challenging this philosophy can be. But try you must. And be it a friend, a family member, a former business associate or the neighbor whose cat keeps using your flower bed as a litter box, treat them as you would wish to be treated and your life will be the one of depth and meaning. It will be you that rests with the satisfaction of knowing you are strong enough to do the right thing which so very rarely is the easy thing.

Anniversaries

Inspiration or obligation? Good question. I think our lives these days are full of sometimes tedious and onerous obligations and adding one more to the pile of promises to keep is cause for groans of despair. Who has the time, the energy, and the desire to tend to every Hallmark holiday that rolls around? And I must confess that while I am nuts for Holidays like Christmas and Easter, the contrived nature of many occasions makes my skin crawl.

Anniversaries however feel like a horse of a different color. They are a celebration of something rare and wonderful. Whether you believe the meeting of your mate to be divinely inspired or it involved online assistance, I believe it to be among the most worthy things in life to celebrate. In fact, I would go so far as to say that any sort of anniversary is a praiseworthy event. Whether you are celebrating the day you started your business, the day you began your spiritual journey or the day you broke ground on your dream home, taking a moment to pause and be proud can't be a bad thing. We all have enough to worry about so let's find reasons to put worry away for just a moment and enjoy the wonder of it all. The wonder of our efforts, accomplishments and inspirations made real. We all take ourselves to the woodshed on a regular basis when things go wrong, so I suggest that just occasionally we pause to acknowledge and celebrate what has gone right.

Play dates

Whose idea was this exactly? And when did simply playing with friends come to be a Play Date. I wish I could write that term surround by flowers and ladybugs because it is so gooey and cutesy. To be sure when I was growing up we played with friends, hung out in the neighborhood and played on numerous dates throughout the year. But this term Play Date is a relative newcomer to the lexicon of childrearing. Wikipedia defines a Play Date as "an arranged appointment for children to get together to play for a few hours." Is it just me or is there something slightly oxymoronic about an "arranged appointment to play?" I think in part I resent the term because I imagine that a Play Date implies that I'm supposed to bake cookies, lead crafts projects, fire pottery, have the soccer field mowed and ready and serve a picnic lunch inspired by Martha Stewart herself prepared and laid out on a brightly checkered table cloth. And I am certain my cynical tone gives away the fact that I'm not doing any of that. Not even a little bit interested. Don't get me wrong, I LOVE caring for my children. It's is my life's greatest passion, but I'm not big on entertaining them. I think the most precious thing about childhood is its carefree, impulsive, and unfettered nature. But I see so many kids with schedules so rigid and rigorous it would make being a Marine look whimsical. Childhood is so precious and fleeting. Dare I suggest that we put the Day Planners away, and simply plan to enjoy our days?

Holiday Warmth and Connection

First and foremost my hat is off to any couple that in spite of some family unease are opening their homes and celebrating the Holidays together. If all your family members don't give you credit for your willingness, make sure you both toast each other and give yourself acknowledgment for playing equal parts Holiday Host and Family referee perhaps. Extended families contain members you do get along with and members you don't get along with. I think that on some level we all have this Norman Rockwell picture in our minds eye of what the Thanksgiving experience is supposed to resemble and I don't need to tell you that it rarely, if ever, looks quite so quaint and charming. I personally feel privileged to say that for many years, when my grandmother was still alive, I was fortunate enough to experience this Holiday as I believe it was meant to be. Family members gathered together and regardless of different personalities and walks of life we shared a contentedness and celebrated it together on that day. Since she has passed, the wheels have fallen off the cart of custom and tradition as it were and we have descended into nothing short of pure, unadulterated dysfunction. I share this because it has made me realize that every family needs a leader and in many cases a hero, a strong force to guide, encourage and expect the best out of each and every one of us. It's as though that person provides the compass bearing that we all are guided by and drawn toward at this time of year. We look to them and their vision and desire of what can and should be and it gives us what we all crave; A sense of warmth and contentedness. There are ALWAYS going to be those moments when family finds themselves thrust into each other's company at this time of year and we end up inwardly stupefied at how it could possibly be that we share genetic material with "these people." So knowing that some weird uncle or sulking Goth obsessed teenager is a given in every family equation, my question is whether or not you as a couple feel up to taking on the challenge of being that rallying point, that example, that force that upholds custom, tradition and the inescapable value of family bonds.

If you are up to the task my hat is off to you both. The world needs more brave souls like you. But if you'd rather just provide the space, the ovens, and the kiddie table than the rallying cry for your entire clan, then keep in mind that it is just a single day. And we can put up with anything for a day. This is not the time to engage with your surly brother-in-law or your endlessly complaining cousin. If you have family members that want to call attention to themselves by sulking in the corner or looking for conflict, do your best to act pleasant and like a grown-up even if it means seeming oblivious to their nonsense. So it's one of two things in mind. Either choose to be that source of strength, belief and certainty or fly a Swiss flag on your front porch and just be a neutral zone for everyone to gather in for the day. Whichever you choose, you're doing a wonderful thing and I believe you are to be commended for it. And if all else fails, there's nothing like some really strong eggnog to help the situation along, especially if your goal is not to remember the entire sordid experience the next morning. Bottom line whether you choose A or B, keep a sense of humor and continue to set the example whether you think anyone is watching or not.

ANYTHING but Regret!

As a general rule, it seems that when people are struggling with their first steps as investors or just making their first basic decisions and choices, what is most often at play is a fear of failure, especially when they are short on cash and have a family to provide for. Even though a lot of Real Estate education may already be in place and even though successful investors may surround them and talk about their success, they see taking action as risking something. Most often that "risk" they fear is the horror of falling short in someone else's eyes or their own. They fear not knocking it out of the park, or not being successful while "Risking" the criticism and judgment of themselves or others. But I would contend that what they "risk" by not acting and moving forward is that worst of all evils…regret. It has been my personal credo of sorts for as long as I can remember that I can live with anything, but I CANNOT live with regret. I simply cannot imagine anything worse. In fact, I believe this so completely that I had it tattooed on my body as a daily reminder to live and breathe that very conviction. Now while I'm not going to suggest permanently inking yourself, I am going to suggest committing, somewhere inside of yourself, to the belief that Failure is child's play when measured up against the unforgivable entertainment of Regret.

Even though these investors around you may be talking about their successes and making you feel as if they are wasting your time; perhaps it would be to your benefit to read this back to yourself a time or two as it is possible that if, in fact, they are having success you may want to open your ears to their yakking and hear what they have to say. Not to put too fine a point on it, but perhaps they feel as though they are wasting their time talking to you who can't seem to get off first base and give this a go. I don't think you as a new investor earned the right to this attitude. But when push comes to shove, I think that what is needed is to tune out all the Noise going on in your head. Decide what you want and go get it. I completely respect that you have a family depending on you and that you take that responsibility so deeply to heart. You have NO idea just how deeply I esteem any sense of duty and care one has for family. But your family members are counting on you not just to provide an income, but to provide the leadership and courage that they grow and learn from. On a personal level I know how brilliant and capable we all are and that this limbo is a waste of time and self. Those you love benefit immeasurably more from you living and breathing your life and your potential. Anyone can earn a dollar. Not anyone can inspire, encourage and create a life of richness and meaning.

"We are very near greatness: one step and we are safe; can we not take the leap?" Ralph Waldo Emerson

The Elephant in the Room

It is always a tricky situation when other family members borrow a considerable sum of money from parents. Especially when those family members are struggling financially but then become stable earning a good income, and appear to be living and spending without regard to the unpaid debt.

This is a tricky situation to be sure and some very volatile and problematic elements are involved in these scenarios. Namely family and money. Otherwise known as oil and water in my book as I'm pretty convinced the two should never be mixed. So, do you address it head on and risk hurting the relationship or just drop it and live with the frustration?

While there are always two sides to every story, there are certainly some consistent truths that I believe apply. First, there is a profound difference between getting involved in an investment which as we all know involves the risk of loss, and loaning a friend or a family member money to help them out of a bind or during a particularly difficult time. I would first want to be very clear on knowing how the loan is perceived. Is it investing or loaning? Personally I believe that these situations are so predisposed to intense conflict that I would never loan family money...I would just give it to them. No strings, ties or expectations attached.

So even though there may be worry about the situation, I would first want to know EXACTLY where the parents stand. Without question, I would have a conversation with them prior to opening up any discourse with any other family member. Make sure you have a very clear picture of their expectations around repayment of the debt as well as their true and honest feelings about the unresolved nature of it. The parents are adults and don't necessarily need anyone fighting their battles for them. Having said that, if the parents are being taken advantage of, or deceived in any way, I deeply believe that not speaking up in the face of something which is wrong, unpleasant or involves potential conflict, as a course of action is an unforgivable alternative to courage.

As well, should something be said to these family members at the risk of hurting that relationship? The reality is the relationship has already been badly damaged. Actually saying something may be the only chance you all stand at FIXING the unpleasant nature of that which remains unspoken. I personally believe it is nearly impossible to have a relationship where there is no respect. If you have lost respect for these family members because they are ignoring and/or avoiding the debt to the parents, what exactly are you trying to salvage by not speaking up and saying something?

What I can assure you of is that there is no such thing as ignoring these sort of tensions. And when conflict involves families the emotions are so deep and the stakes are so high that it is literally impossible as well as unacceptable to just say, "Whatever. It's none of my business." This isn't a matter of they like to watch football on Sundays and you'd rather not. These are core and concerning issues of integrity, respect and character.

Your feelings of frustration with and disappointment in these family members aren't exactly building blocks for cherished family memories and laughs around the Thanksgiving table. They are seeds that will sow nothing but bitterness and disdain in the coming years. But here is what you need to be prepared for: by saying something in a situation like this you run a very good risk of seemingly making things worse. Yet I would contend that in the long run, remaining silent is far more damaging and debilitating than any immediate upheaval that may follow you calling attention to the elephant in the room. Yes, that preposterously large animal, with dollar signs all over it, taking up far too much space in this relationship.

Now...lest I make it sound like you should confront family with guns a blazing and ready to rumble I would advocate something much different. If you determine, after speaking with the parents, that something ought to be said, the very best way to start that conversation is with copious amounts of compassion and empathy. EVEN IF YOU DON'T FEEL THAT WAY. Because the quickest way to conflict is to put somebody on the defensive. You might want to begin by saying to your family member or members "hey, I know you and your family have been through some really tough times lately...boy we've all gotten beaten up in the last couple of years! But mom and dad are really struggling and I was hoping we could put our heads together to help them get to a better place." Is that your responsibility? No. Did you borrow the money and not pay it back? No. But the chances of family engaging in a way that creates resolve vs. revolt are far higher if they don't feel blamed, called out or feel like the villain in the situation. For as much as you may be right, encouraging the best in your family member vs. pointing out their shortcomings is ALWAYS both more effective and productive. If you help them feel able to solve the problem vs. merely focusing on their irresponsibility in creating it, they will come away better people rather than angry and likely making YOU the bad guy. So first ask if you can help them make it right and set blame and wrong-doing aside at the onset of the discussion. When I start to feel righteous and therefore frustrated by a situation, I try to remind myself that there are ALWAYS two sides to a story. This doesn't mean their actions or lack thereof are right, but I find that keeping that in mind usually helps me find a way toward a discussion rather than a confrontation.

So pursue knowing the parents story, then work at knowing your family's narrative and insert your own perspective, strength and principles. It is then that your entire family stands the best possible chance at a happy ending.

The Caboose of the Santa Train

Honestly, I do go a little bit crazy at Christmas time. As we roll the clock to each New Year I continually vow to do the Holidays better next year with family, friends, and the all-around busyness. I vow to be more organized, to get things done earlier, and to be more strategic and purposeful about what we are doing. I plan to actually enjoy the splendor of the Season and all that it offers and means, and every year I fail epically. I find myself stressed out, behind on everything and largely incapable of relaxing into the sentiments of the Season.

As some of you know our oldest daughter has a birthday on Christmas Eve and if I had a dollar for every person who has shared their personal horror story of who they know that has a Christmas birthday and how awful it is, we would have her college tuition to an Ivy League school comfortably funded by now. But as I took all this in during her young years, it inspired me to go above and beyond each year to make sure that her birthday was separate and special and that she never felt slighted, over-looked or lumped in with the Christmas theme. So just add that endeavor to the list of things to accomplish during December. And now we are expecting our fourth child with a due date of December 16th. Phenomenal family planning on our part, but it has pushed me to that wonderful point of allowing the busyness to fall away and to focus on perspective.

What is really, truly important? That it all gets done with lavish flair and I come out looking like some sort of mini Martha Stewart or that I spend time loving and enjoying my family? I have even found that when I plan Holiday experiences or outings with the best of intentions for creating a keepsake moment or memory, there are times when the lack of spontaneity makes it feel insincere and unenjoyed. It is as though I am just checking something off my Holiday to-do list rather than really, truly settling into the Joy of the experience that is unfolding around me, yet without me. I can remember sharing with a friend the experience of a few months after our first child was born when getting to that point of being so utterly and completely exhausted that I didn't give a shit anymore. What a stunningly freeing sensation that was! So what if the laundry isn't done? So what if the house is messy or dinner is delivered in a pizza box? In the scheme of what truly matters in life where exactly does dusting and decorating fall? And the answer is; let it fall. Let those things that don't truly matter fall away to a place where they get none of your time or attention and you will enjoy an amazingly freeing sensation.

Make a list of the most important things to YOU during the Holidays and focus there. For some it might be making homemade cookies and gifts. Others would just as soon go through the entire month without ever turning on the oven and that would seem like a gift all by itself. The point is to decide what is truly important and ENJOYABLE to you and let the rest of it head to the caboose of the Santa Train. If you enjoy the experience of giving a beautifully wrapped gift to people, go ahead and spend twenty minutes wrapping each gift. But if you'd prefer to never see a roll of wrapping paper or a piece of tape then as my step-son says, "there are entire industries devoted to solving that problem." The solution could be as close as the twelve year old neighbor girl that would LOVE to earn some

Christmas money by wrapping your gifts for $0.25 apiece. For me, certain things like decorating the house and the tree are a chore to get through, but I love the effects and it is deeply important to me to "give" that warmth and experience to my family. So from that perspective it matters mightily and I will do it no matter how many times the bottom third of the lights go out on the tree that we got soaking wet going out and cutting ourselves. I might secretly pine for 1-800-faketrees, but I won't go there because of what it means to my kids, and so it matters to me. So save some money to hire a housekeeper for a few hours and spend a Sunday covering the kitchen in frosting and flour knowing that you have help coming to clean up the mess. There are things we can do that take the stress out of Holiday tasks but above all I would encourage you to give yourself a moment to find the perspective in it all. Ask yourself what truly matters and is important to you during this special time of year and focus your energies, heart and intention there. And don't then allow those experiences and shared moments to be tainted by some never ending "to-do list" that keeps running through your mind. It doesn't deserve the space.

What DOES deserve your heart and mind are those you love. And you giving yourself the freedom and permission to enjoy the magic of the moments as they come without the burden of performing to unrealistic expectations is the very best gift you can give to those you cherish. So give it a shot this Christmas. There is nothing to lose and a world of magic and wonder to be gained by you allowing yourself to relax and enjoy this most special time of year.

We silently long to feel valued and to offer something of importance that will, in ways large are small, somehow make a difference.

The Economy of Precious

I have, let's just call them...issues around any frame of mind that suggests that staying home with kids isn't work...hard work. We would never say that a 3rd grade teacher doesn't work and SHE gets to go home at 3:00 or thereabouts. But moms are tasked with the role of teacher, nurse, chef, errand runner, interior decorator, housekeeper, bookkeeper, office manager, organizing guru, social planner, party planner, gardener, etc., etc., etc., and all these jobs are being done for the bargain price of...nothing. (But the benefits package is to die for!)

If some wonderful soul volunteers at a soup kitchen one afternoon a week would we dare believe that they didn't work, just because it was a labor of love rather than a paid form of employment? Of course not! And if that same "volunteer" worked 14 hours a day, 7 days a week every single day of the year without so much as a lunch break, we would consider that person the second coming of Mother Theresa. Yet still, some stubborn, and dare I say ignorant folks including husbands, continue to resist looking on the raising of children as work. And if we were to put this on a scale of importance to our lives, our well-being and even society as a whole, there isn't a job out there that could be considered to be of greater or more profound consequence. I believe it was Lee Iacocca, CEO of Chrysler that was quoted as saying, "I can have all the money in the world, but if I fail my children, I have accomplished nothing of consequence in this life."

But alas, just like with any job there are people…parents that should be fired. They are lazy, disinterested, and occasionally incompetent. But if being a parent is the work that you love then that is exactly what you should be doing. I have two of my absolute dearest friends who have owned and run day-care centers. One ran a center affiliated with her church and the other owned and ran a private in-home daycare. And for as much as I esteem these women in my life, I am not, and never will be a fan of day-care. As far as I am concerned, it is and always will be a woefully poor substitute for the warmth and nurturing that children receive from loving, attentive parents. I have been in and around various day-care environments and while I recognize that many of them do a fine job, at the end of the day, it is not and never will be the same as mom. Now, I am of course creating this discourse around some alarmingly broad assumptions. I am assuming that if your heart's desire is to be home and raising your kids that you would approach that calling with passion, dedication and devotion. If that's not the case, then your children may, in fact, be better off with a quality day-care provider. But it drives me just this side of crazy when I hear parents insisting that they drop little Johnny off at day-care because he needs the socialization. Unless you're making a habit of employing babysitters named Sony, Panasonic or Magnavox, this is utter nonsense and I'm putting that as politely as possible.

I would say that for anyone who WANTS to be the one home raising their children I would hope that spouses would value their children's well-being enough to sit down and discuss a strategy that would allow themselves to serve their family in this way. The average cost of day-care for 2 children, full-time is $250-$300 per week. And if parents don't consider their children infinitely more valuable than that I don't really know what to say or where to begin. So how do care providers make money at this rate? Um...that would be volume. And I for one don't ever want my children to be part of someone's economy of scale. The thought of dropping my children off at a day-care center literally brings me to tears and would shatter my heart into a million dusty and distraught pieces. But I also fully acknowledge that that is my husbands and my personal value system speaking. I have readily and willingly acknowledged that if a woman has a career she is passionate about then I would never want or expect her to fall on the altar of sacrificing that for her children as they will ultimately be the one's paying the price of that regret and discontent. As well, there are extremely difficult circumstances that families are forced to reckon with. I can only encourage parents to sit down together and figure out a way to allow that which is most dear and precious to you to receive all that you have to give. If they aren't worth it, I cannot imagine what is.

I WISH THERE WERE MORE "HANDICAPPED" PEOPLE...

So it's Sunday morning and Greg and I are heading to the zoo with the kids. And of course, living in Seattle and knowing that its about 45 degrees and cloudy out, a stop at Starbucks is in order. Oh, who am I kidding…a Starbucks stop is always in order and has nothing to do with the weather. So Greg pulls up and I run in to grab our drinks. As it turns out, the after church crowd has gathered at this particular Starbuck's and there is an insanely long line. Ah well, it's not like it's an option to go without, so I begrudgingly get in line. Then a young man comes up and gets in line behind me and I notice that this young man happens to have Down's syndrome. I will tell you that back in High School I was in the Honor Society and part of the requirements for the organization included some sort of community service. My choice was always the Special Olympics and I will confess it is 100% because of the kids with Down's syndrome. They are some of the happiest, most loving, most accepting people God has ever created and my experiences with them were pure joy.

But even with a 'disability' these kids (and adults) always know if people are uncomfortable around them. So often 'normal' people feel awkward and don't want to stand too close simply because they are ill at ease. So between a smile and the fact that he could tell I didn't mind standing right next to him, after a minute or two he taps me gently, showing me his zippered bag and asks if he can buy me a drink. And so our conversation begins. I tell him, "no thank you," that he doesn't need to do that and immediately ask him what his favorite drink is. He says it's a mocha and that he usually gets the 16 ounce, but today can only get the 12 ounce. So by this time I've waited my way up to the front of the line, order my drinks, plus a 16 ounce mocha for Zack. Right about now, Zack's dad walks up and says, "What are you up to Zack?" And I get to assure his dad that Zack is "just hitting on the ladies and has somehow done such a good job that he has *me* buying *his* drink." This gets a kind smile out of dad who goes to sit down again allowing Zack and me to continue our conversation.

So as any Starbuck's devotee will tell you, placing your drink order, even with a line, is the speediest part of the process. Waiting for your actual drink to be made is the larger act of patience (or addiction, whichever you prefer). So Zack and I move over to wait for our drinks and continue our chat. In short order some custom crafted mocha order with white chocolate, extra foam and no whip cream or some such thing comes up and Zack reaches for the "mocha." I find myself only too happy to tell him that that drink is someone else's and we need to wait a bit longer. Which means I get to talk to Zack for at least another minute or two. In which time I get to discover that he graduated from Shorecrest High School in 2004 and that his sister, Brook's, favorite drink is a tall latte with extra foam. I even go so far as to point out the fact that there are a number of police officers inside the Starbuck's meeting for coffee and humorously ask Zack what he's done and why are all the cops here? He laughs, completely getting the joke and I laugh, not because it was funny but because he is making me so happy. Through our entire conversation, Zack never stops smiling and looks me in the eye continuously. He doesn't know awkwardness or insincerity. Everything is pure.

I'll be honest with you. I hadn't had the best week. But there were certainly a couple of high points and Zack, the most remarkable among them. I walked out of that Starbuck's feeling both happy and hopeful. Happy for the smile that is on my face and how rewarding such a brief encounter can be, and hopeful because Zack reminds me, without any effort on his part, of what is still good and special and wonderful in the world. And I walk out the door wondering what exactly does it say that we label Zack as the one with the "handicap." I can't think of the last time someone offered to buy my latte or made me feel so good just by being there. And I know that the rest of us who are "normal" can do so much better, be so much better, and offer so much more. So we eventually get our drinks, I shake Zack's hand and tell him that I hope to run into him again sometime soon. I say that a lot in passing. I don't think I have ever meant it so much.

I Miss You...

I'm one of the lucky ones. One of those amazingly fortunate people who always looked forward to Thanksgiving rather than wondering how on earth I share genetic material with the people I find myself surrounded by. And mind you that isn't a statement of better or worse; it's just a statement of different. Sometimes *drastically* different. I was fortunate because I had the most amazing grandmother a girl could ask for. Nothing about her life was showy or boisterous or big, but she is still one of the most amazing people I have ever met. And while she always created the most amazing meal on Thanksgiving what she really created were the most amazing moments and memories.

For years we spent Thanksgiving up at my Grandmother's house and it was the most wonderful, joyous, relaxing, affirming day you can imagine. My grandmother loved Thanksgiving and it showed in everything from the place cards, to the days of preparation, to the mess of dirty dishes afterwards. She smiled through every part of it and never seemed flustered or stressed or even slightly overwhelmed. Of course we would all bring our various contributions to the feast, but the lion's share was left in her loving hands and so we didn't just end up eating turkey we ended up savoring the entire experience. And even when we all felt stuffed full of conversation and laughter, we were always up for another heaping plate of wonderful. Often we would all find a corner to crash in for the night and look forward to trekking out to cut Christmas trees the next day. The weather was always perfectly awful and I wouldn't have wanted it any other way. My Grandmother brought such joy to this holiday and I miss her wisdom, energy and grace terribly. When we lost her it left a terrible void in our family and we have all tried to quietly go about creating our own Thanksgiving traditions knowing full well and good that it will never be the same. To be perfectly honest, there have been some rifts in our family and I think often on the fact that if she was still with us she'd put everything to rights. She was never afraid to dive into difficulty and so often I find myself wondering what she would do. How she would handle these strains and troubles and disconnectedness. She was like a warm fire that just drew everybody to her and without her energy and strength, we've somehow all been adrift for years now. There has been no focus, no center, and no "home" where everybody's hearts are at peace and love and laughter are always on the menu. I don't know how to solve it, but I know in my heart she would have. But in the spirit of Thanks, I am so grateful for the example she set. She gave me a picture rich with colors, tastes, smells and soul satisfying experiences. So now I am throwing myself into rebuilding for my own family an equally warm and rich tradition.

So while I will continue to work my way toward a meal, a table setting and an experience that matches the glorious pictures in my mind, I am Thankful for the fact that today I have everything I need. My husband, my kids...my family. The real stuff, the good stuff, the stuff that my Grandmother showed me how to savor, appreciate and enjoy. She continues to be my example and my inspiration. So right here and right now, I am Thankful for the enduring gifts that she Gave to me and I wish you all endless helpings of Joy on this most special and meaningful Holiday.

I'm Being Bullied by a Dead Bird

For those of you who are Turkey Roasting, potato mashing, gravy making authorities my troubles will either have you sympathizing with my plight, or finding moderate humor in my ineptitude. Today I picked up our Thanksgiving Turkey. A free range, vegetarian fed, antibiotic and hormone free 25 lb. hen turkey. With all that going for it, I can't help but think it should have landed in a more capable kitchen than mine.

I have poured through Holiday magazines all promising a fuss free, stress free Thanksgiving experience replete with menus, timetables, make ahead options and creative ambiance that would leave Martha Stewart speechless. And I have realized that despite all of my ambitious intentions, nothing that comes out of my oven or off of my stove is going to measure up.

I have flipped through page after page of glossy intimidation all vowing to deliver me to the promised land of the perfect Thanksgiving Holiday. It wasn't until I was completely overwhelmed with information and input that I realized I wasn't doing myself any favors. To brine or not to brine? Should you cover the bird with seasoned and soaked cheesecloth or is that a waste of time and cheese, or cloth, or whatever that stuff is made of exactly? Should you stuff the bird or does that just dry it out because you have to cook it for longer? Alas, there are no easy answers but there *are,* I have discovered, an endless number of opinions. What I do know is that the best turkey I ever had was fried. I remember my sister-in-law who is from New Orleans, bringing us the experience of frying the turkey and when I first heard of this travesty, I only half-jokingly quipped, "do you people have to fry everything?" Well thank heavens the answer is yes! If you haven't tried it you simply must at some point. I guarantee it will be the best bird you've ever had. What it does lack however is that ritual of roasting a turkey in the oven. The smell, the warmth, the age old tradition. The Norman Rockwellness of it all...

But still those visions of fall splendor and a bountiful feast taunt my perfectionist self. I found myself walking around the grocery store today muttering to myself, "I don't know what the *#!* I'm doing." And in that moment I realized I was being bullied by a dead bird. Bullied into the belief that Thanksgiving needed to look, smell and taste a certain way. While I may have visions of a perfectly moist turkey, lumpless gravy and delightfully fluffy mashed potatoes my chances of achieving such a success are honestly slim to none. My mom did give me some homemade cranberry relish today so I know that at least something on the table will be divine. Hell, with enough cranberry sauce anything can taste pretty good. It's like the Thanksgiving version of ketchup. So I've decided to fight back. To fight my own expectations of Holiday grandeur. Because while today had me buying everything from birds to brussel sprouts I realize that all the ingredients I need for the "perfect" holiday can't be put in paper or plastic. The ingredients for the perfect Holiday are my husband, my children and my family.

What I *do* know I can serve up is warmth and togetherness. I can make endless helpings of love, laughter and top it all off with a dessert of lifelong memories. Greg will carve the turkey and serve it with a side of perspective and gratitude. He's good at that. And our kids...our family will continue to create a tradition rich with all the good stuff. The gravy of life and love. So regardless of how this bird turns out, it won't have gotten the better of me. I'm saving that for what…for who, truly matters.

Prioritizing the True & the Real

Okay, this is a topic of monumental proportions and it is also a HIGHLY personal decision. So allow me to begin on territory that I feel very much assured of: I may have railed about the fact before that it is a colossal pet peeve of mine when people say things along the lines of , "she or he doesn't work, she or he stays home with the kids." And to be perfectly honest, women are some of the biggest offenders when it comes to throwing around phrases that are thoughtless at best and terribly ignorant at the worst. I would be left in utter disbelief if you were to tell me that any amount of time home with a son or daughter have felt akin to an extended vacation. My guess is that that time is at once, one of the most challenging, exhausting, and immensely rewarding experiences of your lives. So let's not do ourselves the disservice of not calling it what it is…work. Just because you love your job, otherwise known as your child or children, doesn't mean that you aren't working yourself like never before. Truth be told, I have known a number of individuals who went "back to work," and very candidly acknowledged that the motivation was that it was a hell of a lot easier than staying home. I have even met several women that work as full time nannies but have their own kids in daycare because taking care of other people's kids is far less stressful than the high stakes and responsibility of raising their own. Go figure.

I emphasize this only because I believe that our society on the whole has done a miserable job of esteeming raising children as one of the most influential, valuable and critical "jobs" imaginable. Large companies throw monstrous sums of money at research and development and what is raising children if not research and development at its most indispensable level?

I belabor this point only because I want you to ask yourselves as parents whether a father or a mother if your stressing over going back to "work" is coming from unmet desires inside of you or is it coming from a flawed set of misguided expectations?

Now having said that, if there is a part of you, after months or years at home with your children, that yearns for another part of your life and who you are to be challenged and ignited then that's a different conversation. I believe with my whole heart that the best parents are those that feel fulfilled in their lives and their relationships. I was recently having a conversation with several women, none of whom I knew very well, and one of them said that, "I think all married women feel stifled to some degree." And I felt so profoundly grateful that I couldn't identify in the least with her stated sentiment. So the last thing I would want is a mother or a father wrestling with this feeling of being "stifled" because you made the choice to be home with your child or children. I can think of few things more harmful than raising kids while carrying around the burden of resentment for an unfulfilled life.

So ask yourselves first and foremost, what do YOU want in this scenario? What feels the best and most true to who you are and what you both want for your life and family? Your own answers to this question is your best path. YOU may both wrestle with this decision, but I will admit that my bias leans very much toward the fact that these years with your children are fleeting and irretrievable. Life will not offer you the opportunity for a do-over where their childhood is concerned. Many things in life will wait, but the wonder and magic of childhood is not one of them. Children will laugh, cry, fall down, get up and want and need you near for so short a period of time in the scheme of things that I cannot think of a single thing I would trade those moments for. I suppose I should throw in my addendum here that making sure that the two of you as a couple have a healthy, loving, passionate, connected relationship and that it should be on the top of your list. If you resemble at all most of the new parents I know, I would encourage you to devote any additional time and energy you have to one another.

Parenthood can be an all-consuming endeavor and I owe my husband a debt of love and gratitude for always prioritizing this as the most true and real and important part of our lives. So do some soul searching to discover what decisions feel the best and most right to you both without cluttering your heart and mind with the expectations of family, friends or society in general. Tune out all the white noise and focus on what is best for each of you as an individual, you as a couple and you as parents, and craft your life and commitments around those truths. We tend to forget, that our lives are not blueprints off the rack. They are meant to be custom crafted and handmade works of art. So husbands and wives talk it through. Think on where your hearts truly are and create your days and moments around that which you hold most dear.

Follow YOUR Heart

Ah yes, the ever troubling "Group Think" and YOU. Let me give this the thought and attention it deserves. YOU found a home that YOU love and your family's luke warm response has stopped you from moving ahead. Your family is important to you, but who precisely is buying and living in this house? If the answer remains you, are you sure this is really a dilemma? If the answer remains you, then buy the damn house.

Now if this was a communal living arrangement they might all be entitled to their uncensored opinions, but aside from a few pockets in Utah, I haven't heard of such a thing in a good long while. In all seriousness, you need to allow this to be as simple as it is. If you love this home then that is really all that matters. You can politely nod as the rest of your clan plays the role of architect, interior designer and sage real estate investor, but what matters here is what YOU want. This is your home, you will be living here and perhaps raising a family here and if the space feels good and right and warm to you then look no further. Don't ask, don't poll, and above all, don't question your own desires and instincts.

Greg and I are expecting another baby this December and the question gets asked daily, "have you thought of any names yet?" Sure we've thought about it, but do you think that for five seconds I'm going to put our thoughts on something so personal out there for public comment? No way! Why would I subject myself to everybody's horror story about someone they knew in grades school with that name, or what it reminds them of, or the fact that they were once arrested for being drunk and disorderly by a cop with that very name? Not a chance. Our child, our choice, and I can value other people without being required to need or want their opinion on all things.

For all of its revolutionary effect on our society, social media seems to have conditioned us all to seek and in more critical cases, need the approval of others on so many various and sundry aspects of life. We post the ins and outs of our lives and decisions up for all of our "friends" to comment on. Now while I can see the many benefits of connecting and engaging with people, when we decide to lobotomize the decision making part of our persona in favor or some sort of group consensus we have just jumped onto a hamster wheel that we will be running on and relying on indefinitely.

 I think that being a good decision maker is one of the hallmarks of being a grown up. It is a skill that evolves over time along with our wisdom, our maturity and sense of assuredness in who and what we are.   In case you were wondering, I do realize the hole I am seemingly digging for myself. When I suggest that your family's opinions shouldn't trump your own, why in the world would you be in the least bit attentive to my take on the matter? The reality is that much as we love and adore them, family is rarely an impartial sounding board. Often their best intentions can actually add complications and an unhealthy urge to please.   As my husband is fond of saying, things have a way of looking much more clear and definitive from a 30,000 foot elevation versus the emotional muddle that we all seem to experience when we are right in the thick of things.

Having said that, if family members are the funding source for you to buy this home that does change things a bit. It certainly entitles them to an opinion if nothing else. As well, if you do have family members that are pretty savvy when it comes to real estate or construction, and they are speaking up about the three inches of water in the crawl space, or the addition that was never permitted much less built to code, then this is an entirely different proposition and in such a case I would strongly encourage you to take notice of their thoughts and expertise. You might love the old world charm of the sloping foundation, but listen to your Uncle Sal when he tries to warn you off of your impulsive attachment to the white picket fenced wonder that just happens to sit on a four lane arterial.

Bottom line is, when it simply becomes a matter of too many opinions, value your own and don't apologize for them. If you have resources that are simply piping up in the hopes of saving you not just money, but your future sanity, then listen intently. In the end, have faith in the fact that your home is about the hearts that dwell there. I am certain that at the end of the day, regardless of your family's opinions about the house, they will be showing up to see YOU. A house is about dollars a home is about heart, so follow yours and the rest will take care of itself...

Maverick Black Sheep

I have good news and bad news for people who for their entire lives have been labeled as "black sheep" by their families. First and foremost, know that being the "black sheep" is a shockingly common affliction among entrepreneurs. So at this point in my life, if I was to look at the herd of sheep that I spend my days amongst, the vast majority of them are not of the white as the driven snow variety.

Entrepreneurship is still seen as the road less traveled. The path of the impulsive and the occasionally unwise. It still caries images of uncertainty and lacks the stability of the good old American dream of eventually working your way toward a sunny porch and a pension. Is this picture changing? Every Enron brings us a bit closer to the true story. Corporate America is not who and what you should be trusting your fate and your future to. But the fact remains that in the here and now, entrepreneurs are still the risk takers, the unconventional pursuers of dreams and destiny and more often than not their maverick nature earns them the dubious distinction of the family "black sheep."

I think we all share a basic definition of the "black sheep" as being the one in the family who doesn't follow suit, toe the line or fit in in ways that feel expected or presumed by others in the family (usually mom and dad). They are the "rebels" among a group of family members where the idea of being normal, and living up to expectations, be they spoken or assumed, is part of your obligation as offspring. Regardless of years of owning successful businesses, marrying wonderful spouses, etc. the feeling of being a disappointment to them remains.

To be fair, I think that there are times when a family's expectations begin as a lovingly misguided attempt to see their children grow up and be happy and successful. But rarely then is the bridge gapped between wanting good and right things for your children and realizing that they will only be happy and successful if not just allowed, but encouraged to pursue that which THEY are passionate about. If our children are allowed to follow their own intrigue, curiosity and heart's desire, then happiness, the ultimate "success," is sure to follow. It is one thing to expect things such as honesty, kindness, responsibility, work ethic, etc. from our kids. Those are character traits that every human being should value, practice and aspire to. But to suggest that we can predetermine the path that best suits another human being is throwing effort after foolishness.

I remember years ago in a post-graduate psychology class learning of the term "identified patient." This referred to a family counseling scenario where the family would present the trouble maker, the black sheep, the rebellious child in the family as the source of angst, frustration and conflict. But ironically this "identified patient" was often the only one in the family that was showing or acknowledging the FAMILY'S dysfunction. Often times, the issue wasn't the problem child. Rather, that child was akin to the canary in the coal mine pointing to a dilemma far more complicated than the fact that little Joey keeps sneaking out the window at night. I share this not to take an emotional issue and make it academic, but for what it's worth, there's a darn good chance that your "black sheep" label is a moniker that speaks to the fact that you're likely the most authentic, honest, and "normal" person in your little clan.

For reasons that I have yet to thoroughly understand, nearly all children seem to have an innate desire to want to please their parents and win their approval. To a certain degree I think this is our instinctive wiring that guides us toward learning good and right behaviors. However, this goes well beyond bear cubs learning to mimic exactly what berries mama bear eats in the woods. Too often we are afflicted with our own complexity and any parent that denies their children love and acceptance if they don't fit a certain mold or live up to predetermined expectations should be ashamed of themselves. Every time I see this scenario I wish I could take the weight of this terrible burden off of the innocent shoulders and place it squarely back where it belongs. With the parents who never gave their children the peace of mind and heart of knowing that they are loved NO MATTER WHAT. To know that you are not being measured, graded or compared. To know that love and acceptance are your birth rite, not your task to go about winning and achieving. To know that the uniqueness of you will be honored and embraced, rather than judged and condemned. This SHOULD be the way of things. And if unfortunately it's not, find a way to realize that this is not about your responsibility to measure up; it is about every parent's responsibility to revel in the wonders of who their children, no matter what their age, truly are.

So the solution to not always feeling like a disappointment to your family is to spend your time around those that encourage and embrace who you are. And ultimately, if you can work your way to that enlightened place of loving your parents freely and unconditionally without the taint of hurt and frustration, then you have just put something unspeakably precious back into this world and that is a thing as pure and white and glorious as I can imagine.

Friendships and Claiming the

Very Best in Yourself

I feel as though I need to tread lightly here. I think friendships are both an honor and a responsibility and should be revered as such. Having said that, the people we spend time with can have a profound influence on our lives, our beliefs and even our actions. We are all well aware of this where it concerns teenagers so I'm not sure when exactly we stop realizing the importance and the impact of who we spend our time with. If teenagers spend time with peers that plan on going to college, they are more likely to do so themselves. Conversely, if they fall in with what we affectionately refer to as the "wrong crowd," we are more likely to be posting bail than we are to be applying for academic scholarships. Not dissimilarly it has been shown that couples who spend time around people who are divorced are more likely to end up so themselves. If this is an acceptable option for those we spend time with we are more permissive and accepting of it as an option available to us.

Perhaps it is assumed that as we mature we become more resolute about who we are and less susceptible to the influence of others. But my vote is that we purposely remain susceptible to the influence of others, we just make a tremendous effort to choose those "others" wisely. I don't think there is a time in our lives where we shouldn't be extremely conscious of the friendships we maintain and the company we keep. Do we surround ourselves with people that challenge and inspire us? Do we spend our time with people that have the courage and self-esteem to hold us accountable for not just doing our best, but being our best? Do we spend time with people who "raise the bar" of possibility in our lives and encourage us to be exceptional, honest, hard-working, respectful, devoted, inspired and alive? Or does our crowd spend more time watching Sport Center than watching an amazing sunset or their kids playing or with their nose in an inspiring book? Understand, this is not about claiming or feeling that you are "better" than anybody else, this is about claiming the very best *in yourself.*

This hits especially close to home as I have watched those I know and love gravitate toward spending time with people who don't just accept, but encourage less than extraordinary character, so I am trying to check my sensitivity at the door and come at this with both emotional and intellectual considerations. On a lighter note, I remember my very best friend through high school, and I mean inseparable, go to the restroom together and spend every waking minute together kind of friends, calling and getting in touch with me years after we had graduated. I grew up in New York, but had gone off to California for college and she had stayed pretty close to home. But I remember getting this call from someone who used to be as familiar to me as my own self and her saying she had been at the Cold Spring Tavern on Friday night and "Kristin Smith came in and you wouldn't believe what she was wearing." I am sitting there on the other end of the phone thinking, "I cannot believe this conversation. I literally have nothing in common with this person anymore." Not only could I not in my wildest nightmares imagine still spending my time at a high school hang-out, the thought of giving one second of care or concern to what an old classmate was wearing was a level of smallness that literally sent chills down my spine.

I think that it's part of a natural rhythm that certain people come into our lives for a time and that perhaps we grow, change directions and move on. But I also know people who have friendships that have been a center piece of their lives since they were five years old and when I hear of such relationships I cannot help but dwell on what an amazing gift such a bond would be.

But I think the bottom line where it concerns friendships of many years, would involve you asking yourselves, "Are my friends purposing to move and create their lives in a positive direction?" I don't care what the direction is, but is it centered on strength, character and promise? Do they encourage, inspire and push you toward your best and most exceptional self? If you have determined that averageness is not an option in your life, it is abundantly important that you surround yourselves with like-minded people because living a mediocre mindset is about as contagious as the common cold. If you don't want to catch it, the best defense is to avoid it at all cost.

So ask yourself if these friendship relationships are an exchange, as Greg would say, of encouragement and faith in one another. You don't have to *do* the same things, but I believe you must *value* the same things such as honesty, integrity, memories, experiences, laughter, intention, and inspiration. These are the things to have in common and preserve. If you determine that the answer is "no" this is not an exchange then I don't think a deep discussion or any kind of drama is in order. No hard work is necessary. You will just naturally move in different directions. But if you used to share these ideas and ideals and you feel as though friends have drifted, then I think you have a responsibility as a friend to be a steadfast example and show them the way back to what they once were.

So make on honest evaluation of what your friendships are now and what they once were. "Time is at once the most valuable and perishable of all our possessions." Keep this ever and always in mind, WHO we spend our time with is one of the most important decisions we make. Do not ever cheat yourself of the life you were meant to live by spending this most precious resource unwisely.

"I Wish"...

I just recently had discussions with two different couples about how they decided before they were married to not have children. It wasn't what they were about or what they wanted. But, lately after a couple of years of marriage one spouse changed their mind and was dropping hints. These couples loved each other dearly but now don't know what to do. I thought it just uncanny that these same two discussions happened so close together.

I'm not sure at what age theses couples were when they got married, but as people, we all grow, change and develop with each passing year. Assuming that personal evolution is in a positive direction, I think this is a wonderful part of human nature. I also think it is a wonderful part of great relationships. That ability to not just watch your spouse mature, but to encourage them to become in all ways, the most amazing version of themselves they are capable of being. It isn't just normal to want to grow and discover ourselves, but would be a vast disappointment if who we were at 25 was exactly the same person looking back at us in the mirror at 35.

Greg has changed in a multitude of ways since I met him and we were married. Homes, life, career focus, town we live in, you name it have changed. It would be much easier for me to list what hasn't changed in our lives rather than what has. But one thing in particular that hasn't changed and never will is that I love him. And part of loving him is wanting him to be happy and having few parameters on what that needs to look like. Many of you know of my deep aversion to carrying regret in my life and I cannot imagine the sense of regret that would weigh on my soul if I didn't support Greg in what made him feel the most happy, fulfilled, challenged, productive and alive. And I can say this all with ease of mind and heart because I know he feels and does the very same for me in a hundred different ways. Having said that, kids are a game changer in every way imaginable. There isn't one aspect of life that remains unaffected when children are added to our heart and life equation. For most people those changes are not just endured, but rather embraced. Children become the most unimaginably magical stuff of life. Our smiles become bigger, our joy becomes greater, our memories become richer and our love touches on something we never imagined to be real or possible.

But is this everybody's experience? No. And for those couples who make the conscious choice to not have children I have to respect that. Most especially because the thought of someone bringing a child into this world swaddled in resentment and obligation is a thought that makes my heart ache. And if this would be the sentiment that an innocent baby was brought into...I can imagine little that would carry more devastating consequences. I have actually found that most people who choose to not have kids are well aware of the fact that it is a somewhat "selfish" agenda on their part. They want to go where they want to go, do what they want to do, travel when and where the mood strikes and remain largely unencumbered by the responsibility of little ones. Children would throw an unwelcome wrench into their lifestyle and personal program. And once again,

I have to respect that sort of core honesty they seem to have with themselves and others.

But while I know many people that are "childless by choice" and I love them dearly, I will admit that my fondness for them does create a pang inside of me where I wish they knew. I wish they knew what they were missing. I wish they knew what it felt like to hold their own child in their arms and know that they are "the one" to that child. The one given the unimaginable gift of being there to nurture, protect, and love them with a strength that is so deep and fierce it defies explanation. I wish they knew the feeling of having their heart so consumed with love that it literally ached inside because they never imagined something so precious, so pure and so desperately dear would ever be a part of their lives. I wish they knew what laughter and joy and moments felt like when they see the world through the eyes of their own child. It's as though you've been watching this amazing movie in black and white and never noticed how brilliant and full and rich it could be when you added color…when you added kids. I wish they knew how profoundly deep their love and respect for their spouse becomes when seeing them not just as a person, but as a parent. I wish they knew all that I could never find the words to say. Words that would describe, express, or even remotely convey feelings that are connected to parts of their hearts and souls that aren't bound by the confines and limitations of language. I wish I could help them feel, for just a single precious second, what this sort of life, love, joy and laughter feels like not just in the moment, but in a way that feeds your soul endlessly. But alas I cannot. And as the responsibility of kids would be theirs, so must the choice be as well.

But I think that the greatest tragedy of all is when I meet or talk to people that had such horrendous childhoods themselves that they swear off the idea and desire of ever being parents themselves. And in my own mind I fight against the rage that the actions of their own miserable parents have not just taken their childhood from them, but made them desperately afraid of the joy that could be theirs for the taking. They haven't just denied them the past they should have had, but the future they deserve as well.

So after all that, I'm not sure how to help these parents except to say Everest, our oldest child was a "surprise." And I remember well after she came the almost panicked feeling that set in of, "oh my God, what if we had never done this!" The love and joy were so overwhelming that the awareness that I might have missed this scared me to death. So, while I will always respect people making conscious, heart-felt decisions for their lives, I will also encourage you to really take some time to consider this. Because I can imagine few tragedies greater than looking back, when it's too late and saying "I wish…"

The Strength of the Human Spirit

For what it may be worth, the "moral dilemma" of letting any property; homes, businesses, land, rental property, commercial property, personal property, etc. go back to the bank is one that is being shared by millions these days. While I can't vouch for how many of those millions who have sent property back to the bank feel angst about doing so, I can guarantee that in this, none of you are alone. As of 2010, 2.87 million US households received foreclosure filings and in that same year the number of homes actually repossessed reached the 1 million mark. Obviously that figure has done nothing but continue to grow. Do I throw this out simply because misery loves company? Not really. But I do think it is important to keep in mind that the place of loss so many are in is shared by scores of hard-working, contentious, and morally upstanding people.

It is estimated that over 50% of U.S. mortgages have a negative equity position so this leaves owners here, there and everywhere with precisely the same moral dilemma. Do I work myself to the breaking point to keep up with this agreement because I signed a contract with the bank and it's important to me to honor that, or do I cut my losses and let it go? After watching the banking industry respond to the meltdown that began in 2008 I can tell you that I personally feel little attachment to any bank's wellbeing. I see homeowners killing themselves to stay current on upside down mortgages, but I haven't seen a single bank sweating out the moral dilemma of how we do everything in their power to keep people in their homes. Getting a loan modification is nearly a full time job and all things considered they are few and far between. Refinancing? An option if you still have A-1 credit which is about as common as sightings of the Loch Ness Monster. In other words, banks feel absolutely no moral obligation to the people and families they serve so feelings of moral obligation to an institution are, in my opinion, admirable, but misguided. This is an industry that at the highest levels, sought out every opportunity to take advantage of people for profit.

You are operating under an ethical code and I admire that. Banks...not so much. They are operating under the law and regulations and even then, just barely. They aren't losing sleep over taking people's houses back so please don't be losing sleep over holding up your end of a losing bargain. Are there consequences? Sure. And that's reasonable and fair. Foreclosure will make a ruthless mess of your credit. But that's part of the deal. You have in fact not held up your end of the deal and those are the consequences. But in my mind, so be it. A decade from now my guess is that the banking industry will right itself and both the industry and society will hold largely nonjudgmental opinions about the financial traumas that took place between 2008 and ???? So while I wouldn't begin to dream of speculating about when we will raise the Titanic known as the banking industry, I do believe that it is widely known that this time, with all its chaos and confusion isn't a failure in people, it is a failure in policy.

PLEASE know that I am not advocating or encouraging a lack of responsibility on my part or anybody else's part. But I am advocating that owners really, truly assess where their most important responsibilities lie. If owners are putting their families through extreme financial hardship and suffering greatly because of their efforts to stay current on upside down mortgages that their lender has refused to modify, I believe their primary responsibility in that situation is to the health and happiness of their families, not to their lender. There is a movie that a friend put me onto called "Inside Job". I highly recommend that everyone watch it. It is a documentary type film that lays bare, much of what has happened and why we have all experienced and are still in the midst of an economic apocalypse. But for as frustrating and futile as things may feel right now, please don't misinterpret my disenchantment with government and industry for a lack of faith and belief. I will always believe that we live in the finest country in the world. That hard work and doing the "right thing" does matter and always will and that the strength of the human spirit with all its heart and courage and relentless hope is alive and well. These are just uncharted waters and it's going to take us all a while to find safe harbor.

If you happen to be living in a small community or anywhere and worried about what sort of chatter might be going on about the struggles of what you and so many have been dealing with...f*#k 'em! Not a very lady like sentiment I know, but I have NO patience or tolerance for gossipy, cowardly, judgmental people, nor should anyone. If these kinds of people haven't asked you about your dilemma directly, they have no business talking about it at all. If they do feel the need to talk over the fence about your troubles...so be it. If they feel the need to have those downright neighborly conversations with nothing to go on but ignorance and innuendo...please reference above sentiment. Good people, working hard and trying with every fiber of their being to do right by one another and their families are in my heart and mind the very best kind of people. So try not to give the time of day, or even a minute of your life over to worrying about what small people think, say or do. You will never change them so just put your heart and energy into things of true, real and deep importance. The rest will take care of itself.

An Intelligent and Open-Minded Interest

There is a reason that the common caution of not talking about politics or religion exists. In my opinion any trepidation towards engaging is well founded where these subjects are concerned. As adamant as I am about being honest and direct in relationships when something of moral or ethical consequence is at stake, I admittedly have a somewhat different view of politics. Why are politics any different? I think at the bottom line that people's views and beliefs in this particular matter are so fraught with opinions that are inextricably laced with emotions that you are more likely to find a mine field than any sort of common ground. For reasons that have yet to be deciphered, political discussions can rarely be had with open-minded diplomacy and thoughtful consideration of one another's viewpoints. More often than not normally sane and intelligent people turn into mouth frothing, head-spinning lunatics when you confront or disagree with them on a political issue. I'm personally a talk-radio junkie. I listen to it all the time and am well aware of which hosts lean which direction on the political spectrum and so I absorb their thoughts and contributions with this solid awareness in mind. I have little patience for people that hear an opinion or a belief and in lemming like fashion instantly adopt it as their own generally with some sort of bizarre proprietary pride. Personally I grew up an Army brat and will proudly admit to a strong belief and deep esteem for my country and those who selflessly serve it. Having said that, I would consider myself a political independent and I have voted for both democratic and republican presidents in the past. So I think it is not only possible, but would put forth that part of a respect for this amazing country is taking an intelligent and open-minded interest in her politics and welfare.

If you feel as though an individual could engage in a political discussion with level headed tolerance then what a fascinating conversation you could have. But the risk/reward ratio where politics are concerned is rarely, if ever, a balanced equation. The reward is a great discussion among intellectual equals. The risk is something just this side of a personal nuclear meltdown. Hardly a scenario you would take odds on in Las Vegas. An individual may have a benign desire to engage in an interesting discussion with a good friend, but that state of mind generally lasts about as long as a politician's good intentions. Please don't take this as a criticism of anyone as it is almost an involuntary insanity that sets in the minute we verbally walk down this path. But for as much as I applaud the wisdom of its avoidance I do believe it is appropriate to draw certain lines in the sand, cement, or across the coffee table.

I remember an experience in a post-graduate psychology class years ago. So let's begin with the given that this is a class of reasonably intelligent people sharing a common interest in both education and the human condition. So we are having a discussion about how people identify so strongly with their heritage and this young gal pipes up and announces that every time she travels abroad she's embarrassed to be an American. I wanted to crawl across the desks and smack the ignorance and hypocrisy right out of her. Did it never in any given moment occur to her, what a rare and wonderful land she lives in that as a young woman she is not only free to say this, regardless of how uninformed and offensive it is, but she is also a young woman working toward a graduate degree in a world where 90% of the population couldn't imagine such an inconceivable honor? How about a one-way ticket to North Korea where she could spend some time thinking on that particular view point? I couldn't care less what her political views are, but the minute she played her hand and announced that she had no respect for the fact that she had the freedom to hold and voice those views I wrote her off for the immature entitled girl that she was.

You can loathe politicians and despise a given agenda, but the minute you attach that mindset to a disdain for your country, I've lost my tolerance. In other words, there is a time to avoid political discussions for the sake of an important and treasured friendship. But there is also a point at which differences can escalate to the point where a mutual respect between people, not just ideas, is difficult to come by.

So rather than doing the avoidance dance any longer, I would just tell your friend head on that you value and cherish the friendship and would rather not "go there" as you are committed to the relationship lasting far longer than the current season of political ad campaigns.

The Beauty and the

Beast of Entrepreneurship

Stay committed, focused on task, and follow through! Oh this one is easy…Adderall. No, all joking and prescription medications aside, it is a widely accepted dilemma that the attention span of children and young adults is about equal to that of the common house cat. In other words, they have none. I certainly don't mean to criticize, but it truly is a symptom to be contended with no matter what your age. Kids and young adults have grown up in a world of fast-paced TV, instant messaging, video games and various and sundry other means of either watching or achieving a nearly instantaneous outcome.

So regardless of your age, you are going to have to teach yourself discipline. I will readily admit that many entrepreneurs are Big Picture people and that is a gift…truly. But in order to achieve the big picture you need to be able to execute a plan. And that takes time, patience and devotion. The allure of finding the deal and the rush that can come from a successful negotiation are experiences that are the lifeblood of the real estate entrepreneur, but all that happens in between is equally as important if not equally as exhilarating. How amazing to be a professional football player that walks onto the field in front of tens of thousands of screaming fans. But that only happens about a dozen times a year. The rest of the job is the far less glamorous time spent in the weight room and at practice. But game day never comes if you don't put in all the other effort. Clearly I could take this analogy too far, but you certainly get the idea. Consider all the more mundane details of entrepreneurship to be the work-outs that dread them or not, are essential to your success.

I've mentioned Greg's passion for lists in the past and it is such a powerful tool it bears mentioning again. Decide what time of day you want to take your medicine so to speak and schedule the adrenaline free tasks for those times. If you need to just "get them over with," make a list of your morning "chores." If your most inspired and creative times are in the morning use that time and space to plan, call, create and tend to the more enticing aspects of your business but be sure that you've set aside a couple of hours later in the day to write bird letters, call your accountant, write a detailed business plan…etc., etc. It is the beauty and the beast of entrepreneurship. You are your own boss but without that outside influence and set of defined expectations so many people do flounder. But if you're going to do this thing, you need to wear ALL the hats. You are the superstar salesman but you're also assigned to accounting and the mailroom occasionally. If you need accountability create it for yourself. Find a friend or fellow entrepreneur whom you respect to help keep you on the straight and narrow. If you are just utterly loathe to deal with the details you may want to consider taking on a partner with a somewhat opposite skill set, or hire someone to manage the details for you. Because make no mistake about it, a business that doesn't tend to the details will last about as long as a carton of milk.

There is an intriguing book that one of Greg's students put me on to called "The E Myth" and it's certainly worth your time. It acknowledges that every small business needs an entrepreneur, a manager and a technician and that lucky you need to learn to be all of them. If your internal dialog says "yeah, but I'm an ideas guy... I like to dream big and just go for it" then you are not truly an entrepreneur. Worst case scenario you tend to be one of those souls that are drawn to every multi-level market scheme ever created because of the rush of success they sell or alternatively, perhaps you are better off in a corporate think tank where you just get to brainstorm amazing ideas and allow other talented staff to follow through with the implementation. But if you truly want to not just consider yourself an entrepreneur, but actually *be* one then you absolutely must tap into your inner manager and technician identities. The good news is that all of these skills can be learned but as with any worthwhile endeavor their mastery requires focus, effort and education. As they say in the golf world, "drive for show and put for dough." In other words, it's wonderfully impressive if you can drive the ball 300+ yards straight down the fairway, but unless you're willing to put in the time on the greens mastering the touch, the subtly and the precision, neither golf nor entrepreneurship is truly your game.

Women and "Having It All"

Let's get to the heart of the matter and define what "having it all" for a woman means. First are you allowing society and the latest woman's magazine to insist that the path to enlightened womanhood is only to be found through a high powered career, a supportive yet progressive husband, two kids, a golden retriever and a Range Rover? Or have you sat down to think about who YOU are, what makes YOU happy and just exactly what do YOU want out of life... *your* life.

Truth be told, I think that women are so phenomenally critical of one another that we make it a bitterly difficult task to find our way in life. To date in life I have experienced all of the following; The career woman looks down on the stay at home mom as selling herself short and failing in her duty to contribute to the empowerment of women. She casts her in a shadow of tame domesticity and intellectual inferiority. According to her, stay at home moms lead trivial lives focused on meal planning, kid's activities and domestic bliss and simply have no idea what it takes to be a "working mother." All the while she is feeling a powerful undercurrent of guilt and remorse because of all the soccer games she has missed and the fact that she herself has never once volunteered to chaperone a field trip and was left with vicariously seeing her child's laughter and wonder in the pictures the nanny took. On the flip side, the stay at home moms can consider themselves morally superior because they are prioritizing their children and their families above all else and are therefore among the ethically elite. They are devoted and self-less and carry their PTO involvement around like a badge of honor looking down on those moms who's kids go to after school care and have to order hot lunch because their moms don't take the time to make them one. But in some of their quiet moments they resent all that they have "given up" and occasionally yearn for the intellectual obligation of a report due, or the excitement of a critical deadline or pivotal lunch meeting.

And the net effect of all this seems to be that rather than just acknowledging that we as women ALL so often feel torn, confused, overwhelmed and uncertain, we just get bitchy. Women can run the gamut from being subtly disparaging to downright vicious and to be honest I've yet to meet a man that can be as cruel and condescending as an insecure women. If her boobs are better than yours, they're fake. If she's thinner than you she must be bulimic. If she's got a better job than you she slept her way there. If she throws a better party than you she must have hired someone else to do it. It's truly insane and something I have never quite been able to wrap my mind around. To be sure there are those women that are confident and secure enough to encourage, uplift and embrace and I feel deeply blessed to have a few of those in my life. We don't judge each other, we just acknowledge that we're all doing our best, regardless of what that looks like and love, support and encourage each other. So women give yourself that freedom. Try as best you can to detach yourself from other people's ideas and expectations and ask yourself what you want. Know that you aren't going to change womankind and that any decision you make will likely be met with criticism, prone to being whispered rather than spoken aloud, but what's the alternative? Staying on the hamster wheel, stressed and feeling like a chicken with its head cut off, and trying frantically to run between guilt and obligation?

If you as a woman have a career that you love, give yourself permission to love it and then enjoy balancing that passion with the blessing of your kids. If you as a woman ache every time you leave your kids to run off to a job that is barely tolerable, sit down with your husband and have a heart to heart talk about how you can change your picture so you can be home with them. This certainly doesn't mean you are no longer a "working mom." The average stay at home mom works 97.7 hours a week and if she was compensated would earn over $117,000 per year. Even Oprah says that being a mother is the hardest and most important job in the world. And this is coming from a woman that has achieved nearly unimaginable success in business. If some hybrid is your ideal take some pleasure in knowing that corporate America is slowly but surely coming to an understanding of what women contribute to the workforce and are creating scenarios to accommodate their needs through part time, flex-time and working from home scenarios. But above all DO NOT settle for feeling as though it just is what it is. Is it possible that life may look different once a woman makes an honest evaluation about who she is and what brings her the greatest joy? Yup. But that's kind of the idea anyhow right? "Having it all" requires that she first knows what it "all" looks like. Once a woman knows what her picture is, she should pursue it with passion and without apology. She will benefit, her family will benefit and I can guarantee that her actions will give another woman the implied permission to have the courage to do the very same thing.

Spanking

A common question that is often on the minds of new parents to be is the question of spanking especially when one parent grows up being spanked and the other does not. The first thought that comes to my mind is that they should have engaged in a discussion about spanking before they were married much less before they decided to have a baby. Because as far as I'm concerned this is a deal breaker. This is one of those topics for me that has no gray area, no middle ground and no room for a difference of opinion. At best, spanking is a fallout of laziness or ignorance and at worse, it is a byproduct of anger on a much deeper level. If I was dating a man and it got serious enough to start having discussions about marriage and family and it became clear to me that he was in the cavemanesque camp of "if you spare the rod, you spoil the child," we would need to go our separate ways. When two people are already married and a baby is on the way, I truly hope they can both sit down and have a truly meaningful discussion on this subject before baby comes.

I am certain there are many things these new parents, as adults, do differently than their parents did, so why, of all the influences this one needs to remain is an argument that makes no logical sense to me. Don't ask yourself if your parents spanked you as a kid or not, ask yourselves, does it seem right or sane to hit a child. I believe with my whole heart that my God given job description as a parent is to love and protect my kids, not to hurt or hit them. I am mystified by the fact that if you haul off and hit another adult…that's assault. If you smack another adult on the butt, well, that equals a sexual harassment lawsuit. Yet somehow there are groups of parents out there that for reasons that defy explanation, believe that inflicting these same behaviors on a small, helpless child is righteous.

I am all in favor of raising kids with a sense of discipline and respect but to believe that the way I achieve that is with a belt or a wooden spoon is a misguided belief system of epic proportions. It has been proven time and time again that kids who are spanked are more likely to be aggressive themselves. So parents, discuss this reality with each other. If your reasoning is that you want your children to be well behaved, swatting them will more likely put them on the fast track toward the precise opposite. Another undeniable truth is the fact that the greatest leverage you will ever have with your children is love. And I don't mean leverage in the sense that you give love and take it away to manipulate them into good behavior like small puppets on strings. Unconditional love should be every child's birthright. What I mean by leverage is that the absolute love and embrace that you give your children will motivate them infinitely more to do the right thing than the fear of being spanked. The feeling of disappointing you will always sting far more than any physical harm or hurt you could inflict.

There are numerous wonderful books that can shed more light on this topic if that interests you, but at the end of the day, parents need to be steady and strong. It is on both of them to be informed together and to work together to find different ways and means to raise their kids without the option of spanking. Is it harder in many ways once you take this option off the table? You bet. But I have never in my life found the easier path to yield the better result. There's the right way and then there's the easy way. For what it's worth, we have three amazing kids, but I still threaten to buy a dog in the hopes of having some living creature in the house that listens to me.

Congratulations to all new parents and best of luck!

In-Laws

It is a dilemma that has existed since the dawn of time without a singular solution that could possibly suffice for all situations and relationships. As much as we can all howl with laughter as we watch "Meet the Parents," the realities can often be less than a laughing matter. Stereotypes aside, in my experience I know more people that struggle with the tension found in some In-Law relationships than not. So, what to do, what to do...

First and foremost, acknowledge that blending lives and backgrounds is a complicated process where at times we need to be bold and at other times circumstances require us to tread very lightly. But the fact of the matter is that when you marry someone, you marry the whole of that person. And their life, their history, and their family are all part of what you take on when you get married. Each and every one of us is a product of all that has come before. When I married Greg he already had two children and I remember in all my euphoric naiveté believing that because I loved Greg, I would just naturally have a loving relationship with his kids as well. Not so. What I realized in fairly short order, was that his kids are individuals in their own right and I needed to build a relationship with them around who *they* were and what *they* meant to me, not around what Greg meant to me.

So I would encourage you, for your sake as a couple, to try to find some common ground with your in-laws. Find something of value in the relationship and allow that to be the focal point. For example, perhaps you and they have drastically different personalities and belief systems, but they are wonderful loving grandparents. Super! Focus there. If however they lack any redeeming qualities and they are truly doing damage to your family and your relationship as a couple, you have to either literally or figuratively put some distance between yourselves and them. As husband and wife your first responsibility is to one another and you both have an obligation to guard your relationship against harm and continual discord. Any loving parent would want happiness for their children, not constant conflict and friction so keep this in mind as the two of you work to create a UNITED front as it relates to these and all relationships. It never ceases to fascinate and amaze me how powerful family relationships are. And for better or for worse, they continue to be a force for either good or evil in our lives. For what it's worth, take some really good mental notes on this situation so that the two of you can reference them in the future in order to both be the world's best in-laws when the time comes.

Perception in the Moment

I whole heartedly believe that "balance" lies in the perception of what you are doing. I often hear parents talk in terms of "sacrifices" they make for their kids. I can tell you with absolute certainty that I have never in my life sacrificed anything for my kids. Sacrifice implies denial or giving up of something you desire in exchange for something or someone else. There is nothing I have ever done or "given up" for my kids that I wasn't completely and entirely willing to forego. Anything I give or do for them brings so much joy that I never compare it to some alternative notion of what I could be doing instead. Giving to them and doing for them brings me such happiness that the word sacrifice truly isn't part of my lexicon. My hope is that as an entrepreneur you are doing what you love to do. Understand that never means you love everything about your chosen endeavor, but the big picture is something you are not just committed to but are passionate about. So if you are working hard to build a future for your family I'm going to suggest you don't perceive that as a sacrifice, but rather a privilege; A privilege to do what you love while building a life and a future for your family and teaching your kids a great work ethic to boot. But also realize that life is what is happening every single day and it needs to be embraced in all its chaos and craziness. It isn't a matter of awaiting the "benefit" of some Norman Rockwell moment in the future. The benefits are everywhere around you every single day and you deserve to notice and enjoy them. There are times around the dinner table where chaos and craziness reign supreme and I could either feel frustrated and fed up or make the choice to notice it and savor it for all and everything that it is. It's our life, happening right now, in this moment of complete pandemonium. Life doesn't just happen during a well-planned weekend or a trip to Disneyland. It is happening every single day all around you so find the beauty and the joy in the life and the living and never underestimate the value of a sense of humor. In the corporate world people toil long and hard for a great "benefits" package. Every single day I notice the "benefits package," that I have been blessed with and often times, it has spaghetti sauce in its hair.

Romance and Passion

What constitutes romance and passion in a relationship? It is a good question and the answer is simple. Yet simple is not to be confused with easy. First I think we need to arrive at an understanding of what romance and passion in a relationship is. To be sure, men and women will likely have anywhere from somewhat to drastically different views about what speaks of romance and passion to them, but the bottom line is, both matter and need to be tended to. And the bottom line is that you need to prioritize especially if your life is filled with work and kids seven days a week. You need to believe and make sure that you and your spouse know that your shared relationship is the number one priority in your lives. Not work, not golf and not friends. Give each other the number one spot at all times. I think people often fall into the trap of feeling as though that which they most value must therefore be the recipient of the majority of their time and attention. Not so. Letting someone know they are at the center of your life and joy does not take candlelight, bubble bath and rose petals. In fact, the thought of something this cliché makes my skin crawl. I have always told Greg that I would rather have him bring me flowers on a random Wednesday in May than on Valentine's Day along with every other soul out there who succumbs to this annual obligation.

It really is the little things. A tender touch, a text that just says, "I love you," offering to pick up dinner on the way home, or actually mailing the one you love a card that thanks them for being such a great parent and telling them how much you appreciate their irreplaceable role in your life and family. These small things are the lifeblood that continues to feed and nourish a relationship. Also for most women, nothing is more alluring to them than seeing their husband be a great dad. For men, I think at a very basic level, all men desire Appreciation, Respect and Sex. Notice I didn't say that's all they need, but I did say that all men need it. A tricky but true difference. Greg deserves to know how deeply I appreciate how hard he works and how seriously he takes providing for his family. Nobody wants to believe they burned up 60 hours for nothing of consequence or value. He deserves to know that I respect his incredible abilities, talents and work ethic. And when we go out on Friday night, even if what sounds most appealing to me is sweats and take-out after a long week, I'm going to get dressed up and go out to dinner and enjoy my husband. No matter how busy things get you MUST set aside time for the two of you to be together not as business partners or parents, but as a couple. Set it aside every week and DON'T TOUCH IT! Make this commitment to each other utterly sacred.

At the end of the day, at the end of it all, our relationships are all we have. They are not just something that matters, they are everything that matters. So neglecting this garden along the way will leave you with a hunger for love and connection that cannot be fed. We all fall short but therein lies the beauty of a committed relationship. It is willing to wait for you to water it, but it is never to be taken for granted. We are only as good as what we give, so make a list of small things that you can do for one another and make a habit of prioritizing those small acts of kindness. I can promise there is nothing in a seven day sixty hour work week that is more rewarding than the 60 seconds it takes to say, "I love you."

Saying "NO"

Ah, I feel for people who are always playing catch up and who never seem to "get on top of it" or "gain ground". For years I suffered from the exact same affliction and to date, I can tell you with absolute certainty that the only sure fire cure to "feeling buried by it all" is developing the ability to say, "no." I have tried remedies ranging from avoidance, to over achievement to flat out evasion. And after so many years spent practicing the above mentioned tactics and so many more, I have realized that the only way to feel in control of your life is to actually be in control of your life. Now there is a difference between having "five more things dumped on your to-do list," and jobs, tasks or experiences you have willfully and wantingly signed up for. The former are obligations you would much rather be without.

So, the antidote to this feeling is so simple, but it takes an astonishing amount of practice. And I will fall toward that phrase that became part of our culture during the Reagan era I believe, "just say no." If it's good enough for drugs, it's good enough for those of us who are addicted to trying to please everybody by doing everything. The reality I would ask you to think on is that every time you begrudgingly or not, say "yes," to something, you are, by default saying "no," to something else you could be using that time for. And you simply must get to the point where you value your time with such a sense of preciousness and urgency that saying "no" to those things which don't add to your life, your joy, your memories or your bottom line is something you can do without conflict or apology. If I am being asked to work procurement for the school's fundraising auction I need to weigh that against the other things I could be doing with my time and energy. If I am being asked to rewrite a business procurement letter for a client just because they'd rather have me do it than they…the answer is simple yet polite. "I'm afraid I don't have time to do it for you, but I'd love to take a quick peek at it once you've finished your draft. "No" is not a synonym for rude, abrupt or selfish. Rather it is a statement of focus, priorities and intention. For what it's worth, I have found that once you develop the ability to say "no" people begin to respect and value your "yes," in much more meaningful and profound ways. If they know how deliberate you are about how and where you spend your time, when you do say "yes" they will realize and enjoy the fact that it is delivered with sincerity and whole heartedness rather than a sense of resentful obligation.

So start small and keep in mind that as with all things, practice makes perfect. Work at saying "no" to that which frustrates and overwhelms you, and saying "yes" to that which rewards you with laughter, momentum and accomplishment of something of value. I can guarantee that overcoming the fear of saying "no" is nothing compared to wrestling with the regret of wasted time. May the force be with you.

Individuality and True Friendship

Many of us have friends that we care deeply about but realize that sometimes there are fundamental differences present that are hard to respect. So is it possible to keep friendships when you don't agree on certain things? Not only is it possible, but I can't imagine it being otherwise. I have yet to meet anybody, husband and family included where agreement is the order of the day, every day. But the key is to acknowledge how those differences can be an opportunity for growth and learning rather than conflict and discord. I have very dear friends that I would consider myself very unlike in terms of the way we go about our lives. Do I find myself at odds with this at times? You bet. But during those times I try to backtrack to the big picture. Are they good people? Do they bring qualities of value and perspective to the relationship? Does their moral compass align with your own?

Having said this I also believe that any real relationship, by definition, tolerates honesty and openness. If friendship means we need to agree with each other all the time or to keep quiet when we don't agree then I'm not of a mind to call that sort of relationship a friendship. Under those guidelines we can call ourselves acquaintances, or cocktail companions, but not friends. I remember one time watching a friend begin to lose her marriage because of a grown daughter who was living with them with her young children. Now I can see an endless number of ways that this could have been a tremendously positive experience, but the daughter was bringing absolutely nothing to the table. She was creating enormous conflict between her mother, my dear friend, and her husband (who was not her dad). Her mom was married to a terrific man who truly didn't ask for anything unreasonable but still the grown daughter continued to be a source of discontent in the relationship. I was involved not only as someone who cared deeply but my friend had also asked me to drive her granddaughter to school each day, etc., all catering to a grown daughter who was doing nothing but selfishly ruining her mother's relationship and happiness. I wrote my friend a heartfelt letter that expressed what I was seeing unfold and my care and concern for her. It was direct and on point and to her enormous credit she took it for what it was. A statement of both my strong beliefs and my deep concern for her. Certainly this doesn't mean that we need to call urgent attention to every difference. Relationships allow room for individuality and contrasts, but true friendships also allow for honesty and complete candor when something of substance or great consequence is amiss.

I will also say there are some differences I could simply never abide by. Examples would be mistreating a spouse or children and racism. If I found myself in a friendship where those fundamental principles were at odds I would need to move on, but who we vote for on Election Day, whether we attend what church and where on Sundays and whether we opt for paper or plastic at the grocery store...vive la différence!

Feedback Loop of Accountability

This has actually been a real and true education for me. And I want to sympathize with anyone's desire to walk that razor's edge occasionally to reach beyond their comfort zone. I have to admit that I came by an ability to get out of my comfort zone by default. I married Greg. And he is truly a person who wouldn't know how to do anything but take the road less traveled. His very nature is to push and reach for that which would be outside of most people's field of vision. Not because it isn't possible, but simply because they don't see it. I have said many times that since being with Greg I haven't seen my comfort zone in so long that I don't even know where it is any longer. And I mean that sincerely. I don't know what "normal" looks like anymore. A "normal" work week, a "normal" schedule, a "normal" life and pace. But I hope you don't detect even a hint of wistfulness in my tone because there truly isn't any. I honestly cannot imagine my life any other way.

So my point is that I have realized over time that for most people an enormously large part of pushing themselves for more; more life, more laughter, more experiences, more memories, is accountability. Having someone that genuinely and consistently expects more from you than perhaps you even expect from yourself in your life; someone to check in with, be challenged by and even answer to is valuable beyond measure. Now you're on the hook for your inaction, reluctance and fear. We can find a way to justify anything to ourselves but can we really find a way to justify it to somebody else? I can offer myself a million and five reasons for why I didn't accomplish something this week, but do I have that honest, expectant feedback system that is just going to look at me with an eyebrow raised in disgust and say, "really?" Is that the best you can do? All you have to offer? Is it the effort that you'd be proud to write home about? This needs to be someone that can encourage you but will never pander to excuses and inaction. Be it friends, a spouse, a business partner or a mentor most of us need not just a source of support and encouragement, but an occasional kick in the ass or at least the threat of one.

If you think about it, I'm not sure when most of us made the decision that we no longer needed that feedback system. When kids are in school they are encouraged but not without expectation of a level of performance and accomplishment. Entrepreneurs almost by definition have excused themselves from that feedback loop of accountability, but we all need it. And we need it in all things. It keeps us from falling back into old habits. We need to be accountable for our accomplishments, our efforts, our intentions and our behavior. So if you are struggling to push yourself out of that comfort zone and beyond, find someone that truly wants the best for you and give them permission to give you a shove either occasionally or consistently. But speaking from experience, once you take a walk on that wild side of possibility and courage, you will never again want to walk the road of least resistance. Life is best and most vibrantly lived when we dare to do more than we ever imagined possible.

People Skills

Very emphatically I will say the ability to read other people is fantastically important and will certainly pay dividends in life and business when we develop that skill to a great degree of competence. They have actually proven that "successful" people and entrepreneurs have an innate ability to "read" other people and to interpret their facial expressions and body language with a high degree of accuracy. Whether the setting is personal or professional we need to consider other people the "environment" we are working in. Being aware of their temperament, disposition, warmth, sincerity or lack thereof are all highly relevant factors. Just as knowing if you were in a forest, desert or alpine environment would alter everything from your dress to your behavior, so too should you develop the ability to immerse yourself in the environment of others and allow those surroundings (so to speak) to determine your behavior to a large degree. The good news is these skills can certainly be learned and developed as an expertise. At the minimum "reading" other people is a sign of consideration and awareness and at its maximum it can be one of the most essential ingredients determining business success or failure. So what is the best way to improve these skills if you feel as though they aren't naturally your strongest suit? Consistent work and focused attention. We were once highly intuitive creatures, but to some degree we've gotten out of the habit of allowing our instinct to serve us. What does your gut tell you about how this person may be feeling or responding to you? Then adapt. This is an entire area of discipline and study, but I think that at its most basic level, if we just paid better attention, so often that would suffice. It drives me nuts to have a conversation where you can just tell that the other party isn't really listening. Instead they are spending their time thinking about what they are going to say or contribute next and are just waiting for someone to take a breath so they can insert their next insightful, intelligent and overly opinionated point. And as tedious as it may sound, this is a case of practice makes perfect. The more we put ourselves in situations with other people and discipline ourselves to focus, listen and react accordingly the better we are going to become and the better our "results" will be.

Now as far as how other people perceive you, here I want to be quite a bit more cautious. While I think it is important to be aware of how others perceive us, I think it is far more important to feel as though we are worthy, comfortable and sincere about conveying who we are. For those of us that have shaken the restraints of trying to please others, I can tell you the act of pleasing is far different from the act of caring. Caring shows itself as an extension of you and what YOU are. Pleasing is forced, artificial and a direct path to exhaustion and disappointment. So while I am very much in favor of developing the ability to "read" others, I would also emphatically state that your first responsibility is to develop yourself and confidence in the wonderful fact that THAT is all and everything you were ever intended to be. If you are being truly and genuinely yourself, I believe that people appreciate sincerity and respond to it with warmth and reciprocation. And if they don't, I can unequivocally guarantee that you are better off without them anyhow. I don't mean to sound like your personal cheerleader toward self-affirmation, but I DO know that concerning yourself with what other people think of you is akin to being on a hamster wheel running your legs off to nowhere. A lot of effort with absolutely no return.

"It Depends"

Okay! Fasten your seat belts because one way or another you're going to be in for a bumpy ride. But who doesn't like a good roller coaster every now and then? Do you tolerate the unruly kids of friends or relatives? Should you step in and say something? This is a topic where I am going to frustrate you to no end by saying that to some degree, "it depends." If you are over at the home of friends or family, I would steer clear of disciplining their kids. If you're in their environment, on their turf so to speak, it's really not territory where you can lay down the law and let everyone under the age of twelve know that there is a new Sheriff in town. However having said that, if you are left "in charge" for a period of time, go ahead and take charge. Likewise, if you see anything truly inappropriate, like a four year old watching "Night of the Living Dead," or something unsafe like a toddler about to char a hand medium-well on the backyard grill, then I think you have an obligation to step in regardless of the potential fall-out. I would however offer the appropriate parent the benefit of the doubt though and say something to them. I remember a time when my father-in-law commented to my husband on the fact that our then two year old son wasn't a particularly astute listener. In fact, he was pretty darn good at ignoring us. And my father-in-law said something about it to my husband. I personally reacted only because as the Mom, I felt as though I was the one that should be primarily held accountable for my son's behavior or lack thereof. Whether I like it or not, my father-in-law was spot on correct, I just didn't want my husband taking the heat for something I felt was my responsibility. Shortly after that I bought a shock collar for our son and his behavior has improved dramatically. All kidding aside, tread lightly when in other people's homes and if something is concerningly amiss at least try to give the appropriate parent the opportunity to step in.

BUT, what if you are either out in public or friends and family are at your home? Take the reins and let the ruffians have it! When I have other kids in my home, they follow my rules. Plain and simple. I'm not setting out to be the second incarnation of the Grinch who stole Christmas but I am going to be firm and unapologetic for any expectations I do have. We had some dear friends visit us at our place in Arizona and with their being a pool in the backyard I was adamant with kids and parents alike that even though there is an alarm system, NO kids go into the backyard without an adult. Well our friends little guy got numerous tutorials and reminders but still wasn't taking this too seriously. Nor were his parents. So the next time he set the alarm off I unabashedly took matters into my own hands and handled it with a very calm but meaningful "time out." The bigger problem was that his behavior potentially cleared the way for other kids to break the rules as well. Monkey see, monkey do as it were. Rest assured, if the tables were turned, I would have NO problem with them putting out similar enforcement measures with our kids in their home. To be sure, I do think that having one set of guidelines is really important and you better be as ready to discipline your own children as you are lying in wait for someone else's because they've been getting on your nerves for the last four years. If my kids are truly out of line, I appreciate someone stepping in in that moment as it really does "take a village" and I can honestly say I am under no protective, hyper-sensitive delusions that my children are flawless, blameless and consistently lovely creatures in word and deed. I do however think there are positive ways to approach other people's children when discipline is needed that will win you not just the fondness of the kids, but the other parent's eternal gratitude. I recently saw this masterfully done on a trip I took with my daughter and some of her school mates for a competition in Tennessee. One of the dad's on the trip is a super involved parent and has tremendous rapport with all the kids in the class. And there were a couple of occasions on the trip where I saw him step in and do an inspiring job of correcting certain kids. We were at dinner one night and a younger sibling kept banging his silverware on the table. His mom half-heartedly asked him to stop a goodly number of times, but as kids will sometimes do, he persisted. So this dad very subtly stepped in and put an end to the oh so annoying behavior by kindly, but very determinedly telling him he needed to stop...now. I also noticed him very tactfully pull one of the boys aside on a different occasion and engage in a conversation that was heavy on the concepts of choices vs. consequences. Let's face it, for reasons that defy explanation, often times the same words from a different voice can have a remarkably immediate impact. But this dad always corrects the kids with intent but no anger and balances this out with such frequent support and encouragement of them all that I find his evenhanded involvement not only reasonable, but welcome.

So, if you're in someone else's home realize that you may just have to bite your lip when the little darlings start acting like trolls. I could spend hours on a soap box of how lazy parenting is ruining kids but that's a story for another day. But if they are in public or your home...be measured, but firm and don't hesitate in the least to lay down your law. After all, someone's got to...

269

Whose Celebration!?

There are numerous things I have never understood and over the top birthday parties when a baby turns one has made my list of things I would consider to be borderline baffling. I suppose I should offer a confession that when it comes to celebrations (birthdays, Christmas etc.) I don't throw much energy at them until my kids are at an age where they are likely to remember said event. In fact, the first two Christmases after our third child was born the only reason we got him any Christmas gifts was because our oldest daughter would have certainly sensed something was amiss if Santa didn't bring anything for her brother. So let's just say he got numerous "practical" gifts so that I was getting things he needed while primarily catering to my oldest daughter's sense of awe, wonder and belief.

When it comes to celebrating a child's first birthday, I think we have done a woeful job of misplacing where, precisely the celebration belongs. So I have long said that the people who deserve to celebrate when a baby turns one; are the parents. That beautiful bundle of joy hasn't done anything in this last year other than feed off your endless supply of love, nurturing, sustenance, cooing, cuddling, sleepless nights and attentions to his or her every single whine, whimper or need. You have been a single minded dispenser of care, concern, and attention at every turn. You have done it wantingly, willfully and blissfully with nothing to show for it but the soul sustaining joy of a smile or a giggle. What an amazing job YOU have done. And I mean YOU so why exactly does the party have an Elmo theme?

If you want to celebrate, and I would emphatically encourage you to do so, make plans to go out to dinner with your husband or do something relaxing together...just the two of you. I don't need to remind you that the two of you made the baby and have selflessly poured yourself into his or her well-being for the last year, so it is really the both of you that deserve the "celebration." I believe this so deeply that I have put my money where my mouth is in trying to encourage this philosophy. I have a cousin who when their first child turned one, I called HER parents and asked if they would mind having their grandson overnight (they were thrilled!) Then I called a lovely little Bed and Breakfast and made dinner and overnight reservations for them (on us) and they had an unforgettable time celebrating their son's birthday and there wasn't a balloon or a party hat within 100 yards.

Now understand that if you want to have a small family get together and make a cake for your child to dive into and have lots of wonderful pictures to show for the memories, I'm all in favor of such a thing. Just be sensible and realize that throwing a big themed bash with elaborate gifts and preparations is, in my mind, putting effort, energy and attention in the wrong direction. You don't need to make yourself crazy or break the bank to ensure that you remember your child's first birthday with fondness and great joy. I have often said that people aren't getting married anymore, they are having weddings. I think it may be these same people that hire party planners and dancing

271

ponies when their child turns one. Don't even get me started on the garbage bag...I mean goodie bag trend. But in all seriousness, try to keep it simple and I think that as time goes by you'll find that focusing on your family and not on a party is going to create the most treasured, enduring memories you could imagine.

Becoming a Step-Dad

Do you have to have your head examined when someone you are serious about already has two kids? No. Do you need to make sure it's screwed on good and straight? Yes. What I mean by that is that this is a situation you need to approach with your eyes wide open and give it the respect and consideration that it deserves. I believe that in matters of love and life mates, we need to let our hearts lead the way, but this is an instance where your head definitely needs to be in the game as well...big time. Is this an incredibly challenging state of affairs? You bet. But it can also be incredibly rewarding. I am convinced that the very best way to approach this is to ask yourself first and foremost, could this be the person I would love to spend the rest of my life with? When kids are involved I don't have time to hear, "well she's really nice, we have fun together and she actually likes football." If that is as infatuated as you are at this point...move on. If however, you would walk down the aisle tomorrow save your caution around the fact that she has kids then the two of you can look forward to some long and meaningful conversations at this point. Does she want to get married? Do you want more kids? Does she? Does she have primary custody? Is their dad involved in their lives and if so what kind of factor/influence is he? How will she align herself in matters of parenting and discipline? Is she willing to create a united front with you or does she feel that the parenting needs to be left to her because she's their mom? I believe strongly that if she wants to be with you, but doesn't want you to have some say and influence with the kids that is an enormous red flag. Did she introduce you to her kids right away or did she protectively wait to expose them to any relationship until it was fairly serious? I hate to see parents that parade a laundry list of boyfriends and girlfriends through their children's lives. I think it goes far beyond irresponsible and borders on cruel. But I digress.

To make matters even more challenging, western society has done a bang-up job of vilifying the step-parent role. You need look no farther than Cinderella, Snow White, Hansel & Gretel, etc., etc. to realize that those of us that have taken this on aren't starting on an even playing field. I don't say this to put anyone off, but personally speaking I can say that I wish I had been better prepared. Where my naiveté left off, other people's perceptions took over. So keep in mind that if you want a B+ in the step-dad department you are going to have to seriously over achieve. Is it a challenge worthy of your efforts? It can be that and then some. But in this situation, ignorance provides little bliss.

On the truly positive side, I actually think you are in a position of having wonderful vision and insight about the woman you are serious about that most people lack for quite some time in relationships. You get to see what type of mother she is. How she treats and responds to her kids. Her morals and ethics around family and those relationships and this can, for you, be akin to fast forwarding the movie and getting a glimpse at the really good stuff long before most people would enjoy such a benefit. As well, I know with my whole heart that often times, being and becoming a parent brings out the very best in people and it could well be that she is, in fact, the person you are drawn to today because of the fact that she has kids and life has asked her to grow and become in those ways. But now it will ask the same of you. As I've mentioned before, her kids are people in their own right with feelings, emotions and dispositions that belong uniquely to them and you will need to forge a relationship with them independent of their mother. This is a complicated, complex situation to be sure, but what I can tell you is that Greg's kids have been an ENORMOUS blessing in my life. Has it always been easy? Hell no! But has it been worthwhile? Utterly and completely. At heart I'm a romantic and I do believe that love...real love conquers all. But I also know that you owe it to yourself and her to be as aware and sure of yourself as possible as you go down this path. After all, there are extra hearts at stake in the matter and they are the most tender of all.

Isolation, Self-Confidence,

And Depression

First and foremost when someone has a few true, close friends, they are fortunate indeed and can consider themselves blessed. For better or for worse, social media has led us down the path of thinking that we are capable of having 452 friends. We're not and we don't. But in my opinion, when someone has even a couple of solid, loyal, honest friends, but feels isolated perhaps they are just not allowing themselves to reach out to them. Allow those friends the opportunity to be friends not just in word, but in deed as well. All my life I have been fiercely independent and loathe to ask anyone for help with anything. It's like it goes against my very DNA to reach out and ask anyone for anything, including those closest to me. But I can tell you that I'm a work in progress on this point and am trying to change this stubborn, overly resolute part of who I am. With time and maturity I have realized how honored I feel when those I love and care about call on me and allow me the privilege of truly being a friend. And so who am I to not allow for the give and take that is the hallmark of true friendship. So I would ask everyone to look at whether or not they are asking and allowing their friends to truly be their friends. If you feel isolated and alone, look at what you are putting out into the world and ask if you are allowing yourself to be open, approachable, and yes, vulnerable. The more we offer of ourselves with unguarded sincerity the more we will receive in like kind from those around us. There was a TED speech that Greg had me watch one time that was like a well-placed arrow aimed directly at the heart of who I am. It challenged me then and continues to vex and challenge me now because I know it is the answer I just have yet to master the message. It may be something you want to watch and listen to oh...I don't know, a hundred and four times perhaps.

As far as depression goes, allow me to say that having brushed up against this kind of darkness in my life I take it more seriously than you could possibly imagine. When Greg was "away" I came to an awareness that individuals in common culture can have a couple bad days and lament over happy hour at the local watering hole that they are "so depressed." If you have experienced or known anyone who has battled true depression in all its gripping and unshakable despair you will never use the phrase, "I'm so depressed," in casual conversation again. Having said that, any MD, Ph.D. or therapist worth their salt will tell you that you can no more talk yourself out of depression than you can talk yourself out of a heart attack or being diabetic. This is 100% a medical issue and needs to be respected as such. The wonderful news though is that there is a world of treatment options available and we owe it to ourselves and our loved ones to seek them out unabashedly if we are struggling in this way.

Now the topic of self-confidence is a tricky discussion to be sure. It is my firm belief that every parent's primary responsibility in life is to allow their children to know they are completely, utterly and unconditionally loved. While this should be every child's birthright, we all know there is much that can happen along the way to uproot this garden and that for some, it was never planted in the first place. So if self-confidence wasn't given to us, how do we go about giving it to ourselves? I would refer you to the wildly successfully Nike advertising campaign and say, "Just Do It." Ah, but easier said than done you say. Of course it is, just like everything else in life. And if I leave Nike out of this, the best advice I can give to anyone is to find and explore your spirituality. Each one of us here on Earth has a purpose and a reason. Each one of us is an act of Divine Inspiration and Heavenly achievement. I'm not going to tell you what your belief system should be but if you are struggling with self-confidence, it is a pretty safe bet that you lack one. And this isn't a criticism, it is a calling. A calling to become acquainted with just how necessary, unique and priceless you are in this world. What right do you have to deny or belittle what a matchless and singular creation you are? I don't believe one can live with awareness in this world and not acknowledge a higher power. I, and everyone you know, could tell you how special you are until the cows come home and you will always find a way to talk yourself out of such assertions. But go ahead and tell God that he made a mistake...I dare you. Try telling Him that you aren't absolutely everything he intended...just not yet. His purpose for you is your "verse" as Greg would say and how you can find the wherewithal, to doubt His perfect work...you, is an argument I would love to hear. It is the one embrace that never wavers and I would encourage you to seek it out. The entire world will look different once you allow the certainty of how meaningful and intentional you are to soak in and allow the garden to grow in all its glory.

Communication; a Lifelong Priority

Ah yes, Mars and Venus are at it again. First allow me to compliment anyone who takes communicating with their spouse seriously. Because it is, in fact, an enormous component of healthy, thriving marriages and relationships. More often than not we hear the same worn out record playing over and over again about how women want to talk about their feelings and men simply would rather chew on broken glass. I think this is selling both sides short quite frankly with gross over simplifications.

I suppose I should first make the confession that in our relationship Greg is the FAR better communicator. I tend to grind on everything on the inside and try to sort it all out myself which is at best unhealthy and at worst disastrous if we're talking about the importance of good communication. So I can tell you what I think is right, only because I have expert qualifications brought about by learning so many things the hard way. But I suppose the point is that spouses need to meet each other where they are. They both need to acknowledge exactly what their communication styles are then work to find ways to honor one another's personalities while keeping the lines of communication as free, easy and open as humanly possible. By way of an example I mentioned that Greg is much more apt to want to dive in and talk about things, but over the years he has learned to respect the fact that when I get REALLY upset I completely shut down. I don't say a word for fear that in a moment of being hurt or angry I will say something that I don't mean but can't take back. So he has realized that at times I need that pause and space to process through things. But then I owe him the exchange of sitting down and working it through once the tidal wave of emotions has subsided.

Having said that, I think men often get a bad rap about being insensitive because women can be so coy about verbalizing things directly and simply. Simple and direct. This for the most part is a man's language. If I was to go on a trip to Zimbabwe I wouldn't expect them to understand English. So don't expect a man to speak Woman. Or vice versa for that matter. Women shouldn't torture men with zingers like, "if you really cared about me you would know what was wrong," or "if you really loved me you would understand how I feel," or anything else of this breed or derivation. I personally realized long ago that I have this wonderful, willing husband that just wants to make me happy so for God's sake, just tell him Shauna! Tell him what you want. Tell him what you need. Tell him how you feel. Tell him what to get you for your Birthday. Now I don't say this as a free pass for men to be lazy and inattentive. I say it as a baseline that in relationship communication being forthright and upfront is a really good place to start. Now on the flip side, it drives me to just this side of crazy and back when I hear men complaining about women "nagging." If men listened and reacted to what their partner was saying there would be no such thing as nagging. The problem isn't that she keeps saying something over and over again; the problem is that you didn't listen and take action in the first place.

So the bottom line here is that in long term relationships I believe that for BOTH parties, one of the most important aspects of good communication is trust. Do I trust this person to be honest and straightforward? Do I trust this person with my deepest feelings, sensitivities and vulnerabilities? Do I trust this person to always support, encourage and defend me? Do I trust that what I say and share will always be honored and respected? If these elements are in place I think that so many of the other "problems" tend to fall away. To be sure, we need to allow for individual differences and there is room for every personal nuance and idiosyncrasy once the basics of love, trust and respect have defined the playing field. But do keep in mind that sorting all this out is part of the journey. One of the most beautiful things about a long term relationship is the privilege of growing to know someone in every deep and wonderful way imaginable. What do they most enjoy, what makes them laugh, what presses their buttons and what makes them feel, angry, afraid or deeply and completely loved?

So do you need to have it figured out within the next four months? Absolutely not, but you both need to keep caring about it enough to make communication and one another, a lifelong priority.

Life without Purpose or Direction

So many feel like life is going 110 mph without any purpose or direction. Allow me to reassure you that you are not alone and have some stunning company. If I had a dollar for every person I know who has at least felt this way, if not lived this way, I would have a second home in Fiji by now. Said a better way, don't beat yourself up for this space you find yourself in because we've all been there. In fact, some of us, for better or for worse, know the lay of the land pretty well. And when you find yourself in this space, it's a bit like polishing off an entire quart of Ben & Jerry's as though it was a single serving that never even had time to melt. You need to just forgive yourself for allowing life and all of its incessant, seemingly urgent demands get the better of you and of your time. Then take a deep breath and hit the "reset" button.

But the solution is not only remarkably effective, it's darn cheap. Greg is a fanatic about making lists and it is one of the simplest, yet most astonishingly effective tools I have ever witnessed. In fact, what it's worth in the world of efficiency cannot be rivaled. Case in point, if I go into the grocery store with a list, I'm in and out in 20 minutes. If I wander in without one, I'm doomed to wander the aisles for a solid 45 minutes hoping that I will catch sight of something that jogs my memory and reminds me of what it is exactly that we needed. If I start my day with a list my productivity increases tenfold. I'm no longer wasting time and energy wondering what it was that needed to get done or whether or not I got the marketing flyer sent or the Thank You notes dropped in the mail. Now for all of the emphatic urging I can give you about writing lists, I'm still not very disciplined about it but I am committed to being far more so. But in the same breath I would also like to ask you to drill down on precisely what about the busyness is truly unsettling you. I recently went through a wave at my kids school where we went from birthday parties, to Portfolio Nights, to Graduation parties (for Kindergarten!) to a teacher's baby shower and I felt as though my involvement in all this barely allowed me to come up for air. But what I realized was that I wasn't frustrated by the fact that I was trying to create a memorable Baby Boy themed shower to include cake pops that I was determined to perfect regardless of the fact that I had never done it before. What truly bothered me was that I didn't feel as though I had the time to devote to these things because so many other things were now being neglected. I might actually enjoy figuring out how to work with fondant and make something really special for my daughter's birthday if I didn't feel so conflicted about all the other "more productive" stuff that wasn't getting my time and attention. So do pay attention to what about the busyness most disconcerts you. Is it what you are *actually* doing, or is it other people's expectations you are battling about what you "should" be doing.

Now, want to, versus need to aside, likely your list will seem heavy on the trivial, seemingly insignificant stuff that is currently weighing you down with "busy." But this "stuff" that can seem to clog our day and our life is often times the stuff of life. As odd as it may sound, make an effort to find meaning in the mundane. If the kids need haircuts, I go to the shop that one of the mom's at their school owns. And while I'm checking something off my list I'm connecting with someone in my children's lives and letting her know that I value this relationship. If it's something as tedious as changing the oil in your car, bring a book, return phone calls, or clear out your Inbox. THEN the most important part is to cross these nuisance things off your list and give yourself credit for the accomplishment. I used to be surprised by the range of entries Greg would put on his lists. Some were huge, urgent, behemoth tasks but he would also write down the simplest things and cross those off the list as well. And I realized there is unspoken genius in the sense of accomplishment that this provides regardless of how plebeian or profound the task happened to be. But here is the heart of the matter. Make it absolutely non-negotiable to put something on your list each day that feels significant and important to what you deeply value and hold most dear. Don't put picking up the dry cleaning and organizing the garage on the list before you've added in a lunch date with a dear friend, or that weekend trip you've been meaning to schedule for the last two years. Don't ever let the day-to-day, be more important than tending to your heart's desire. It's up to you to allow what matters to truly matter and that means making time for it...making time for you.

Family Discord

Long standing family "issues" have a way of coming out especially during Holidays. Like it or not, the reality is that big waves around those long standing family issues, already exist. It's really just a matter of whether or not you or anyone else in the family is willing to acknowledge that they're already on the high seas. Then the follow-on question is are all family members interested in finding safe harbor or do they all want to keep pretending that the white caps and swells don't exist?

Truth be told, I may be unqualified to answer this question. Do I believe that in certain times and in certain situations discretion is the better part of valor? Absolutely. Do I have a tendency to rise to that calling where family discord is concerned? Not hardly. And I am ready and willing to admit that there may be occasions among family where rocking the boat is unwise. But I think I'd rather be considered unwise than unwilling to tackle an issue and say, "this situation is a mess, but I care about it and want to work to fix it." To be sure this is not license to offend anybody or autocratically decide that you are the one who's got it all figured out and point the finger at everybody else's flaws and dysfunction. If you're going to call attention to the fact that the family ark is taking on water, I implore you to be as open minded as humanly possible. The best I can give you is the reassurance that I truly believe that if your heart is in the right place of wanting things to be better for all concerned, then I would always opt for trying to resolve issues versus trying to avoid the fallout that may result from speaking your mind. The reality is that if your relationships do not allow for candor and openness, they really aren't relationships at all.

I will never forget a time when my brother-in-law challenged me during a bit of a storm to ask myself, "Do I find value in this relationship?" And as simple as the question may sound, give it its due. If these are connections that truly do have value to you, then invest yourself in them. Give them your time, your attention, your thoughts, opinions and your energy. And be ready to honor the input that others offer. Whether you agree with their take on things or not should not be the initial focus. Consider it a given, that people are much more willing to listen if they, themselves feel as though they are being heard.

In recent years I have had to contend, for the first time in my life with family friction and I can sincerely sympathize with how stressful and downright heart wrenching it can be. But I will tell you that I have taken away from the difficulty some powerful lessons about how I will handle things in my own immediate family as the years go by. In my situation, I SO wish that my parents would stand up and say, "Okay, this family is being torn apart and enough is enough. Be at our house next Sunday at 10:00 sharp and we are going to get to the bottom of all this. Nobody leaves until we feel like a family again." I find the recent conflict in my own family to be especially hard because my Grandmother who was in every way the matriarch of this family, not to mention one of the most extraordinary women I have ever met, wouldn't have put up with this nonsense for a nanosecond and I miss her strength, guidance and influence on us all just terribly.

The world needs more people who are willing to dive in and give a damn. Is it going to help the situation? Who knows. But what I do know is that if you arrive at the decision that these relationships do indeed have value, then invest in their worth. I realized long ago that I cannot control anybody other than myself and my actions. And so I need to be unshakably certain that *my* actions are in keeping with a sense of courage and conviction. I need to be willing to do what I believe to be the right thing regardless of what unpleasant consequences or criticism may come my way. There is no question in my mind that I would always rather live with the criticism of others, than being disappointed in myself for not having the care or courage to hold fast and steer through the storm.

Here's to wishing you smoother sailing ahead!

Letting the Big Picture

Make the Decision

What do you do when a friend borrows a sum of money from you, let's say $500.00, and weeks turn into months and it's never mentioned let alone repaid? What do you say? Uugh! I loathe these scenarios! Certainly not because you've done anything wrong, but rather because these situations are so damn awkward. Perhaps I can give you clarity about one thing and that is that while you may be wistfully toying with the idea that perhaps this friend has innocently forgotten that they owe you money...they haven't. Five hundred dollars isn't exactly along the lines of you buying their favorite microbrew at Happy Hour because they forgot their wallet. It's a lot of money and there isn't a chance that it just slipped their mind.

So where does this leave you? With a flakey friend and an uncomfortable situation on your hands. What always most aggravates me about scenarios like this is that while YOU haven't done anything wrong, YOU'RE the one feeling frustrated and conflicted about the situation. Something is just egregiously bass ackwards about that but there you have it. So the way I see it you can choose Door A or Door B.

Door A follows the sage like wisdom that you don't LOAN money to a friend or family member in need you GIVE it to them. If you can't afford to give it away for nothing more than the good karma that you're putting out in the Universe then don't do it. Don't even think about doing it unless you can be truly detached from any expectations of having the money paid back. I will also caution that for as sound as this principle is, it can still impact relationships and create an underlying current of disappointment. So before you go this route make good and sure that you truly have it in you to acknowledge that even the best of us, yourself included, could use a little grace now and then and what a privilege that perhaps you can provide that for someone you care about. I have also found that with this scenario it is often better to give it as a "gift" of paid rent or some such thing. Or even put the cash in one of those money holder cards and give it so it cements the fact in both your minds that this is a gift and that payback is not just unexpected, but unwelcome. Can you retroactively go back and make the intellectual amendment to consider your $500 a kindhearted donation from you to a friend in need? More power to you if you are able, but I would consider that a mental adjustment of heroic proportions as that wasn't the agreed or original expectation.

Door B involves you saying something to your friend realizing full well that the future of your relationship may hang in the balance of his response. If this friend says they don't have the money to pay you back right now, their next statement should be a definitive commitment as to when they *will* pay it back. Call them what you will, goals, deadlines, ultimatums or expectations, but the reality of the human psyche is that we don't function well without them. Leaving it open ended that this friend will pay you back "when they get the money" is a commitment that has little weight and less meaning. But I would ask you to look on this as an opportunity for your friendship to either deepen in its respect or for you to leave something and someone behind that isn't worth your time much less your frustration. There was an instance not long ago where parents were buying materials for a project the kids were involved in at school. One of the boys in the class had parents who volunteered to pick up the items for the entire class and then they let us all know our share of the expense. To be fair it was a nominal amount; under $10.00 but a couple of parents neglected to pay them back right away and they sent out a very polite reminder email about the money that was due. Needless to say, I was one of those being reminded and I was mortified. I felt truly awful that my absent-mindedness put them in a position where they had to ask *me* for money I owed *them*. I don't care if it's $10 or $1000 it isn't right. So I immediately put the cash in a card along with a Starbucks gift card worth more than the amount of money I owed them and most importantly an extremely sincere apology for having dropped the ball. They were, of course, appreciative, but once again, it was my mistake and therefore on me to try to make it right. So trivial as this example is, if once you bring it to his attention, your friend goes out of his way to make it right and OVERDELIVERS in terms of what is due, then your friendship will surely strengthen in its mutual respect and appreciation. If however your friend acts unaffected by the quandary he has created or worse yet, somehow entitled to your charitable giving then the friendship is most likely doomed. The bright spot however would be that if, indeed something of this insensitive sort is his response, this is a person that will undoubtedly continue to take advantage of you. Hard as it may be, you are far better off to put an end to the relationship now as what it will "cost" you in terms of not just dollars, but stress and heartache in the future is a price I can only hope you are unwilling to pay.

For matters where money is not the object, there is a Door Number 3 if you will. Some of you know that I have been very involved in horses all my life. Many years ago a horse of mine had to undergo a colic surgery and needed a lot of layup time to just heal and recover. I had a new baby and an enormous amount going on and we asked some very good friends of ours, who had a lovely horse facility, if they would care for him and allow him to rehab at their farm. We of course paid them just as we would if he was elsewhere, but it was an enormous mental relief to me to know that he was being cared for and looked after by a friend and someone I trusted. To make a long story short when the time came that life settled and I was ready to start riding again, I brought Max to an equestrian center Greg and I had bought and I cannot begin to explain the sense of crushing shock and distress that followed. Max, my pride and joy that was my first "baby" of sorts came off the horse trailer nearly 300 pounds underweight, uncared for, unkempt and looking like absolute shit. This is a magnificent animal that was worth a phenomenal amount of money and here he was looking like an animal that you'd be hard pressed to spend a nickel on at auction. My first emotion was being bitterly upset with myself. Max was my horse, my baby, my responsibility and I had let him down dreadfully. I hadn't paid close enough attention to his well-being and he had suffered tremendously because of it. And while I will never be able to shake the feeling that I let this splendid animal and loyal friend down, I was beyond disappointed in the fact that friends and people I had trusted had treated him and their responsibility with such negligence and carelessness. But here's the Door #3. I had to decide then and there that the past and future relationship I had with these friends was more important to me than what had happened and I never said a single word to them about it. Not one. What was there to be gained? There was no money that was to be paid back, no reasonable "compensation" for what happened. So I made the decision that ultimately Max was my responsibility and that I was the one who had fallen short. These friends didn't owe me, I owed Max for letting him down so unspeakably. Do I consider this the literal truth? No, not really. But in the interest of our friendship combined with my own personal guilt, this is the path I chose and things have worked out for the best. So keep in mind that money is pretty cut and dry. It's precise and relatively free of "interpretation" but other scenarios where friends disappoint you and let you down things aren't quite as simple. So commit to trying your best to let the Big Picture make the decision rather than any immediate emotions you may be feeling. I don't always manage these scenarios with Solomonic wisdom, but I'll continue to give it the college try and hope you do too.

Couples and Risk Tolerance

 A frequent question I am asked by entrepreneurial couples over and over in some form at events we have done is the question of risk tolerance in business. Often husbands are much more willing to take chances than wives. Rest assured many entrepreneurial couples are trying to do this dance but how do they address this difference without being driven apart? Most couples I know, Greg and myself included have had to deal with the issue of "risk tolerance" in some fashion and have had to work our way to common ground and a mutual understanding.

More often than not one partner in a business or marriage has a greater ability to handle and live with risk and uncertainty than the other. This can create problems in a relationship. To be fair, I do believe that business partners need to be more like minded in this regard than marriage partners and since you mention this difference exists between you and your husband, versus your business partner, I tend to expect a wider berth. In other words, I actually think these differences are quite healthy in a marriage relationship, but can be much more concerning and consequential within business partnerships. I think that most relationships truly benefit from a balance that can be stuck when differences are both respected and embraced.

If we want to get anthropological about this, men were the ones out hunting large animals, succeeding on a combination of risk taking, strength and adrenaline. Women were more apt to be gathering, tending to and raising children. Have we evolved? Of course we have, but my point is we come by these differences in instincts and skill sets genetically and that's a good thing. Both were necessary for survival then as they are now believe it or not. Everything needs a balance. A ying and yang as it were. And where marriage and especially families are concerned, these differences are the ingredients for the finest recipes of all. But the key is that the aspects of what both a husband and a wife bring to the table are respected and valued for how essential they are. A husband's ease with chance and uncertainty can be absolutely necessary to drive business and financial success in a forward direction. It can also be the spontaneity and spirit that adds incredible moments and experiences to your repertoire of life stories and adventures. But at the same time your husband needs to value what your steadiness and stability contribute to the relationship and family. You are likely the influence that keeps his actions risky versus reckless. Greg is all emotion and I adore this about him, but sometimes in life a more tempered and measured response is needed far more than a fiery and impetuous one. I can love Greg for his willingness to walk the razor's edge but he also appreciates and respects the fact that there are certain basics and givens that I need in my life. I can cope with an extreme amount of unknown and anxiety in life if our core foundation, our home, our family and those basics needs never feel threatened.

In all honesty this has been quite a learning process for me. I had what you would consider a pretty darn conservative upbringing so it has only been through my relationship with Greg that I have learned to not just tolerate, but to embrace a very unconventional life. On the flip side I believe that in both life and business certain times call for subtly, tact, and a certain amount of diplomacy. Not generally the realm of the risk taker. A velvet hand can often times be far more effective than a hammer. Patience and grace can often be far more becoming than insistence and immediate action. I will never forget a wonderful statement I remember hearing Dr. Phil make about his wife. His comment was, "I make the living and she makes the life worth living." The comment spoke volumes about his appreciation for the color, the tenderness, care and the joy that she brings to their life and family. I also remember hearing the female CEO of a Fortune 500 company being interviewed and asked the secret to her success. Her answer; "I never tried to be a man." In other words, she brought her compassion, warmth and femininity to the table and feels she was successful not in spite of it, but rather because of it.

To some degree the bottom line is, "do you trust your husband?" Do you trust that he will never do anything that would threaten the well-being of what is truly important in your life? Do you trust that he will respect and appreciate that the temperament and qualities you bring to the table of life are every bit as valuable as the ones he brings to the mix? In a thousand lifetimes I cannot imagine asking Greg to get a corporate 8:00 to 5:00 job so that we could have a more predictable, anticipated life. In the same breath, he should never insist that I change who I am and that there are certain givens that I need to feel safe and assured. Have we both come to the middle? Absolutely. And in the end, I know we are both far better for the influence of one another

It's time to get rid of the "Good"

Now at first this sounds a bizarre and relatively unwise proposition. We all long for what is good. A good spouse or significant other, a good job, good investments, good kids, good grades, a good 401-k, good friends, a good vacation, a good bottle of wine, a good golf score, good hair, a good book and occasionally a good movie. By all accounts, good, seems an impressive goal worthy of our efforts and attention. But odd as it may sound, I have learned across time and experience that good is often our greatest mistake.

Time and again I have both watched and experienced how we hang onto good with a vice grip of possessive pride. If we have earned or achieved good we tend to feel satisfied, grateful and protective of the status or experience we have earned. And perhaps rightly so. Good is certainly worth appreciating and nothing to take carelessly for granted. However, I have found that it can be that thing, that experience, that state of mind that keeps us fearfully unwilling to reach for more. More? If things are good, what kind of self-indulgent, entitled person wants more all the time? I do. And so should you.

More money? More cars? More house? More toys? Nope. I'm talking about more life, more memories, more abundance, more connection, more purpose, more spirituality, more impact, more time spent reveling in not merely what is good, but rather that which we would dare describe as great. More often than not we feel so grateful for good that pursuing something grander is a risk we are relatively unwilling to take. For some the notion that we deserve the extraordinary takes an enormous amount of mental rewiring. Not many of us can boast an internal dialog that insists we are worthy of absolute abundance in all things. The vast majority of us consider ourselves "lucky" if things are good and dare not temp the fates to ask or expect more. As a result I have found that time and time again, the comfort of good is what keeps us from letting go and reaching for a life of utterly amazing.

If we quit a "good" job to pursue our passion our life might not exactly resemble that of Richard Branson. What if we end up with the decidedly unglamorous reality of struggling to pay rent or make a mortgage payment? If we demand an extraordinary relationship are we going to risk upending the good one we have and making a righteous mess of things or do we dare to become amazing to and for those we love? Do we accept being content with our tidy cul de sac house or does the dream of ten acres with horses or a house on the lake call us like a siren song that we remain afraid to answer? Do we feel satisfied with partners or employees being good or do we expect them to be exceptional? The reality is, good is something we consider to be within our grasp if we are willing to work hard and dedicate ourselves accordingly. But extraordinary is a horse of an entirely different color. And extraordinary never, ever happens without risk. Without risking letting go of comfort, complacency, ease and those things which could rightly be described as good and free falling toward that which is inspired, exceptional and uncommon.

Our oldest daughter was distraught when we moved to Arizona. Growing up as an Army brat moving was a common occurrence in my life but not at all familiar in hers. The notion of a new and very different school, meeting people and making new friends, adjusting to entirely different surroundings…none of this was on her radar screen as being changes she wanted any part in. Her life, her school, her friends were good. And this new adventure wasn't merely a hard sell, she went into it kicking and screaming.

And I don't blame her one bit. Having moved so many times myself, I knew in my heart of hearts that she would be absolutely fine. But she didn't know or feel any of my certainty. She was understandably scared and resentful of the risk we were asking her to take. We were asking her to free fall into an absolute unknown and trust only in what WE knew to be true. And she did it. She fell grasping and grabbing into an entirely new life and what she got a hold of was an experience of profound joy and belonging. She became part of a school, a life, a belief and support system of the most remarkable and astonishing kind. She has friends that aren't merely good friends, they are heroic, no matter what, weather any storm with you, kind of friends. She spends every single day in the midst of an extraordinary experience and I can promise you that forever more in her mind, good will never be good-enough.

For the rest of us life often throws us unwelcome curve balls that force us toward new and different decisions. And just as often we must make deliberate, somewhat terrifying choices in order to earn the extraordinary. So consider perhaps that those curve balls, those upending unwelcome experiences are the greatest gift you've ever been given. A chance to reach for something you never would have believed in before. And those times in our life when we choose with courage…those cross-roads where we surrender to the safety of good or risk it all for the possibility of the extraordinary. These are the times that define us. There never is and never will be anything wrong with good. But oddly it is the unlikely culprit in keeping our life, our story, from what it has the ability to become. Letting go is always a daunting, uneasy experience. But it is absolutely essential if we want to grab a life of astonishing instead.

The Time of your Life

So we have as a family, recently returned from an oh so busy, but wonderful trip to visit family. The focal point of our escapade was a long awaited and much anticipated 60/80 celebration for my husband's parents. Celebrating their 60th anniversary and 80th birthdays which conveniently fell a month apart allowing us the opportunity for one Big Bash to revel in.

So allow me to admit that the lead-up to this adventure was manic. Getting five kids packed up and ready for any eventuality of experience in the Northwest seems to require more baggage than an Everest expedition. And not a Sherpa, or yak in sight. So the dubious beast of burden label applied to Greg and myself and when you're trying to cover the basis for everything from a three month old infant to a fourteen year-old, not a single effort can be duplicated. Nobody wears the same size t-shirt or tennis shoes and apparently accessories for a newly minted nine year old are not optional attire, but an absolute must. To say we packed everything but the kitchen sink is to grossly underestimate the scale and scope of our inventory. Now I must admit that I am the world's worst packer. I don't hate it, I LOATHE it. With every fiber of my being I resent the horrid activity. Why…because I'm awful at it. I fret about everything from beach balls to Band aids and every little thing in between. The notion of travelling across Europe with nothing more than a backpack is, I am convinced, fictitious folly as surely, it couldn't possibly be done. But truth be told, I long for such a thing. The idea of being whimsically unencumbered by all the stuff we stuff into our lives.

Now that I have made my confessions of traveling ineptitude, what exactly is the point of my ramble? The point is that as I took in all the experiences over the weekend celebrating my husband's parents, I realized that exploding suitcases, abandoned naps and a diet of ice cream and s'mores weren't worthy of a second thought. In the midst of utter, wonderful chaos, we tend to find what matters. It is when we peel back our trivial concerns and mundane cares that life, and the moments we will remember forever reveal themselves to our waiting hearts. If we allow lesser concerns to seize our focus we lose the magic of the moment. And life doesn't have a DVR feature. We cannot replay moments of laughter and delight. We cannot rewind the magic of watching our kids discover or understand something new and impossibly amazing. We can't redo the hug we gave, the sunshine we felt, or the crunch of the leaves we walked on. There is a vast difference between merely doing something and truly experiencing something. Experiencing something in that special, indescribable way that makes it ours forever. And those memories and moments are the soul food that feeds our need for joy across a lifetime.

As a somewhat odd case in point, I absolutely hate sand. Despise it really. As a clean freak, it assaults my sensibilities to the point of irrational aversion. But we spent the entire weekend at my brother and sister-in-laws spectacular beach house. And everybody was living in the water and on the beach. Boat rides, inner tubing, clam digging. Sand was in buckets, little britches and everywhere in between. And if I obsessed over the irritation inducing sand invasion, I would have missed all the good stuff. The giggles, the fun, the exploration, exhilaration and absolute delight that surrounded us all. We weren't there to worry about nonsense, we were there to celebrate two utterly spectacular people. We were there, together to enjoy one another, to revel in the relationships, the adventure, the planned celebration and the spontaneous joys that tumbled into our memories forevermore. So the moral of my story is that if we are waiting around for it all to be "right" we are doing ourselves the worst kind of wrong. We need to give ourselves the gift of laughter and loved ones. The gift of taking a risk and watching what comes from our courage. If we become fixated on the work we are missing, the text messages we aren't checking, the presentation going perfectly, the date going flawlessly, the kid's clothes adorably matching, having good hair for endless iPhone snapshots, or whether or not the burgers are organic grass-fed beef on gluten-free buns then life in all its messy, imperfect, wonderful beauty will slip through our fingers. I don't know about you, but I'd rather smile as I watch the sand slip through my children's toes, knowing that it couldn't possibly get better than this very moment, right here, right now. And when we allow ourselves the joy captured in the here and now, we claim as ours, forevermore, that moment to add to the storybook of our heart.

Avatar Advice?

When I first saw the movie Avatar I will say I enjoyed it. It wasn't an "OMG, that's the most amazing movie I've ever seen!" kind of thing, but it was certainly entertaining. But there was a scene in the movie that left me with that head cocked, "huh?" sort of expression on my face. A movie moment that was intended to be poignant but to me seemed awkward and oddly placed. But for some curious reason I have pondered it over time and the phrase that at one time seemed peculiar I now realize is deeply profound.

Okay, okay. So the scene I am referring to is where Jake and Neytiri look at each other and speak the phrase, "I see you" to one another. This phrase is also mentioned earlier in the movie as an expression that the Na'Vi people speak to each other often. By the way, in case you're wondering, I am not an Avatar junkie and I did need to look those names up on the internet. But Avatar devotee or not, we would all do well to think of the last time our attention and deliberate focus earned us the right to look someone dead in the eye and say "I see you" and absolutely and truly mean it. There is no question we all know an impressive number of people. Friends, family, associates, acquaintances. Spouses, children, teachers, co-workers, sisters and brothers. Our lives are chock full of all kinds of people. Too many people perhaps? But how many of them do we intensely know in that soulful, sincere, naked kind of way. Naked in that you see another stripped of all the pretenses that life has layered on over years of pretending. Free of the armor of appearances, expectations and impressions that weigh on our soul to the point where I wonder how many of us would even recognize what is truly the essence of us anymore. So often the person we were born to be is a strangely far cry from the one that life and circumstance have insisted we become.

There are piles of people that talk about the undeniable power of authenticity, myself included. I will beat that drum all day long and believe in it fiercely. But for as much as each of us can and should fight, demand and courageously claim our authentic selves, it is worthwhile to keep in mind that even such a noble task could be vastly improved upon. When is the last time we paused in our personal pursuits for a moment and seized the time to look into someone else's heart? I'm not talking about a mental note that says she would love flowers or he would love a carefree round of golf. Those are activities. And while thoughtful and generous in nature they aren't the gift I am asking us all to consider giving. When is the last time we looked at and into the very soul of someone we love and said, "I see you" and in those words we spoke the truth of the deepest kind of understanding. What would it feel like to you, to me, to each other, to realize that someone sees the heart of who we are and embraces that Us in an "I love you and I'm never letting go" kind of way. You don't need to act, impress or achieve in order to earn my affection. I see you, and you is enough for me.

There is an entire industry devoted to "self-help" of every conceivable kind. Help that promises to correct our faulty thinking and damaged self-worth. After absorbing the recommended remedy we will then be triumphantly ushered onto the path of personal enlightenment and professional high achievement. I however would contend that if from the beginning we felt seen and adored for simply and wonderfully who we are, our turmoil would cease to exist. For as much as we all love our children in that "walk in front of a bus without a second thought" kind of a way, are we making sure our kids understand that they, and they alone own our hearts? It is all too easy to send messages that WHAT we love are good grades, good manners, and their proficiency on the piano or that kick ass scholarship they earned. Every day I mess this up. Giving my kids accolades for what they DO. I need to make certain that the voice they hear from me embraces who they are and perhaps I can at least limit their need for the self-help aisle at Barnes at Noble at some future date

Now I hope it will come as no surprise that I remain adamantly in favor of the passionate pursuit of high achievement. But once again, I want to talk about nouns not verbs. What if occasionally we took the spotlight off of what we DO and instead took the time to realize who our loved ones ARE. How many men have I met that climb the corporate ladder and chase achievement when they'd rather be a high school football coach, or a hunting guide, a bush pilot or crafting a fabulous microbrew. On the flip side, I've met countless numbers of men who have the heart and ambition to change the world, but are slave to job they can scarcely endure for the admirable sake of paying a mortgage and putting food on the table. When we truly SEE someone, it becomes impossible to allow them to choose between their passion and paying the bills. When we see into another's soul we are obligated to honor who they are, and insist relentlessly on a life without compromise. Similarly, how many women have I met who crave feeling powerful and accomplished in the business arena because they think that is what the world, and most especially other women, will be impressed by. Yet in their heart of hearts, they long to be "just a mom" yet survey says this isn't nearly flashy, sexy or remarkable enough. Then we dive into the deep end of hypocrisy when a woman pursues a job she loves and muffle our disgust over how she is doing irreparable harm to her unfortunate offspring. We are besieged by expectations that we can and should "do it all." And as a result, men and women alike suffer from being "jack of all and Master of none." We thrash around in our life doing a little of this and a little of that and ultimately making a righteous mess of things. Sure we are doing many things but not a one of them are we doing brilliantly. Am I suggesting we are incapable of taking on a multitude of roles in our life? Perish the thought. But I will argue to the ends of the earth that if what you DO isn't purposefully woven to a part of who you ARE then life will be endlessly frustrating versus infinitely inspiring.

So what if we took these words off of the Big Screen and chose to try? What if we chose to give someone the greatest of all gifts? The gift of looking at them with all their fears, their failures, their hopes, their dreams, their insecurities and their wildest imaginings. What if we chose to reach into the deepest being and most urgent longing of those we love? What if we chose to grab hold of the silent truths of those we adore and drag those hidden heartbeats into the safety of our tender care? What if we could have someone truly believe that THEY are seen and that WHO they are is so much more than enough? What if we purposed to see those we love in that absolute and unconditional way? This extraordinary and uncommon kind of love gives us the freedom to live fearlessly. And when we live fearlessly everything…EVERYTHING changes.

Do you agape?

Stating the Obvious

So the other evening Everest, our oldest, took her siblings for a walk on the golf course. Upon returning Everest told me about how she observed her two year old brother, Cor, standing with his hands in his pockets. Now a toddler standing with his hands in his pockets is about the cutest visual I can imagine; unexpected and charming in a heartwarming kind of way. So Everest asked him, "Cor, what do you have in your pockets?" His dead pan answer was "hands". Now we all know that children are literal. They take everything at uncomplicated face value and while we can say that perhaps nuance and subtleties escape them, there is something wildly refreshing in the fact that they don't analyze everything to death. They say what they think and take you at your word, so the matter of fact response of our two year old got me thinking about those things that should, in fact, be obvious. We seem to have drifted carelessly away from them.

Say please and thank you. This seems something we are constantly coaching our children to remember, but I have witnessed an astonishing number of adults that seem to have forgotten this utterance. Are we so preoccupied with our thoughts, our to-do list, our obligations and our appointments that we can't focus on the most basic of courtesies? "Please". A single word that invokes the humility of a request which is always swallowed far better than a demand. And "thank you." Two simple words that acknowledge our appreciation for an act, an effort or a service. I have never met a single person that doesn't appreciate feeling appreciated. Bottom line, whether it is out in the world at large, with your spouse, your children, your business partner or your barber these two remarks go a long way.

Look people in the eye when you speak to them. For reasons I haven't completely explored, this seems to be a tougher task. I'm not sure why we shy away from looking others in the eye and acknowledging them in a focused, intentional way. And I feel certain we can all agree this is only getting worse. With all of us keeping our eyes and therefore our attention on our smart phones, we have dumbed down our experience of one another. Every time I see someone order anything from lunch to a latte without so much as a glance at the person helping them I feel angry and exasperated all at once. Anytime my kids speak to an adult I insist they look them in the eye – not at their shuffling feet or the buttons on their shirt. We are all profoundly visual creatures. It is what draws our attention and ignites our thoughts. So the reality is that when you look someone in the eye, it is a profoundly simple way of saying, "you matter." What you are saying, what you are doing, what you are feeling…it matters, and I am always interested in such a thing as that.

Gentlemen. Call me frivolous, old-fashioned or anything else you like, but guys should open the door for gals. Not just their gal…any gal. I am both stunned and disappointed with how little of this small but meaningful effort I see. And ladies. Part of the problem is that we've stopped expecting it. If you are going out with a guy and he can't manage to open a car door, a restaurant door or any other variety of entry, or exit devices, might I suggest you stand there until he does, or find a different date? I remember being at a dinner with another couple one time and the husband had been raised in the Carolina's. I got up to go grab something and he got up too and helped pull my chair out. It literally took me a moment to process what he was doing. If I hadn't just stood up, I would have fallen off my chair I was so surprised. Pleasantly surprised. At Everest's school all the kids in the eighth grade participate in an etiquette dance. Yes, etiquette. A concept nearly as endangered as Siberian Tigers. They are actually graded on everything from basic ball room dance to which side the bread plate is on. Now we've slid so far that full tilt etiquette is asking a lot of people. So let's just go for the basics; men, open the door for women and moms teach your boys to do so.

Pick up a pen. Now I am all in favor of emails, texting, Facebook posts and messages, Instagram, etc. They are terrific tools that facilitate businesses, communication and connectivity. But they never have, and never will replace the written word. The hand written word to be more precise. No email or messaging medium will ever upstage the elegant impact of picking up a pen and putting our thoughts, our sentiments, our appreciation, our congratulations to paper. If someone gives to you, if they give you time or substance, WRITE a thank you note. This goes for our kids too. If our children receive a gift, once it is opened, they aren't allowed to play with it, touch it, taste or wear it until they WRITE a thank you note. Gratitude should be the priority, not playtime, and appreciation is a learned behavior. From the time they can scribble with a magenta colored crayon, this can and should be expected. If someone goes out of their way in service, action or effort, acknowledge it. Milestones, accomplishments or simply the time to actually write our love, admiration or appreciation will never be anything less than time wonderfully and beautifully spent. It is an age old effort of significance, sincerity, and depth that will continue to endure across time and space. I would stage an avid argument that it is far MORE meaningful today than it has ever been because it is so painfully uncommon. We all know that anything rare has immense value. Taking the time and effort to reach out to one another in such an intentional, personal way is both rare and profoundly important.

There are always two sides to every story. They may not be equal. Right and wrong do, in fact, exist. But understanding one another is never a wasted endeavor.

If someone is thoughtful enough to invite you to something, be thoughtful enough to RSVP.

Our lives and obligations can be all-consuming. So awareness of others takes a focused, even disciplined, effort. Be aware of the lives and experiences swirling around you. You have the ability to simply make someone's day or the power to change their lives just because you chose to care.

If you wouldn't say something in another's presence, it is safe to say it shouldn't be said at all.

Distance allows shockingly false bravado from those who would more realistically qualify as cowards.

As fiercely loyal to and immensely fond of our opinions as we are, they are just that...opinions.

True facts rarely present themselves outside of calculus class. Most everything else is subject to interpretation. Being interested in another's viewpoint just might improve your own.

Anything done or said in anger is most likely a choice you will regret.

If you borrow something, return it better than you found it.

Be the most generous person you know.

Don't just do enough. Over deliver in absolutely everything you do.

If you are picking somebody's brain over lunch or dinner, pick up the tab.

And as my kids remind me, if someone says, "guess what?" Guess; don't just say "what?"

To be sure I am a work in progress on all of these fronts and so many more we could expound upon. But I would like to think that the moral of my story is that no matter how often I come up short, I will always be working in the belief that I can be better, do better and give more. And I hope it is obvious to us all that pursuing better is a challenge worth rising to.